To: DOTTIE INGIIS
A VERY SPECIAL
FRIEND - SPECIAL
IN MANY WAYS -
BUT ESPECIALLY
TO US BECAUSE WE
THINK ALIKE ABOUT
SO MANY THINGS.

With deep affection -
Warren Taylor Knightong
June 20, 1998

BOOK # 24

HOBBY HORSE RIDER

From the Writings of

LILBURN ADKIN KINGSBURY
1884 - 1983

Edited by Warren Taylor Kingsbury, Ed.D.

Published by Timestream,® Inc.
Oakland, California

HOBBY HORSE RIDER

Autobiographical excerpts from writings of Lilburn Adkin Kingsbury
focusing on the hobbies he rode.

Editor: Warren Taylor Kingsbury
Publisher: Warren Taylor Vaughan III
Editorial Assistant: Rosanne Lyles Armijo
Cover design: Rosanne Lyles Armijo
Printing: Walsworth Pub. Co., Marceline, MO

Published by Timestream,® Inc.
Oakland, California
info@timestream.com
www.timestream.com

ISBN 1-890709-01-8

Library of Congress Catalog Card Number: 98-84382

First Edition
9 8 7 6 5 4 3 2 1

Timestream is a registered trademark of Timestream, Inc.
Printed in the United States of America
June 1998

To my wife of 68 years

Madeleine Huppert Kingsbury

without whose unfaltering love, understanding and
encouragement, this book would never have been completed.

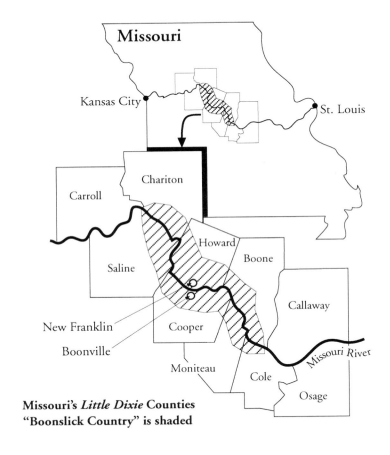

**Missouri's *Little Dixie* Counties
"Boonslick Country" is shaded**

Foreword

Now that he is dead and gone, it cannot do much harm to his memory to say that his time might have been better employed in weightier labors. He however was apt to ride his hobby his own way ... though it did now and then kick up the dust a little in the eyes of his neighbors, and grieve the spirit of some friends for whom he felt the most deference and affection.

From: *Washington Irving's Rip Van Winkle*

This book, *Hobby Horse Rider*, was really written by my bachelor uncle Lilburn Adkin Kingsbury. He was born October 14, 1884 at Fairview, the Kingsbury home built by slave labor about 1834, in the heart of Missouri's historic Boonslick Country. From his parents he inherited the orchard/farm and lived there until taken to the hospital shortly before his death on July 1, 1983.

As a young school boy, Lilburn began to write letters. This became a life-long hobby. Many of his relatives and friends with whom he corresponded found his letters so enjoyable they couldn't bear to destroy them. Many of these found their way back to Lilburn. In the 1930s he began to retain carbon copies of letters written to family and friends. This accumulation of more than 3,500 pages which he gave me just before he died, describes many of his hobby horse rides.

I have attempted to link a number of his interests together in a connective time sequence interspersed with some of his humorous, often shrewd observations and philosophical comments about the outlandish behaviors of himself and the people he interacted with during his long and busy life. These captured with poignance some of the joys and tragedies of his family and the Boonslick Country.

My links are italicized. The excerpts are from Lilburn's letters, speech manuscripts, articles for organizational journals and bulletins, newspaper articles and columns.

Some of his relatives and friends did indeed say, "His time might have been better employed in weightier labors." They thought he should pay more attention to the Fairview orchard/farm, to his insurance business, and to church and community activities. After some years of trying to change him, they accepted him as he was.

The versatility and wide range of his talents brought him the admiration and respect of all who knew him. Boonslickians came to address him affectionately as "Mr. Lib." By the time he was 75, he had become a "living legend." He was the subject of many magazine and newspaper articles with headings such as: "A Living History Book." "Writes It Like It Was." "Mark Twain of Mid-Missouri," "Country Gentleman" and "Howard County Historian."

In a sense, Lilburn's letter-writing was the lead horse in his hobby horse stable. In writing to many people at home and abroad, he spiced his writing with amusing anecdotes about his pursuit of other hobbies, such as:

- *Music - a very important part of his life*
- *Collecting antique furniture*
- *Establishing Fairview as a show place*
- *Collecting early American glass, china and lustreware*
- *Collecting bottles, jugs and clocks*
- *Exploring Howard County graveyards and compiling vital statistics and epitaphs from early pioneer graves*
- *Compilation of folklore songs and stories*
- *Collecting buttons*
- *Developing genealogical records*
- *Talking to clubs and organizations*
- *Writing articles for journals and bulletins*
- *Writing newspaper articles and columns*

It is my hope you will find the reading of my uncle's hobby horse rides a joyous experience. I like to think that in your imagination, you'll gallop along on many of his rides through the back roads and paths of his beloved Boonslick Country.

Warren Taylor Kingsbury
Tempe, Arizona, 1998

Acknowledgements

Foremost of those to whom I am indebted is my editorial assistant, Rosanne Lyles Armijo, owner of Duotype Graphic Services. Her interest in the unique quality of this book and its challenge to her creativity and editorial skills resulted in her giving generously of her time at the expense of her business and valued services as a board member of many community organizations. Her painstaking editing and thoughtful suggestions have enhanced the appeal of this book and her creativity produced the striking Hobby Horse Rider cover. It has been a joy to work with her.

Next, I appreciate the thoughtful review of the manuscript by my daughter, Carol Kingsbury Weed. Her encouragement has kept me going when occurring obstacles made me want to say — "to hell with it."

My thanks to Warren Taylor Vaughan III, who is my cousin twice removed and President of Timestream, Inc., for his help and assistance in the publication of *Hobby Horse Rider*. Also, many thanks to his father, Warren Taylor Vaughan, Jr., M.D., for his help in the tedious task of copyediting.

I am grateful to the *Boonville Daily News*, where as a high school student I used to write for permission to excerpt from the weekly "Lilburn Says" columns written during the last fifty years of Lilburn's life.

I appreciate the helpfulness of Judy Priest, Executive Secretary of Friends of Historic Boonville, for pictures and information about Thespian Hall, oldest surviving theatre west of the Mississippi river.

And James Denny, Missouri State Department of Natural Resources, Jefferson City, for pictures of Lilburn Kingsbury and Fairview.

My thanks also go to Dr. Robert Archibald, President of the Missouri Historical Society of Missouri (St. Louis) for permission to excerpt articles written by Lilburn published in the Society's *Bulletin*.

Thanks to Jody and Ron Lenz for providing the picture of "Rivercene" which they now operate as a delightful and popular bed and breakfast facility.

I appreciate the interest and assistance by Bob Dyer, editor of the Boonslick Historical Society's journal – *Boonslick Heritage*, and offer my thanks to the *Columbia Missourian* and the *Columbia Daily Tribune* for permission to publish photographs belonging to their archives.

Most of Lilburn's writings, genealogical and historical records are housed in the Western Manuscript Division of the Missouri State Historical Society at the University of Missouri - Columbia. I remain indebted to the WHMC-C for permission to publish photographs and exerpts from the *Lilburn A. Kingsbury Collection, 1816-1983*, namely, selections from the Charles van Ravenswaay folders (164-165) and the photograph of Lilburn on page 343.

– WTK

Table of Contents

Table of Contents

Table of Contents

Table of Contents

Chapter One

BROTHER BILLIE IS DEAD!

We have had an unbroken family circle for an unusually long time, but tragedy stalked in last night. Billie is gone.

His body, revolver clasped in his right hand, was found under a towering oak tree in Valhalla Cemetery in Overland Park near St. Louis.

His partner Leo Meistrell's body was found in the locked vault of their offices. He had been shot once in the head, twice in the chest.

So wrote Lilburn Kingsbury to his Cousin Lillian Kingsbury Agnew in Great Falls, Montana on April 8, 1932. The letter continues:

Billie was taking Julia home about 7:25 p.m. She asked him to let her out of the car so she could go see Mrs. Nelson. Billie asked her how long she wanted to stay so he could come by for her on his way home from the office. She thought about ten o'clock. Billie said he would not be long. Julia had wanted to go with him but he told her she'd better not, as it might be cold up there.

Jere called me at six this morning asking that Horace and I come over immediately. We got there as quickly as possible. We learned Billie had not been seen since he left Julia, and Leo Meistrell was also missing. Mrs. Meistrell had talked to her husband at eight o'clock and had called again and had no reply. Julia had gone home earlier with Jere and had also called to tell Billie, but got no answer.

Mrs. Meistrell was quite frantic and so was Julia. The police were called out after midnight, combing country roads and searching for clues in the office and found Leo's hat. Billie had gone up to open his mail, having been away a couple of days. The mail on his desk was unopened. I was in the office with several others and we rattled the vault door, but it never occurred to me it might hold a tragedy. The door was locked from the outside. Mrs. Meistrell and others thought someone should go to the cabin in the Ozarks so Jere and I with others made the 200-mile round trip in less than five hours, but when we got there to the store [at the bridge up the lake from the cabin] we found a message. Horace had phoned and said Leo had been found shot to death in the vault. Leo Meistrell was shot twice in the face and once in the chest, and had fallen on his face. The door was closed and locked.

We found no sign of Billie's car at the lake nor anyone who had seen Billie, so we hurried back (to Boonville). By the time we got there, word had come from St. Louis that a body had been found in a cemetery at Overland Park, as No. 40 enters St. Louis, with a note pinned to it, asking that Mr. J.W. Jamison, a lifelong friend of Billie's, could identify the body, and that H.M. Kingsbury be notified. Details were hard to get, but I think they said the body with two shots through it, had not long been there. Request was made in the note that the body be cremated. Horace, Ernest and two close friends of Billie's have gone to St. Louis. None of the rest of the family will go. The remains or ashes will be returned to Boonville. I do not know what disposition will be made of them.

Mother and Father are bearing up bravely. We are all crushed, but we have been so fortunate through the years. I feel we can only accept this blow in a humble spirit or else be ungrateful for the blessings of the years. All of Billie's children will be home as quickly as transportation can bring them. Julia is wonderfully brave. I think she has feared something like this for a long time.

April 9, 1932:

Dear Cousin Lillian,

An envelope addressed to Horace, mailed from St. Louis, came this morning. It enclosed a parking garage check for Billie's car which Horace and the others had been unable to locate.

There was a short service at the crematory this morning at 11 o'clock attended by Horace, William, and a few close family friends.

It is still undecided just when burial services will be. If there is a service, it will be the Episcopal as Bill would like it, and Billie always thought that burial service was fitting. He didn't care for music at funerals and there will be none. Service, if held, will be at our home. Julia feels she would like to place his ashes in Mount Pleasant, as the lot used to be a part of the farm which Billie always loved. No service before Monday. And then only for family and closest friends.

Father feels terrible and when I came to town a while ago he had gone to bed. We had tried to comfort him with the thought that Billie's mental suffering is all over, but Dad says, "Mine isn't." We know the sympathy of the community is with us for sake of the parents if nothing else.

April 13, 1932:

Dear Cousin Lillian,

And the world goes on! The wheels of our mentalities have spun so fast lately it seems weeks must have elapsed. But we have nothing to do now except settle down to normalcy as much as possible and adjust ourselves to the living without dear old Billie.

Major Irvine was in St. Louis on business Monday and phoned he would bring Billie's ashes as he returned that evening. I suppose you will be interested in every detail which I can think of to enumerate. I don't know why it is so long before the ashes can be sent out after the service which precedes the cremation. They come in a rectangular copper box, 5 x 5 x 9. On one end was engraved the name and date, April 9, 1932. I don't know whether that was to indicate the day of death or date of cremation. He died on the 8th. If it was in error, I kept it to myself, thinking nobody else noticed it. While it makes no difference, I always feel if a date is of any consequence at all in a case of this kind, it should be correct.

William placed the receptacle on top of the desk in the

northeast corner of the parlor. There it reposed until yesterday
afternoon. Some men and women who had just buried their
mother that afternoon had brought in a large hydrangea with
pink blossoms and this was placed on the desk also. On the back
of the piano I had placed a large decoration of redbuds with a
few of the richest peach blossoms I ever saw, and it made that
corner very attractive. Elsewhere in the house we used the spring
garden flowers, narcissi and jonquils. We all live so close together
we were in and out of the home constantly. Julia got so tired of
seeing callers in Boonville that she found relief in coming over to
our house.

Yesterday, all our family were present at noon. The sisters-in-
law brought in and served lunch of ham sandwiches, fruit salad,
watermelon and crabapple pickle, stuffed eggs, coffee, custard
and cake. It was just the same kind of old family party except...
Billie was absent. Not another person but family was present. We
had all thought perhaps we wouldn't feel like eating anything,
but you know what good cooks the girls are, and the food was
most tempting. It seemed a long afternoon when most of us were
not able to sit down for long, nor could we find satisfaction in
walking about. The whole family just shifted around from place
to place in the house and yard except Father and Horace, who
sat in the latter's car and talked the whole time.

In the morning while I was downtown, Rosie and Margaret
found Mother leaning over the little copper box crying her heart
out and saying she just wanted to hold it in her lap. Of course,
there was no reason why she shouldn't and she did. It was a
comfort to her. She heard Father coming into the house and told
them to take it and put it back as she wouldn't have him seeing
her for anything. When the hour came to go over to the cemetery, she asked Horace if she could carry it over there and he told
her "of course you can." I knew Julia desired to do the same
thing, and it was all planned she should. They told me to iron
out the situation. I went in and heard Mother telling Father they
were going to let her carry the box to the cemetery and asking
him if he didn't think that was nice of them. Mother was looking

so pleased, I could hardly tell her Julia wanted to do the same thing, but I did and was pleased when Mother said, "Of course she should." And after Julia and William got in the car to go, I carried the little box out and gave it to them and the procession started.

The lot to which the ashes were committed is right on the driveway, so they stopped the car with Mother and Father in it immediately beside the spot. Father wanted to get out, but finally was persuaded to stay inside.

The place prepared for the box was simply the base upon which will be placed a modest marker. A space for the box was prepared inside the base and a blanket of pink roses, pinkish brown snapdragons and different shaded pyrethus, not very large, perhaps four feet by three, was spread out over it. As the undertaker advanced with his little box, his assistant folded back a part of the flowers so the ashes could be put in place. The flowers fell back in place, and Rev. Gregg used the shortest service he knew. He delivered it very eloquently and I liked it very much.

In spite of the fact it was a private service, there were a great many people and we were glad to have them, or anyone who felt really impelled by love for Billie to come. Julia had said she wanted just his immediate friends and I told her that would include quite a large circle, for there were people who were his friends of whom we knew little. We have learned as the days have passed, people have said Billie had done this or that for them.

Everybody came back to the house, but all of Julia's family returned to Boonville late in the afternoon. I think all of the others stayed for supper and dwindled away gradually until nine o'clock when we went to bed feeling like we had been beaten over the shoulders with a club.

Mother said this morning she and Father felt more reconciled, and I believe all of us are going to be able to get up before the "count of ten" and fight the second round. For a lot of us this is the first round with sorrow we have had.

A safety box, with the name Kingsbury and Meistrel on it was found under the bed in a room at a motel on Highway 66,

30 miles west of Kirkwood, a suburb of St. Louis. Sheriff Groom and a young attorney named Martin went down to recover it. They found it empty except for three documents which were under a secret flap, and in the stove in the room there were charred remains of papers, a few unburned edges indicating the papers were of a legal nature.

From Jefferson City, Billie had mailed a dollar bill to a girl friend of Julia's, who had done some stenographic work for him in Boonville a few days previous. He was fond of her and she of him and she was just crushed to have received it from him in that way. He mailed some sort of paper to Albert Smith [*a cousin*] and a purse containing some money to Judge Fisher, Leo's father-in-law. This was money which belonged to the Meistrell children from sales of the Saturday Evening Post. No doubt Leo had pitched it in the box and Billie found it and returned it. Presumably everything in the box was burned except the three concealed items. Obviously, Billie felt Leo had cheated him and would proceed to cheat others who had dealt with them as partners.

Surely something must have arisen of great provocation to Billie. There had been a failure on Leo's part to live up to the agreement of last August to care for certain obligations he was assuming. Such a lot we don't know and can't understand, but Billie was a fine man. I have always been proud of him and I am proud of him yet. Think what a man he was to have the courage to go through with his suicide after all these hours following Leo's removal from this planet.

Stops in Jefferson City to go through Leo's deposit box and return certain things, doubtless a sorting of the papers at the motel, where he arrived at 1 a.m. and remained until 7 a.m. He arrived at the St. Louis downtown garage, where he parked the car at six after ten, got the check for it and mailed it back to Horace, then took a street car, from which he had to transfer to the Wellston Line leading to Valhalla, and the remainder of the time was consumed in the ride to that destination. At the Boonville filling station where he had his car serviced, at the motel near St. Louis, and at the garage, the attendants noted nothing a bit unusual about him. I can almost see him dropping off the car at the Valhalla entrance and walking briskly along to the great sycamore tree under which he passed into the great unknown, about 200 feet from the gate.

I wonder if Billie didn't have the old Viking legends in mind when he planned all this avenging destruction by fire and entrance to Valhalla.

When he was missing last Friday morning, Mother cried and prayed he might be spared the sufferings which would be involved if he was apprehended. He did not finish the job any too soon, for people would have begun to look for him as soon as the broadcast of nine o'clock became generally known. And by the time he was leaving the car at the garage, requests for his arrest were being radioed.

Well, he was a sweet old thing, and we shall miss him; but if he were terribly unhappy in this life, perhaps it is well it is all over...

I wouldn't feel free to send this sort of detailed letter to anyone except the dearest to us. I felt the exhibitions of mother love were almost too sacred to mention, but you are such an understanding person.

This was Billie's note:

"Have no regrets except for family - all of whom I love dearly. This is the first time my mind has been clear for months. I could feel myself slipping and I do not care to be a drooling lunatic on my family's hands regardless of their affection for me.

"Julia certainly deserved better than this for she was all that could be asked of a wife and more. If I had only listened to her, Leo would never have had a chance to put me where he did. So I square my account with him and take mine. I thought he was afraid to cheat me. I was wrong. He thought I was afraid to kill him. He was wrong.

"Am not writing Julia or any of the children. There is nothing to say which could do any good and I can't say I would not do it again under the same conditions. Will mail receipt for car which is to go to Jere, with his mother's consent."

Chapter Two

YOUR GOLDEN YEARS
I'LL SPEND WITH YOU

On the day of their wedding, April 21, 1872, Robert Taylor Kingsbury carried his bride, Alice Virginia Smith, across the threshold of Fairview, the comfortable big home built by slaves in 1833. The place was a wedding present from his father, Dr. Horace Kingsbury. Soon after, Taylor, as he was commonly known, planted the first commercial apple orchard in Missouri. All seven of their children were born there. Throughout their 50 years of marriage, Fairview had been a happy home free from tragedy and crisis, filled with joyous memories of their growing family, friends and relatives who frequently gathered to celebrate holidays and special occasions.

Fairview was a mile north of New Franklin, the shopping center for those farming the rich Boonslick Country heartland. The town of about 1600 was on a rising slope up from the Missouri River about three miles away. Looking south across the bottom land and the river, one could see Boonville, a town of about 4500 stimulated by riverboat traffic. To get there, one crossed the river by ferry or rode the Missouri, Kansas and Texas Railroad over the bridge.

Lilburn was 38 at the time of his parents' 50th wedding anniversary in 1922. He usually walked a mile south into New Franklin where he was cashier and manager of the Bank of New Franklin. He also had an insurance agency and was active in church and community affairs. A personable, interesting bachelor, he never lacked attractive feminine companionship.

Bank work was keeping him busy. The directors decided to build a new bank building. This and responsibility assumed for promoting and making loans and attracting new depositors ignited his interest in banking.

He spent less time at Fairview. When he told his parents the demands of his work might better be met if he moved to town, it brought a tearful session with his mother. She tearfully lamented, "All your brothers and sisters have gone off and left us. And now you're going to desert us and we'll be all alone in this big house. What will we do?" This so moved Lilburn he vowed he would never abandon them. Their well-being was much on his mind - something needed to be discussed with his siblings after the golden wedding party was over.

Prior to taking major responsibility for planning the golden wedding party, Lilburn, although a loving son, respecting and honoring his parents, had lived a rather fancy-free existence. Both parents idolized him and gave him the run of their comfortable, pleasant home. He had given little thought to the mortality of his parents, taking their continued presence at Fairview as a given.

A golden wedding celebration was indeed a special occasion! Lilburn, the only unmarried child, living at home, undertook to see it was.

On March 7, 1922 Lilburn wrote his Cousin Lillian Kingsbury Agnew of Great Falls, Montana, alerting her and numerous Montana relatives of the golden wedding celebration being planned for his parents.

"Father and Mother are going to have a big party on April 21 to celebrate their golden anniversary, and I hereby extend all of you an invitation to come in for the event, and all accompanying activities. We have not decided on the nature of the affair, except it will be quite a public affair, with everybody invited and no presents. We will have to get our heads together from now on to get all the plans made and effected by that time."

All the children and grandchildren, many relatives and friends were present. One of Grandfather's brothers, Adkin, a prominent Montana rancher who was later honored by being named one of the state's two representatives in the National Cowboy Hall of Fame, and his daughter, Mary, came out for the event.

On May 9, 1922, Lilburn wrote his Cousin Lillian:

"I am sending you a newspaper account of the golden wedding. I have intended doing this sooner, but not until today did I get down to the office for the papers. Ever since Uncle [Adkins Kingsbury] and Mary and Anna Rose and the others came, I have been going, stretched out, on the gay, good-time race track. We haven't had a nickel's worth of sleep. I am exhausted, but hope to recuperate in a day or so by getting a few nights' sound sleep. There hasn't been anything special to do here, but always some place for us young'uns to go and get home late."

CELEBRATE GOLDEN WEDDING ANNIVERSARY

New Franklin News - April 30, 1922:

A day so fair that even fairies could not complain of the loveliness; an old gray brick home surrounded by budding maples; a flowering orchard of pink and white blossoms to the south; waving fields of young wheat and grass to the west, and the old cemetery to the east, added a touch of sacredness and holiness to the occasion - that was the picture one looked upon as they drove to the home of Mr. and Mrs. R.T. Kingsbury last Friday afternoon to participate in the Golden Wedding Anniversary celebration of this highly-respected couple of southern Howard County.

Robert Taylor and Alice Kingsbury at their 50th Wedding Anniversary

Nothing could have brought more happiness to friends and relatives than that day. Fifty years of wedded life, not all sunshine, but so much happiness that it made each one glad to press the hands and kiss the lips of these good people, who along the downward path never failed to help the less fortunate, and who have always lived near their God and found all things well. They are now looking toward the sunset of life, their cares are behind them, but by their presence, true reflections of upright Christian characters, they have helped make the community a better place in which to live.

The old house on this day was at its loveliest. The spacious old rooms with their soft light, abundance of cut flowers, the dining room table (the most attractive of all) with the large wedding cake surrounded by 50 lighted candles, the mingling together of the sons, daughters, grandchildren, relatives and many friends of the bride and groom of 50 years was an occasion long to be remembered.

Mr. and Mrs. Kingsbury are lifelong residents of southern Howard County, their birth places being only a few miles from their present home. They have seven children, five boys and two daughters, all of whom returned to the 'old nest' for this most joyous occasion. They have every right to be justly proud of these children.

Horace M., the eldest, is one of the best known and success-ful (now retired) farmers of Howard County.

The second son, William Wallace, has long been a promi-nent banker and influential citizen of Boonville.

Ernest, the third son, is a prominent and well-to-do citizen of Omaha, Nebraska.

Robert, the fourth son, is a prominent farmer and fruit-grower, his farm adjoining the home place; while Lilburn, the youngest son, is one of our bankers who has played an important role in modernizing banking business in this city.

The oldest daughter, Lillian, is the wife of C.A. Edmonston of New Franklin, and is socially prominent in community activ-ities.

The baby of the family, Anna Rose, is the wife of Will Darneal, a successful businessman in Richmond, Missouri.

About 200 guests were assembled for the occasion and the program was very informal, just as Mr. and Mrs. Kingsbury wanted it to be. The afternoon was spent in social communion, and the renewing of old acquaintances, intermingled with many musical selections rendered by the Culley Orchestra of Boonville. Delicious refreshments were served from the dining room throughout the afternoon.

We congratulate them upon having attained the coveted station in holy wedlock, so often viewed from afar, but so seldom realized. With their present good health, the family chain still unbroken, and bright prospects for many more happy years, they indeed have much for which to be thankful. Their lot is an exception and would it be out of place for us to say, that payment for work well done and faithful servants, has begun on this, the earthly kingdom, while most of us have hopes only in the great beyond."

Lilburn's letter continues . . .

As a hearty eating Kingsbury, I'm sure you wish to know about the refreshments.

We served white brick ice cream with yellow heart in the center - heart of apricot ice - individual cakes iced with yellow icing flavored with orange peel. We engaged a five-piece orchestra with a woman singer. While they are a regular jazz orchestra, besides a lot of jazz, I had them play "Kiss Me Again," "Oh Promise Me," "Mother MaCree," and things like that. The vocalist sang the old song about Maggie, "Silver Threads Among the Gold," "Carry Me Back," etc.

We had no ceremony - no eulogizing remarks from anybody. It was just sort of an "open house."

AFTER THE PARTY WAS OVER

It was not long after house guests departed that life at Fairview resumed its normal living patterns. But soon Alice and Taylor's children and their spouses began discussing how best to assure their elders might live out their lives comfortably in their beloved home.

Discussions culminated in agreement as follows:

1. Lilburn would continue living at Fairview.

2. Lilburn would assume responsibility for supervisory management of the orchard/farm.

3. Lilburn would monitor his parents' well-being and provide for their needs - using income from the orchard/farm for that purpose and any improvements in the property he thought necessary.

4. In return, siblings and spouses agreed to waive any claim upon the property.

5. At the death of both Alice and Taylor, Fairview would become Lilburn's "free and clear."

To Carry Out This Agreement:

1. He had to find and keep a watchful eye on "live-in-help" to do most of the cooking and cleaning.

2. Employ a farmer to live in the tenant cottage and work with the other farm hands.

3. Begin refurbishing the house and grounds so they would be what he wished when the property became his.

GENESIS OF LETTER-WRITING HOBBY

With these responsibilities added to the growing pressures of his banking, insurance and church obligations he continued writing to relatives. In a Lilburn Says column written in 1972 for the Boonville Daily News, he gives the genesis of this hobby:

For more than 80 years my palm has itched to write and receive letters. Scratching it has afforded me immeasurable pleasure.

It began during the romantic days of high school. A young girl classmate and I, though we had never dated, had come to an agreement that we would pretend we were Lord and Lady Earl of English royalty. Of course, there were official edicts I had to communicate to my lady which had to be delivered during school sessions by couriers in seats which separated us. The thrill of doing this was increased by the risk of having our messages intercepted by the teacher.

In 1901, it was no bother for me to walk a mile daily to and from Estill, our post office, to get a letter from and mail one to the prettiest girl in the world who had visited in New Franklin, but now lived 150 cruel miles from me. Old Mr. Grider, clerk in the Tutt store where the post office was in the back corner, used to welcome me at the door to gladden or sadden me - "It's here" or "She done forgot you today." . . .

He goes on to tell of fascinating female correspondents developed in London, Paris and across the United States. He concludes:

"If I ever fail to get letters, I think I shall die."

Lilburn knew, to get letters, he had to write letters. This he did diligently - especially in these years to his Cousin Lillian Agnew. In them, he tells of some new hobby-horses he had saddled, bridled and on which he had galloped away.

One of the first things Lilburn did was to get live-in help. This resulted in employment of Mary Kuhne, a deaf mute woman of about 30. Lilburn wrote of her to his Cousin Lillian as follows:

Mother and Father have been pretty well since the first of the year except for colds. Our girl hired as live-in cook and maid gets better all the time and Mother often laughs after breakfast and says, "She has such a hard day ahead of her." Then Father giggles and says he has too. They spend the day reading, sewing, and picking out nuts, sleeping and just having a good time resting.

Mary Kuhne keeps the house well and Mother has taught her to enunciate quite a number of words. I am sure if one devoted a lot of time to Mary she could be made to speak. She is devoted to Mother and whenever she writes to know anything about Father, calls him "Papa." We feel like we have a jewel.

Lilburn paid increasing attention to making Fairview what he visioned it being when it became his. He quickly began redecorating the place and replacing the furniture with early American antiques. Collecting these antiques was just becoming fashionable in Boonslick Country. Most of the beds, tables, chairs and chests which had been brought from Virginia or Kentucky, or crafted by the skilled woodworkers emigrating into the community, had been sold off years before or given to the Negro help. Much of it at the time was adorning their shanties. Lilburn wrote Lillian Agnew about the new hobby-horse he was riding.

GETTING THE OLD FURNITURE BUG

I don't believe I have written about getting the old furniture bug. I used to laugh at Henry Tindall [*a cousin living in Fayette*] and Sister Julia and everybody else who cared for the old stuff, but one day I bought a piece of it, got varnish remover, and reduced the wood to its natural finish, then refinished it with satin finish and it looked so good, I decided to furnish a room.

I found a double and a single Jenny Lind bed, both beauties which I had a professional workman finish. Then I traded for the pieces of another one and used the turned pieces and the spindles in having a table and window bench made. I cut up more of the spindles and used them to ornament the top and bottom of a screen made of walnut panels. Then old Mr. Furniture Man gave me a foot stool, and I picked up some attractive old chairs, all the little stuff, and an old dresser which I found in Moberly at a second-hand store. The little table I had made has a pedestal which came from wood out of our house when we remodeled. The spindles are from a bed brought from Virginia and the top came from the shelf in Grandfather Kingsbury's old desk. I have found some attractive old picture frames in which I have put prints from old-fashioned pictures. You must have surmised by now that my "stuff" must have over-flowed into another room.

My prize piece is a chest of drawers about 85 years old, of cherry and walnut with ash veneer trimming and glass knobs which I found in Warren County, at the home of a spinster, with whom I have been corresponding in the hope of purchasing more of her things.

Lilburn in his Fairview parlor with some of his antique furniture

Pretty soon I will have the house done over to match the period in which it was built, providing Mother does not pitch me and some of my old stuff, out into the yard. I have had an electric light made using old-fashioned prisms, and also two tall brass candle-sticks which have been adorned with a collar of brass from which to suspend prisms. These are especially attractive. That is how I have spent a good many evenings since the new year. The second room I have started to fix up is to have burnt orange and black draperies and trimmings and will be real gay, festive and loud. After I get these rooms fitted up, I will call them "The Trap," for with them, maybe I can catch a girl. . . .

I'll try to keep you posted on how we're progressing. This year we thought of putting down hardwood - but it is so expensive. I decided I'd see what kind of floor we had down under the paint. So one rainy day, I didn't go to the bank, but got lye and went to work on the front hall. It's about 20 x 6 and I found it a terrible job. Took me about eight hours and by then I didn't have any legs or back left for comfort. The floors in this house are of ash and such a pretty grain. I've just put a coat of shellac on the hall floor tonight, and when it dries, it'll be ready to wax.

A *bedroom in Fairview, the Kingsbury home in New Franklin, Missouri*

In mid-summer, he wrote his cousin:

It's been about all I can do, moving things along at home, and looking after a bank, but just lately my date and I have been going swimming some and "progueing" around at night. This I enjoy and at such times I forget my age and responsibilities.

We had a wonderful drive Sunday evening across the hills to Boonsboro, then on to Lisbon, arriving there just about sunset. Then we came back along the bluffs and watched the sunset reflection in the river. We watched the bright colors fade and the stars come out. And the whippoorwills calling and the frogs singing and the high water splashing against the rocks below, and millions of fireflies lighting the cliffs and woods above us. It was like a dream spot, and we stayed so late, we surely had to "whip up" to get home by midnight. We wished for a stop watch so we could have more time. Now that sounds like serious doings, but coming from me, just pass on over it. I never heard wedding bells ringing up there on the river. But to me, it is the most beautiful spot in the country and I enjoy it as does anybody else with a love of nature. It was so nice Sunday evening I have asked the same girl to go back there with me.

As manager of the bank, Lilburn found himself faced with fore-closing on the Clark Store whose terminally ill owner could no longer manage. Lilburn's store-owning brother-in-law assured Lilburn it could become a successful operation. So, in addition to his other banking responsibilities, insurance business and supervision of the orchard/farm, Lilburn found himself running the store.

Public response to his management was so ego-satisfying that he bought it from the bank and gave it the Kingsbury name. He thought this might provide the escape from the bank he was seeking.

It took little more than a year for his ego to be fully satiated with store involvement. He felt fenced in, unable to find time to ride his hobbies.

NOT BORN TO PULL BOLTS OF GOODS FROM SHELVES

The New Franklin News *of September 26, 1924 announced:*

"Mr. Kingsbury is closing out his store because of other interests which require his entire time."

That wasn't the whole truth, Lilburn told me late in life when I asked him about his experience as a merchant. He said he always had interests to which he wished to devote his entire time but that he soon found the store wasn't one of them. He went on to say:

I discovered I had not been born to the art of pulling bolts of cloth from shelves for discriminating women and then putting them back in place only to have to repeat the performance for another customer.

I couldn't become accustomed to seeing the latest styles of ladies fashionably trimmed hats tried on by women who punished them by pulling a brim up or down trying to make it attractive to their faces. I grew weary of women trying on dress after dress and more often than not leaving the store without buying a thing or even saying, "thank you."

The News *story continued:*

"The entire stock of the Kingsbury Store will be placed on sale in a Quit Business Sale. It is arousing county-wide attention and will no doubt attract people by the hundreds. The people of South Howard County particularly know the goods are fresh stocks offering bargains seldom found in a close out sale.

"Besides the usual and far-reaching reductions ample in themselves to attract hundreds of shoppers, a contest will be inaugurated and many valuable prizes will be awarded during the sale. New stunts will be introduced every few days that will be of great interest. Mr. Kingsbury says this is positively a quit business sale and the big selling event will continue until everything is disposed of."

The following week's News *(October 3, 1924) carried this story:*

"The Quit Business Sale of the Kingsbury store continues to be the talk of the Town and Country and the store is filled daily with eager shoppers.

"Interest is kept at fever heat by the new and unusual stunts concluding with the giving of some useful, worthwhile prizes. Contestants working in the sale for the 10 capital prizes offered by the store at the conclusion of the sale are all distinguishing themselves as hard workers seeking patronage for the store with the hope of securing votes to win some worthwhile prize.

"Wednesday, October 1 was registration day and a great day for the Rustlers, as the contestants were called. Every person registering at the store had 1000 votes to give one of the contestants and every mile one came (up to 30 miles) in order to register, counted another 1000 votes. People were registering from New York, West Virginia, Colorado, Michigan, Kansas, Indiana, Illinois and Iowa. The Rustlers were even waylaying tourists passing through."

The end of the sale was reported on October 17, 1924:

"The Kingsbury Quit Business Sale closed at 3 o'clock this afternoon, every article in the big stock of ladies wear, dry good and gents furnishings having been sold.

"The sale in many respects was the most unique ever held in this section of the country. What contributed more than anything to the complete success of the sale was the interest in buying caused by the Rustlers' Club who were competing for the 10 capital prizes. [First prize was a diamond ring; second, a handsome cedar chest.]

"Of all the stunts, the most interesting was the giving away of the "real live white baby" on Wednesday of this week. It was the talk of the town and at 9:30 of that evening the store and street were blocked with people eager to see the baby and the winner. The doubt among some and curiosity among others as to whether or not a real baby would be given away only added to the interest and the award offered much amusement.

"The baby proved to be a small white pig all dressed up in baby clothes and was won by Mrs. Margaret Robinson.

"With the closing today of its doors, the Kingsbury Store passed out of existence in this city, a fact much regretted by the many friends of the store throughout the Boonslick Country."

When Lilburn and I were discussing his store, I asked him if he had any regrets about closing it. He closed his eyes, pressed the palms of his hands to his cheeks, and was silent, apparently in deep reflection. Then he opened his eyes, dropped his hands, looked roguishly at me, grinned and said,

"Well, yes. I wish now, I'd promised to give away 'two real live babies - one white pig - one black - but that was before desegregation."

ESTABLISHING AN OFFICE

Shortly afterwards, to devote more time to his parents and orchard/farm operations, Lilburn left the bank. He bought the building across the street vacated by the Citizens' Bank when it merged with the Bank of New Franklin. There, he established an office he maintained until his death in 1983. From it, he serviced his insurance customers, handled the Fairview records, stored many of his collectibles, and kept his genealogical and historical records. Unless he was away on a trip, he tried each day to spend some time in his office. These two moves enabled him to fulfill the commitment made to his brothers and sisters of looking after the well-being of their parents.

Lilburn's office in New Franklin

On October 3, 1925 Lilburn wrote Lillian Agnew about this:

The hot days of September played havoc with the Jonathan and other fall apples, preventing them from coloring and they nearly all fell off onto the ground. The winter varieties are falling so badly we are having a terrible waste in harvesting the crop...

I am still antiquing around. These last few weeks, I have added a mahogany table, a mahogany dresser, and the quaintest old brass lamp you can imagine to my collection. Am having the old lamp wired for electricity so its appearance will not be changed. The mahogany furniture has such lovely crochet designs on it. Then I had some footstools made, but instead of a cross-stitch top, I am using a hooked woolen top."

Paralleling Lilburn's interest in furnishing Fairview's interior with antique furniture, glass and china was a desire to embellish the surroundings of the old home. In the text of a talk he gave in 1977 to a Boonville Garden Club, he wrote:

There was a time, 45 years ago, when I was just as enthusiastic and devout a gardener as you are. I was making a formal garden (60 x 20) at one side of my house. There was a large bed in the center with rock walks from three sides to and around it. The walks were bordered with jonquils. As much as possible, I planted perennial flowers: lilies, delphinium, poppies, gaillardia, hollyhocks and iris. Highly esteemed were the "starts" which garden-minded friends gave me to "homestead" a claim on my garden. It was beautiful in its formality for many years - but how informal it is now!

In 1925, the road past my home was christened No. 5 and a concrete road was built. To widen it, they cut off a part of our front yard. They left a terrace across the front, a deep bare surface which seemed unsightly. I conceived the idea of planting iris on that terrace to spell out the name "Kingsbury" using a different variety for each letter, arranging them as much as possible so the colors would harmonize.

It made a beautiful display for years, and people had no trouble finding where the Kingsburys lived.

A GOLDEN YEAR GALLOP

The winter of '26 - '27 was a severe one. Lilburn's parents had resisted Lilburn's attempts to persuade them to go to Florida, where they might get out and around. Spring brightened their lives. Their health improved. They became restless and "put their goin' shoes on." With Lilburn as the chauffeur and his sister Lillian along for the ride, off they went. Lilburn wrote of their "wild ride" to his Cousin Lillian on July 20, 1927.

We have been back home 10 days from that wild ride through Missouri and Arkansas. Toward the last days it became a hurried and distressing trip, but now that all of the wrinkles put in us have been ironed out, we are inclined to renege on our oath that we would never go again, and have even expressed the hope we may yet get to Niagara Falls. In Memphis, mother said she could not eat fresh peaches, for they always "just ruined her." But not many hours later, when I brought some fresh peaches to our room at the hotel, she proceeded to eat two of them. When we got started on our way in the afternoon, she was seized with awful griping.

We were carrying a bottle of Chamberlain's Colic Cure with us and I gave her the prescribed dose for an adult. It was good for her in a way, but she declared I had given her too much, for her stomach burned so badly, she continued to feel quite miserable. We were headed for Sikeston, Missouri, 157 miles and we had a good trip, but ran into a wind and rain storm which worried mother terribly. We pressed on to Sikeston where we intended to rest a day or two and give her a chance to recuperate.

But we were not destined to remain in Sikeston long. We arrived at 8 p.m. and at 6 a.m. mother was up, as was father, and was clamoring to ride on so she could get home as quickly as possible. She looked just awful and was so hot we all knew she had fever, but she wouldn't listen to reason, and we thought it might make matters worse to use force, so away we went, rushing to get the 155 miles to St. Louis in time for her and father to catch a train which would get them home a little quicker than we could drive the distance. Mother was complaining of such pain, we figured a Pullman would be much easier on her. By the time we arrived in St. Louis, I knew she was in no condition to go on a train or anything else, so we just went to a hotel and remained until she was better. The following day, after a good rain in the night, we had a lovely cool day and availed ourselves of it to drive on home and she stood the trip nicely and has been resting and improving ever since.

Father was like castor oil to the rest of us. We would not get to bed at one place before he would have us passing on to the next. Always up by seven and ready for me to drive the car around and load up. And if we made our allotted daily distance in good time he would see no reason why we could not go on to the next big town, 60 or 70 miles further, provided the roads were reported good.

When we got to Hot Springs, the rest of us just struck on him and said we were settled for at least three days, when he said just after we got up to our rooms, "Well, I have seen all of Hot Springs I care to see for a while."

The rest of us enjoyed everything there and have decided it would be a nice place to spend time in the winter, the busy season. It is a town with a permanent population of 16,000 which has accommodation for 25,000 visitors. It had one long crooked main street, and the $12 million worth of bath houses are all in a row on same. There are foreign shops like one sees in Los Angeles and San Francisco, and hotels and cafes by the hundreds. We liked the water very much. There are some 50 springs but the mineral content of the water varies so little in any of them that the difference is negligible. Some of the water is 172 degrees hot, and is drinkable though too hot to hold your hand in.

Our next stopping place of any importance was Memphis, though we did spend a night in Morrillton and went out to see the nurse who had taken such good care of father in the Boonville Hospital. There we found three of the old Boonville nurses and they chatted and took on over dad and seemed very glad to see us. They had gone down there to open up a hospital. We were located so nicely in Memphis that I was hopeful father would catch the like-it from me.

Before we had enough of Memphis, dad decreed we should move on. Next time he wants to take a trip, we shall get him connected with some passing band of gypsies. He thrived on the trip, apparently has regained his customary weight and looks fine. I think he could have gone on indefinitely, provided we did not stop anywhere long. But since he has been home, he has complained of some abrupt shortness of breath when he exercises. This is probably due to excessively high temperatures, as our weather has been pretty warm.

Since I have been home, there has been the hay harvest and plenty of other things to do, some of which are done; some are not.

Chapter Three

STUBBORN AS A MULE?

In 1928 Missouri was known as the Mule Capital of the World. It was estimated the mule population was more than 500,000. The state's rugged mules were stubborn and in demand by the Spanish Army and the French Foreign Legion. The Barnet Mule company in East St. Louis did a thriving business of buying mules and selling them to those military bodies. They made five or six trips a year to Europe. The mules required caretakers. It became "the thing" for recent college graduates to sign on to tend mules on the long trip across the Atlantic.

My college roommate, Roy Basler and I were planning career changes in June when we heard about a trip starting from East St. Louis on July 1. The following weekend we were at my parents' home in Boonville talking with Lilburn, who was a visitor. Things were going well at Fairview. The live-in housekeeper/cook was seeing to his parents' needs. Neither was experiencing serious health problems. The farm foreman was experienced and competent. Lilburn's office secretary could look after his insurance business. Our excitement about the trip was contagious. Lilburn caught our enthusiasm and called Barnet. They were delighted to have him because of his experience working with mules.

Lilburn was then 43 years of age. He was not a handsome man but had an engaging personality. He was about six feet tall with reddish- brown wavy hair. He looked directly at you with bright, blue eyes. His friendly smile reached out and drew you to him. His handclasp was firm and dry. He spoke with a bit of a drawl that aroused interest and held attention. Physically, he was in excellent shape. The farmwork he did was enough to keep his muscles firm and his body trim. Perhaps the following excerpts from an unpublished Lilburn manuscript, based on the diary he kept will enlighten you as to just how stubborn a mule can be! Today (1998) you'll probably be unable to find one in the once "Mule Capital."

Three dozen young men were hired to tend the mules on the 21-day trip from Norfolk to Barcelona. I was the oldest of the group. Most were recent college graduates and had never done a day's work at hard labor in their lives. But they were lured by the promise of free transportation and $1 per day on the outbound voyage. They were yearning for adventure on the ocean and the romance of Spain's sunny towns and black-eyed senoritas. When we assembled for briefing in the Mule Company's offices, disillusionment began to set in.

It came in the person of Tobe Malone, a red-headed Irishman, powerfully robust, like a heavyweight boxer. He was dressed in a blue shirt, and moleskin britches. A heavy hickory cane hung over his arm. Red, as we called him, looked tough; he talked tough and we soon found he was as tough as his looks and talk. He briefed us on the responsibilities we had for our passengers. He had breezed in to where we were assembled and proclaimed: "Boys, this ain't goin' be no picnic we're embarkin' on. Work's goin' to be hard. When we get out to sea and have to get feed out of the hold, it's goin' to be hotter'n' hell. Your food's goin' to be plain, not what you're used to at home perhaps, but you won't starve to death. I've been over 23 times and ain't dead yet. Look at me!"

What we saw was a specimen of red-blooded manhood, two hundred and twenty pounds of it, hard as nails and not an ounce misplaced. Red's keen, blue eyes bespoke vigor; his jaw, determination.

"You'll have wooden bunks with straw mattresses and cotton blankets," he resumed. "Clean when you get 'em and comfortable, if not homelike. Ev'ry man's got to do his work, sick or well. Jus' cause you get seasick ain't no sign your mules is goin' hungry. I want you to get that good." He paused while his steady eyes swung over the group, impaling the edict into our consciousness.

"Any questions?" Red asked. One brave soul wondered, "When do we see the mules?"

Red grinned malevolently, and said, "Follow me." He gave a sweeping come-on sign with his right arm, turned and led us from the company meeting room onto the building's veranda. From there we looked out on the vast expanse of the East St. Louis stockyards. On a long siding, crowded into each of the 50 boxcars were 24 long-eared tail-switching, foot-stomping (mare-jackass progeny) Missouri mules. There were 1200 and it was a breathtaking, staggering sight.

With that, a buzz of questions were thrown at Red. "What do mules eat?" "How on earth do you feed a mule?" "Do mules bite?" "Do mules get seasick?" "How do you keep from getting kicked?" "What do you do with mule shit?" etc., etc., until Red beat on the veranda floor with his big, corked-handled cane and shouted "Silence!" You'll get your answers as we go along. Now I'll show you where you park your asses on the train."

Red led us to the long, impressive train parked in the nearby railroad siding. At the front were two huge diesel locomotives. Hooked behind were 50 bright red stock cars, each with its 24 mules. Then came a day coach, a diner, a Pullman, and a caboose. And who was to occupy the day coach? You're right, it was we "Muleteers" as we soon came to call ourselves. We dumped our knapsacks and duffel bags on the day coach seats and tried to reconcile ourselves to our lot. More than one muleteer wished he had never left home.

The long haul to Norfolk, while speedy, seemed endless. The engines shrieked through towns whose inhabitants gaped or waved at our speeding special which had right-of-way over all other traffic.

One unusual incident of the rail trip remains embedded in my mind. The train halted sometime after midnight to take on water at a tank in the vastness of the Tennessee Mountains. The silence after hours of pounding the rails was intense, unbroken even by the chirp of a cricket. Suddenly, from one of the stock cars came a loud bray - a roisterous "hee haw, hee haw, hee haw!" Whereupon 1199 other mules joined in the chorus of a stock-car prison song which reverberated from peak to peak. It was eerie and the sound rolled and echoed on and on. Never had I heard anything like it. I quivered all over.

Finally, the iron rails led the long train into a Norfolk ware-house at the wharf at which was moored a huge freighter, hungry for a cargo of mules. This was the Italian tramp steamer, Monar-co. She was a dirty old tramp from putting into the bottom hold thousands of tons of coal destined for Italy.

The joint ceremony of loading the mules, and initiating us into the mysteries of the Order of Muleteers, began at 5 p.m. on a broiling hot July 4th afternoon. We found loading 1200 mules on that old tub no Fourth of July picnic. A humidity of nearly 100 degrees didn't help.

As the first mules were run through a long narrow chute extending from boxcar to ship, they were haltered by hands which never before had touched a hard-tail and driven onward and upward over a long brow to the boat deck. From there, they were driven down other brows inside the ship and through long aisles to stalls where other green and tender hands grasped halter ropes and tied the beasts to breastboards.

The progress of the mules was hurried by a score of husky, half-naked sweaty black stevedores stationed along the chutes and aisles. They prodded the animals vigorously. They yelled and swore vociferously at every manifestation of stubbornness. Clatter of hooves on steel floors, shouts and curses of the stevedores and noisy commands of bosses filled the air. The beasts in their stalls, perplexed by strange sights and sounds, brayed and lambasted each other and rumpboards with their hooves. It was utter bed-lam.

We had to work in semi-darkness down on the mule decks, as we fastened halter latches, tied ropes to breastboards, and dodged nipping teeth of spiteful mules. The decks, with no cir-culation of air, seemed like inferno; the night, endless.

Seventeen hours after the first mule had been prodded up the runway, the last one was tied up. Then the ship blasted its depar-ture whistle, the lines were cast off, the tug boats nudged the ship from the pier and guided it through Hampton Roads and past Cape Henry's lightship out to the open sea.

We clambered down the stairs into our bunk room and fell

wearily into our wooden bunks with their lumpy straw mattress-es. Several hours later, into our deep sleep of exhaustion came a growing awareness we were not the only bunk occupants. Some-thing was biting and the bites caused intense itching. After a half hour or so of continuous scratching, some of us took our blan-kets up on deck, examined them closely with our flashlights to make sure they were free of bedbugs, and spread them out on the piled high bales of hay. There we slept until dawn, when Red aroused us for the day's work. First he gave us instructions in the use of the articles he gave each of us.

"This hand-axe is for cuttin' wire on hay bales and for general purposes," he said. "The bucket is for measurin' feed for the mules, for carrying water, for washin' yourself and your clothing, and, if the occasion arises, for bailin' urine and manure out the stalls in the hold. Each of you'd better put a mark on it so you will know it. Your mules are thirsty. Hook your trough over the breastboard as you work along the aisle and run water in with the hose line. Give 'em plenty, boys. Then fill up the aisles with hay. I'm countin' on you handlin' these mules like you would your own property, for better or worse 'til Barcelona do you part."

The decks below were stifling with animal heat. Sweat seemed to pour from every pore of my body. In a few minutes every thread of my clothes was wet. My feet squashed in my shoes, as if I had been wading in puddles. In desperation, I lifted the hose line from the trough and held it up so the water would pour down over my head and down my back. It was more than two hours before I had watered all my mules, broken hay out into the aisles and wearily clambered up to the deck for air. I was one of the first to emerge and hunt out the pump to wash my dirty, grimy body.

At six o'clock every morning the ship provided strangely flavored tea and hard tack for breakfast. But thanks to the gen-erosity of the Spanish Don importing many of the mules, this was augmented by corned beef or pork and beans, scrambled eggs, canned fruit, crackers and imitation jelly - delicacies de-signed to maintain our energy and sustain our morale. Happier muleteers, happier mules, was the idea.

At 11 a.m. the mess boy served the midday meal consisting of macaroni with a tomato-olive dressing, beef and potatoes or beans and sliced onions with spaghetti. Codfish (which the cook laid dry upon a slab of iron and beat vigorously with a heavy sledge hammer before putting the carcass to soak) was dished out to us on Tuesdays and Fridays.

The evening meal at 5 p.m. was a repetition of the noon menu with the addition of soup, which usually contained rice, bits of macaroni, and tripe. It was heavily flavored with garlic. Ancient hard tack with pinhole eyes veiled with cobwebs was plentiful. Often a man and a worm surprised one another sharpening their teeth on the same disk of whetstone bread.

Each of us was given a tin pie pan, a metal cup, a knife, fork and spoon for service at meal time. The bread line filed past the mess boy, who served rations from dishpans in the mess hall. When our food was dished out, Warren, Roy and I usually hunted out a bale of hay to sit for 15 or 20 minutes and compare indignities endured.

As the days passed, stiff, sore muscles, and blistered hands were the ripe "fruits of labor." The sun took its toll of tender skin. Groups gathered on the hay to share their complaints. We compared bruises on body and blows to pride. We shared our reactions to the sameness of the garlicky food, dirtiness of the ship, behavior of the mules and sadism of our bosses. Some of the language used was pungently profane. There was talk of mutiny but two of the group who had made previous trips on the Monarco speedily quelled it.

"Did you ever hear about the time the kid from New York refused to take a feedin' order and the boss smacked his face off?" asked one.

"Yes, And once I seen Red beat a feller in the face for a full half hour for sassin' him," replied the other.

"Did he go back to work then?" inquired the muleteer.

"You better believe it. And with one eye swoll clean shut for a couple of days. Meek as a lamb after that! Don't you guys think for a moment Red ain't man enough to handle you. Lord knows what he could do with that hickory cane."

Shifting the conversation to tragic happenings, the first veteran inquired, "Can you ever forget the trip when the feller got kicked in the head and killed by the so-called gentle mule?"

"God no!" replied the other. "He sure stepped on the gas and went to Kingdom Come in a hurry. It was ter'ble. Pulsatin' life one minute, cold death the next! But talk about horrors! Remember that God-awful storm? A wave that looked a hundred feet high washed across the open deck and knocked down all the hospital stalls like they're building up here now for mules. Some of the mules were killed outright. Some was washed overboard. A feller named Sim got caught 'neath the wreckage. He was mashed up fearful and after a day of horrible suffern' that poor devil's light just flickered out."

"What do they do with the dead on this boat?" asked the curious muleteer.

Red's assistant, who had joined us, answered: "Put 'em overboard, of course. There ain't nothing else to do with 'em. I've helped put four over myself."

"God!" gasped one of the youngest, pale-faced and shuddering. "That's terrible! I'd sure hate to see anything like that."

"Hell!" ejaculated the second boss. "Ain't nobody enjoys it, but I tell you there ain't nothin' else to do."

"Do you have any kind of funeral service?" another asked.

"Sure," rejoined the boss. "First we take the body and wrap it up good in a tarpaulin and tie weights to the head and feet, then lay it right up there on that cabin. The ship's engine stops. They bring out the little book and read a verse. Then we just shove the corpse off and splash, it's all over. The ship don't stop. It just keeps on driftin'. The reason they puts weights on is to make the body sink, though it won't go clean to the bottom. If they didn't put weights on the corpse it would float around on top of the water and look right neglectful."

The Monarco traveled the Southern route to better escape storms. It had no air-conditioning. The only fresh air to reach the

lower decks came through two wind-sails hung in the rigging
above the fore and aft deck hatch openings. The heavy canvas
sails were about 10 feet in diameter. Attached to each sail was a
canvas tube - 24 inches in diameter. The forward progress of the
ship forced air down the tube into the lower decks. As the ocean
air temperature was in the 90s, with high humidity, this provided
little relief. The combination of the summer heat and mule body
heat made the hold temperatures during the day well over 100
degrees.

This hot weather necessitated much extra labor. The heat
produced ailing mules, which had to be moved from the over-
heated decks to the hospital stalls constructed on the top deck.
I was one of the muleteers chosen to spend the time between
feedings at stall building. Others were ordered to prod, drag or
drive the hybrids from the lower decks to the top deck.

It was usually a difficult and spectacular task to move a
stubborn mule. The head boss, Red Malone, would slip a lariat
over the mule's head, grasp the rope in his powerful hands, and
leverage the pulling force against the resistance of the beast. If the
mule hesitated to move forward, Red hurled a crescendo of commands with the rapidity of a Gatling gun.

"Come here a lot of you fellers and swing onto the end of
the lariat," he bellowed. "Now! Pull her damn neck off! Get
behind her Jones! Take my cane! Get behind 'er and hit 'er with
the cane! Knock 'er hind end off! Lay it on 'er rump! Hit 'er! Five
dollars if you break the cane the next lick!"

Raining blow after blow on the rigid hindquarters of the
obstinate mule, Jones made a supreme effort to win the money,
but the cane held firm.

"Hit 'er again!" roared Red. "Lay it on her fast! Faster! Watch
out! She's getting ready to kick. Don't let 'er kick you! Your folk'll
never see you again. Watch out, man! She nearly got you!" Jones
ducked as the hoof whizzed within an inch of his head, and the
mule took off down the   aisle.

The weather cooled. In the stalls on the boat deck, several
dozen mules with white noses deep in metal troughs hooked over

breastboards in front of them, muzzled their oats contentedly.

During this period we were usually free for a couple of hours following lunch. Sometimes there were special assignments. All the water drunk by a mule doesn't emerge as perspiration. There were scuppers in the decks back at the ship walls. They were supposed to carry off the urine. But by the time we had been at sea for about ten days, some of the scuppers clogged up with straw and manure. An ankle deep pool of liquid formed in a depression of the deck. We called it "Lake Urine." The arising aroma would never be mistaken for Chanel #5!

Complaints from those working in that area caused Red to take action. He singled out the two muleteers he thought most sissified and gave them the onerous task of bailing Lake Urine. He sent them down to the mule deck with a couple of water buckets. Up on deck, he lowered a rope with a snap clasp at the end. One of the men standing ankle deep in urine would scoop up a bucket load, pass it to the other to snap into the clasp. Red then would pull it up, let one of us muleteers unsnap the bucket, carry it to the ship's rail and empty it overboard while another moved to Red's side. Occasionally, he would slop a little on us. I never heard him say "Pardon me." On this first bucketful, though, the two boys below, stood there - their faces turning upwards as their eyes followed the bucket up. About two thirds of the way, Red's grip on the rope slipped. He quickly pulled up on it and about half the bucket's contents showered down on the bailer-outers. Red had a devilish look of pleasure on his face as he laughed down at them. To me, the urine-drenched hair and faces were a pathetic sight. Imposing such indignities, however, was to Red, a joyous pastime.

But we did have our pleasant moments. Most of us were crossing the ocean for the first time. It was a new and delightful experience to be sleeping on top of stacked bailed hay on deck with only a star-studded sky for cover, seemingly close enough to tuck under one, watching the sky and moody sea by day and at night watching the luminous of the waves ahead of the ship. We were amazed when a misdirected school of flying fish landed on the deck.

Mules or no mules, the ocean was wonderful when one had time to consider it. At times it was like a lady, sitting serenely with folded hands in a chair and rocking gently. Again, like one writhing in the throes of epilepsy, foaming at the lips. The day winds whipped up the spray and played rainbows with it. Little flying fishes glided like tiny silver planes, then flopped abruptly into the water, as if engine trouble had developed.

And there was always a peaceful satisfaction in the evening, knowing there would be no more work until morning. With the quiet disturbed only by the swish, swish of waves against the ship, it was wonderful to lay on your blanket on the timothy hay, looking up and watching the shooting stars, the flying fish of the heavens.

One thing learned in working with my 35 mules that I hadn't discovered working with our farm mules was that each mule, like humans, is different. By the time our voyage ended, I was identifying characteristics in my mules which reminded me of people I knew. I named one mule Bob for a man in our church who was all smiles to your face, but loved to stab you in the back. His mule namesake opened his mouth smile-like but turn your back on him and he would nip you if he could. Another reddish colored mule I called Red for he seemed to snarl at me like our crew boss. I remember another that looked at me with soulful brown eyes like a girl I once went with named Virginia. This mule I called Ginger. She liked to have her head patted. I found myself telling my many frustrations to some of my more friendly animals. I thought sometimes I saw signs of sympathy.

So on we went, passing through the straits of Gibraltar and along the picturesque coast of Africa with its milk-white villages. A last feeding of corn and oats gave us a feeling of exultation not dampened by a squall of rain. Arching the sky, a marvelous rainbow reflected on the water and its brilliant colors reflected a circle, perfect except where the bow of the ship cut its circumference.

Oran, a great city of Algeria, was a gladsome sight as the ship glided into its harbor and was warped into its berth at the wharf. There, veiled white-robed women mingling with bronze-faced Algerian soldiers in dark blue jackets braided with red, baggy trousers and red fezzes, gave color to an animated picture. There were hybrid costumes, the offspring of American and African fashions. Old horses drew dilapidated phaetons and stanhopes of styles which disappeared from America decades ago. There were big two-wheeled carts drawn by small donkeys hitched tandem. A flute player with little children dancing at his heels. Fresh, interesting sights to my eyes.

Brown-faced men in flowing burnooses, with stout hickory canes, now recognized as the badge of muleteers, soon came alongside to officially receive two hundred mules which were bidden a glad God-speed as we helped run them off the ship.

Trotting briskly and turning their heads from side to side and braying at the strange sights of Africa, these four-legged Beau Gestes of Muledome disappeared over a hill to join the French Foreign Legion.

We were not permitted to go ashore, but the ship was swarmed upon by vendors with chocolates, luscious grapes, cakes, cigarettes, ice cream, wine and beer. After thousands of miles of travel deprived of such, we filled our bellies to near-bursting with tasty luxuries. We matched wits with Arabs in an improvised bazaar on deck until all of their delicacies were bought and the ship put to sea - headed for Barcelona.

Sportive porpoises had been leaping and racing ahead of the ship for several days. Ship-crew members had tried hard to spear one. Finally, one of the sailors, standing on an anchor at the bow, cast a harpoon successfully. His voice rose in an exultant cry. His fellow sailors ran forward excited, all talking at once. They grabbed the harpoon rope and swiftly hauled the big mammal up over the rail and onto the deck. It whistled its groans as the harpoon was cut from its body and flopped about until a sailor jumped astride its body and held it quiescent. He was loudly acclaimed as if his steed had been one of a sheik's wildest Arabians. A carnival spirit spread through the crew. One of them drew a long knife and cut the throat of the animal. Its blood gushed out. With deft hands, the porpoise was butchered, its meat to be hung up and dried, its fat to produce valuable oil. Its opened body revealed a flopping baby porpoise which the sailors nonchalantly cast unharmed into the sea. We watched transfixed!

One of our muleteers was horrified. "They oughtn't to have killed an expectant mother," he proclaimed indignantly.

Another speculated, "Why would they kill a porpoise anyway?" It isn't fit to eat and it's the only friend a sailor has. Why, on an English boat, they'd mob a man who would harm a porpoise."

"Why is it a sailor's friend?" another wanted to know.

"Well, when a body is drowned at sea," came the reply, "the porpoises keep nosing it along and nosing it along until it is tossed up on the beach."

That was our last evening before Barcelona. Our ship was cutting its way through the front yard of one of the Balearic Island sisters. This daughter of Spain, Ibiza, with her chalky peaks dominating expanses of open spaces dotted with scrub pine, looked like a raw-boned peasant clad in a dingy brown dress with spots of mildew. She appeared wan-faced, unsmiling and dreaming.

I couldn't help thinking the glories of the Mediterranean sky and water had been oversung by the poets. But as we watched the sun dip into the sea, the sky blazed with a marvel of indescribable colors. The sea shimmered with opalescent ripples as tiny as overlapping fish scales.

Ibiza, as if aware that strangers were within her gates, flushed with the excitement of choosing the most becoming gown in which to receive them. In the glow of sunset, one seemed to sense changes of expression and graceful movement as Ibiza mirrored herself in the sea and whimsically laid off draperies of pastel shades for those of smoke blue haze, which in turn were replaced with a robe of mauve. The raw-boned peasant stood transformed into a comely Spanish princess who graciously smiled a welcome to her country.

The sky smoked. The sea smiled. A muleteer smiled and said, "The whole blamed works has been so lovely I think I could just praise God and die, if Barcelona were not just over the horizon to the north."

AFTER THE MULES IN ITALY

'Lilburn Says'... a Boonville Daily News *column published February 17, 1975 tells something of his experiences in Italy while the Monarco was in dry dock in Genoa for two weeks.*

Rummaging in my archives the other day, I found a diary of my visits to Italy in 1938, the reward I enjoyed after nursing Missouri mules across the Atlantic to Spain.

From the diary addressed to a favorite "little bit of loveliness," here are some excerpts:

How I yearned for you at Tivoli (a few miles outside of Rome). You would have been delighted to visit the beautiful old Villa d'Este with its magnificent old cypress trees which have never lost their slender lines, its terraces of fountains, hundreds of them, all playing. The cardinals who lived there seemed to have had a flair for feminine figures in bronze with water sprouting from their breasts. One lady had 20 nipples, 16 of them functioning. There were water falls, swans in languid pools. And down the mountainside were grape arbors with luxurious leaves.

Renting a clip-clop [*horse-drawn carriage*] we drove through the little town of Tivoli and around the side and head of a canyon to the opposite side of it for a distant view of the fountains, waterfalls and vineyards. The tile stucco houses of Tivoli, tinted pink, green, buff and azure, crowned the mountain like a hat.

Near Tivoli are the ruins of Hadrian's villa. He was a Roman emperor who lived in the years 78 to 138. Its theaters, temples, baths, etc., are still in a fair state of preservation. Its cypress trees showed no signs of the ravages of the ages. They whispered in

sighs as the wind blew through them. I wished I could understand what tales they told.

In Florence we saw things at the art galleries until we were
pop-eyed and our legs threatened to collapse. Among others in
our party were maiden teachers, and an old man with a young
bride who couldn't understand why they didn't have electric fans
installed. Students pored over guidebooks, looked at the art, then
pored some more.

A fat woman always lagged behind the group but would
catch up just as the guide finished his explanation of a special
piece of art. He had just told us of a marble figure with a funny
head when she overtook us and inquired of him.

"Now, what does this big man represent?"

"Lady, he represents the river Nile and do you know what
these little figures all around him mean?"

"Well," she replied hesitantly, "let me see, they are - they are"

"Lady, I'll help you, they represent the tributaries of the Nile."

She beamed and exclaimed, "Oh, how marvelous!"

A lot of people were listlessly herded on through the galleries,
while others sat and said to the guide, "If there isn't anything
slightly special in the next gallery, I'll stay here until you come
back. The marble people around me here sure do look comfortable sitting or lying down in one place for awhile."

Venice, too, had charms for us, from gondolas to pastries. We
were directed to a pension (boarding house in the United States)
under the clock tower facing St. Mark's Square, the building
dating back to 1495. From its balcony one looked down upon
the Campanile, Doge's Palace at one end of the Square, and
shops and cafes with people enjoying meals or refreshments outside
along the sides and other end. And over all, thousands of pigeons
circling in flight or being fed on the pavement by the people. It
is advisable to carry an umbrella when you walk through the
square.

Our pension was entered from what we would call an alley
and required mounting a flight of 70 steps. It was conducted by
Mrs. Smith. (The name made us feel at home.) She was English

and had been there 44 years. She could switch gears and show speed in speaking many languages. We found ourselves among French, German and American tourists.

Dining country style at a long table, the last to get hold of a dish often got "leavings." One day we had fish and one of us didn't help himself to what was left, a head. Mrs. Smith noting that he had no fish, inquired, "Sir, don't you like fish?" Our disgruntled member replied, "Yes, but don't care especially for the head." "Well, sir, I'll see that you get a tail." She rushed to the kitchen and returned with some of the middle too.

The bathroom was equipped with a long tub of tin with only cold water which felt like it had run over ice. None of us ever took more than one bath and then we wished we had kept our clothes on. The walls and ceiling of the room were decorated so beautifully you wouldn't believe it.

We explored the canals of Venice a couple of hours on a moonlit night when gondola traffic was very heavy. There were small ones with only a young man serenading and loving his sweetheart. Other large ones were gaily decorated with flowers and torches and loaded to the guards with people as if it were a festive occasion with singing, stringed music and laughter. It was too romantic for us, so we disembarked at the Bridge of Sighs and wended our way back to Mrs. Smith's.

Regarding the home voyage on the Monarco, Lilburn wrote in his diary that although devoid of creature comforts, the old freighter did afford opportunity to witness many God-made wonders. A few diary entries follow:

After the first day and there have been twelve since, the ocean has been marvelous, the Atlantic putting to shame the Mediterranean at its smoothest. Since leaving Gibraltar we have sighted no land and only one ship. Nothing but water and sky and the geyser of a mighty whale. The days have been bright with occasional fleecy clouds which serve as a canopy for shade. There is always a comfortable breeze.

While the long trek homeward is griping some of the boys with so much time on their hands, to me it is most enjoyable to spend some time without a single responsibility. I lounge in my steamer chair which I bought in Algiers and read among other things, the "Autobiography of Cellini" and "The Romance of Leonardo da Vinci," each the artistic creator of so many beautiful things we saw in Italy.

Clouds have been wonderful today with their ever-changing shapes of animals, buildings and face profiles. The sea is calm except for a slight swell that rocks the ship as gently as if we were in a cradle. The sun is warm, the breeze balmy. Near noon as I stood at the rail, light was refracted by the water so I could look down at considerable depth and see schools of fish. Flying fish rise gracefully from the sea; some appear no bigger than a silver quarter and fly along like hydroplanes skimming the water until flop! they splash back as if their engines had stopped functioning.

INTO A HURRICANE

A belated ambition of mine was to cross the Atlantic on one of the great liners, the United States, the Queen Elizabeth or the Queen Mary in five days or less. But the nearest I ever came to it was to visit the Queen Elizabeth moored at the pier in New York.

I found myself thinking how different a trip in the lap of luxury would be from the one I took on a mule boat on which I spent twenty-one days going to Algiers, Spain and Italy and eighteen days coming back without so much luxury as a bed sheet for my bunk. But instead of enjoyment of all the creature comforts devised by man on a liner, the old Italian freighter *Monarco* did afford us opportunity and time to witness many God-made wonders.

I kept a diary in which I recorded indelible impressions while sailing on this luxury-starved old freighter. Quoting:

It is mid-afternoon. I am sitting at the stern of the boat from where it looks like we are coming down an incline from the horizon. When I am on the prow it appears that we are sailing up a slight incline. In fact as I look around it seems we are in the middle of a huge saucer. We are making excellent time, the captain tells us, and if we should have smooth sailing the rest of the way we may reach Norfolk sooner than anticipated. We have crossed south of the Azores in latitude about 33 and are headed directly toward the Bermudas where, we are told, we shall strike the Gulf Stream and sail northward with it to our port.

We ran into a shower this morning which didn't amount to much but the resulting rainbow was spectacular. I had always seen an arch but in this instance there was a complete circle of colors broken only by the prow of our ship. For the first time in my life (and incidentally the last) I saw the ends of the rainbow coverage. If it had been true that there is a pot of gold at the end of the rainbow, it would have been on our boat. There was none.

But we were not destined to arrive in Norfolk on time. About a day's run from port, we ran into the disastrous hurricane which had devastated southern Florida and then turned back to sea. For a couple of days our men were all battened down in the hold. As the storm abated and we were allowed on deck, even then the sight of the raging ocean was terrible, awe-inspiring, humbling and yet magnificent.

When the sun came out we discovered we were headed out to sea. The Captain was playing for time, daring not to try to enter the rocky capes which guard Hampton roads.

But directions were righted and we were soon anchored in the harbor. The muleteers dispersed. Few goodbyes were said.

FROM MULES BACK TO HOBBY HORSES

Prior to his mule boat trip, Lilburn had befriended young Charles van Ravenswaay, a son of the Billie Kingsbury's good friends, Dr. and Mrs. Van Ravenswaay. Charles at this time was a student at Washington University in St. Louis. He had become attracted by Lilburn's captivating personality, fascinating story-telling and insatiable interest in people, places and things.

Lilburn saw Charles as a precocious young man with a consuming curiosity about how things came to be what they were. Lilburn became a role model for Charles and they developed a relationship that continued until Lilburn's death.

When Charles would return home to Boonville for weekends and vacations, he would frequently join Lilburn on his antique collecting rides. In between times Lilburn would inform Charles by letter of his antiqueing accomplishments. Excerpts from the first of more than 1000 Lilburn letters saved by Charles follow. Undated, probably written in 1930.

Dear Charles:

Yesterday I drove down to the Hollywood Cafe [in St. Charles] to take up goods that were stalled on the shelves there and to put in fresh stock. This time, I left selections which would appeal, as Miss Clara might say, to "cigarette smokers and liquor drinkers." I had intended taking that corn bottle but forgot it, and now it is just as well since you have "fell" for it.

It was no fun driving down there and back. I determined the next time I go in winter, I shall take the "iron horse" or put on red flannel for motoring. Arriving at the Cafe I immediately ate the vegetable soup, as I was so cold. I visited with the waitresses for a couple of hours while we exchanged stocks, and I enjoyed one of them particularly because she resembled so strongly a girl I was very much in love with about 18 years ago. (I lost her through death after she married somebody else.)

I had to hurry back to sing with Herman Deck, a butcher in Boonville, and I didn't want to sound all tired out against the freshness of his voice. On my return trip I stopped at Mr. Van Huffein's drugstore in Wentzville to see if someone had left the grape pitcher I bargained for three weeks earlier. And then in Wright City I stopped to see the Sino-Lowestoft cream pitcher like the one in the museum, hoping I could overwhelm the old maid with a three or four dollar offer. But she's one of the kind of persons who just make you mad. She "doesn't want to commercialize her possessions" and if she ever did, not needing the money, would ask a good price. When backed against the wall for a price, she says, "Oh! twenty-five or fifty dollars." She said at one time when she broke her leg she would have sold these things because she thought she was going to die, but now it is different. God forgive me the temptation not to trip her last night! I never expect to see her again though she is going to let me know if things get different with her.

I reiterate my appreciation of the evening in your home. I shouldn't have liked anything quite so well as a visit with your Mother and Father and the "children." And it was a wonderful dinner beautifully served.

Chapter Four

WHAT DO YOU KNOW ABOUT THE GREAT DEPRESSION?

Memory fades with the passing years. Perhaps somewhat as women forget the pains of giving birth in the joys of seeing their children develop delightfully, Lilburn's painful memories of the great depression's effects upon the Boonslick Community seem to have eroded with the passage of time and the joy he found riding his hobby horses. This is suggested by his "Lilburn Says -Depression" column in the Boonville Daily News, *April 7, 1975.*

High school, even Central Methodist College students have, over the years, come to ask me to relate incidents of the depression. (One of the benefits of being middle-aged.) They seemed to expect to hear of heart-wrenching experiences suffered by people of New Franklin or myself. But I knew of nothing of the kind. A good percentage of the men in town worked for the railroad and their pay went right on. The government came to the rescue of others. Many geared their living to the rescue of others. Many adjusted their living to the times and made the best of it like Dr. Moser whom I asked last week how he weathered the storm.

"Well," he said, "every morning I would lay a dollar on the table and say to my wife, 'Now, Jessie, make this go as far as you can. Maybe before the day is over, I shall be able to give you another.' Some days the other dollar would materialize, sometimes not. It was remarkable what she did with the first one.

"I had plenty of work but I got so I knew before a man got inside the office he was going to say he needed some work very much but he didn't have any money and hoped I'd credit him until he could lay hands on some. I didn't turn anybody down except a lady who brought an old set of teeth to trade as down payment for a new set! But I felt pinched to pay for new materials which I had to have and ordered. With a dribble of dollars paid me now and then, we managed to get by without any memorable hardships.

"The first good crop year after the depression began, 95 percent of those I had credited came in and paid what they owed. It was wonderful. I wonder sometimes if people are as honest today as then!"

Personally, as I recall, my insurance patrons kept their insurance premiums paid up. If any failed it wasn't enough to make a lasting impression on my mind. I lived in the country where we raised enough of almost everything to supply the table. Other things were to be had in needful quantities. We had a large apple orchard and generally good crops. While prices for apples were low, the crop was large and brought in sufficient funds to pay expenses and buy necessities. Mrs. Robert Kingsbury, my sister-in-law, remembers people who bought a bushel of apples and got mad if we didn't throw in the basket.

So I was fortunate that the depression left no scars on me to show the inquiring students who wanted to know about those "terrible days."

However, there were people who felt knocked down and stomped by depression incidents. I learned this when I casually mentioned to a lady, the inquiring students who had been given the assignment of writing essays about it, whom I had not been able to help.

"You should have sent them to me," she said. "I could have filled their notebooks. It was a nightmarish time for me. My husband and I had made a trade to purchase a farm in 1929. Thinking we had completed arrangements to borrow the money to close the trade, we cashed in every holding we had and made the down payment. However, some other parties were desirous of buying the land, and influence must have been brought to bear on the parties who were to lend us the money. They advised they were unable to let us have it.

"We tried everywhere to get the loan without success. Without it, we were in a position to lose all life savings we had used for the down payment.

"Do you know what I did? I wrote to President Franklin D. Roosevelt telling him of the situation, described the land, related the circumstances which had kept us from getting a loan on the place we had hoped to make home for the rest of our lives, and about us being in a position now to lose everything we had saved.

"To my dying day, I shall revere the memory of President Roosevelt. In our behalf he wired the people who held the old mortgage to be patient, their money would be forthcoming: and to the Federal Reserve Bank in Kansas City to send a representative at once to inspect and appraise the land, to show us every consideration, and if the value of the land supported the amount requested for the loan, to make it immediately. In our estimation, Eleanor and Franklin could never do anything wrong!

"Of course, during the depression it was difficult to sell farm products enough for us to take care of the interest on the loan plus general expenses. We had a hard time, but we made it."

"How long did the depression last?" I asked her.

"For us, until we got into World War II and farm prices began to go up."

The depression had affected millions by 1931. The job my brother Bill Kingsbury expected to return to at the Nashville Tennessean *after a year in Europe was no longer available. He had then been hired to edit the weekly paper Edgar Nelson of Boonville was establishing in Marshall. Lilburn writes of this to Lillian Agnew, September 10, 1931:*

Edgar Nelson has sold his paper in Marshall and that put Bill out of a job. Jere is not returning to school owing to a shortage of funds to maintain his university fraternity life this fall, so there were William, Warren, and Jere all unemployed. The day before Bill left Marshall he learned of a vacancy in the high school English department, so he phoned Warren to come post-haste and apply. The point of it was Warren got located at $150 a month, so unexpectedly they were quite shocked with pleasure. I don't know where Jere is, but a friend hoped to locate him in the oil business in St. Louis. Bill, his mother and father went down to the cabin on the lake last Sunday and expect to be there for some time. Business matters got so stringent in the farm business handled by Billie and his partner that Billie was forced to sell out and did at a great loss and has been terribly upset over it. Personally, I think it was the best thing that ever happened, for running a string of farms can be a constant drain which will dry you up sooner or later and his drying might just as well be now as later.

This foreshadowed Billie's tragic death, and about a year later Lilburn wrote:

With the increase of postage coming up, it behooves me to write all the letters to even up my scores. I suspect a good many letters will be written for that reason. I heard Julia (*Billie's widow*) say she was busy trying to get a good many off. That she had so many the "tax" would amount to a good deal. She is counting the pennies for didn't the Boonville National just turn up its toes last Thursday and keep all the people's money that was therein? She had saved out from investment enough for a year's expenses. This was every cent she had. Fortunately she was selling a piece of property she had in Huntsville. The deal had not been closed and she will have that to fall back on. Of course, Julia is only one of hundreds who were hurt. Luther Lee, Horace Kingsbury, Horace Blankenbaker and Albert Smith all were bank stockholders and, aside from losing the amount of their stock, will be required to put up an equal amount to meet the deficit. Uncle Charles had sold some hogs, banked the money there and given a check on it for more hogs. The check had not been cashed before the close.

There is talk of reorganization but some say they doubt if they can do it for practically every cent can be counted as lost. Reorganization had been practically completed but the Reconstruction Finance Company which had practically agreed to furnish about $150,000, decided to advance only $70,000, and the top blew off.

One of the bank directors got scared and took $10,000 he had in the bank out of the Boonville National and put it in the other Boonville Bank. This move contributed to the decision to close. Well, the directors of the Boonville National were on bond to guarantee the money which the other bank had in the Boonville National, and when the other bank saw this director who had brought his ten grand to them was a signer on the bond, they just proceeded to tie up the $10,000. So the man who tried to protect himself will probably lose anyhow. Some of the other directors on that bond will not be able to pay.

By the spring of 1933, some of Lilburn's nieces and nephews had had to drop out of college, cousins had lost their farms and some friends were jobless. When Work Program Administration jobs were created, those taking them could only work half time so more families could have some income. I think it probable some of the apples from Lilburn's orchard may have found their way to the peddlers on street corners of the big cities.

Charles van Ravenswaay became a beneficiary of the Federal Writers' Program - becoming director of the Showme State's Guide Book.

Roosevelt's election in 1932 launched the depression-fighting New Deal programs which affected the lives of many. Lilburn became a founding committee chairman for the Agricultural Adjustment Act designed to stabilize farm prices in a manner which would assure farmers a profit. He wrote of this to his Cousin Lillian on March 9, 1934:

CORN-HOGGING

Such corn-hogging as I have been doing! We thought when we rounded up the farmers and helped them make out and sign their papers the big job was over. Really, the work is just commencing. In the main office, they have clerks who checked over the papers and marked the errors. I am amazed at my inaccuracies. And what I didn't err on, somebody else seemed to have. We are overhauling all of our 90 applications, correcting what we can. The rest will have to be attended to when we go to see the individuals. We have to go back over the farms of every one of those men, and got underway yesterday afternoon. We appraised five, and as it was muddy, we had to do all of the exploring on foot. We had to go to one end of it to see where the corn had been grown last year and then to the extreme northeast corner to inspect the acres they are renting to the government. So we made a complete circle of the farm with much mud balling up on our shoes. We are hoping for more favorable weather before getting off the hard surface roads and tackling the outlying farms.

We had a meeting a few days ago and decided we would pay ourselves $5 a day for this work, and it will take each of us about 50 days to complete the job. So I am willing to walk over some farm land. If I don't get to do it that way, I might have to walk over some of it behind a plow. Through the CWA, the old orchard at the Agnew place was cut down this winter and cleaned up, quite a saving to the owner and a Godsend to Mr. Baker, who has his fine commercial orchard just up the road, where he fights coddling moths to a finish and the moths have had a harbor for years. The Agnew orchard has not been sprayed or cleaned up for several years. I was in line for aid, but thought they would never get to me, so we had our own men cut down the trees. It is slow, as they allow the men, who aren't worth their salt anyway, to work only 24 hours a week. Unless the owner stands and watches, they cease work and warm and talk around the burning brush pile.

About 25 tobacco growers of the county have formed an association to reduce their tobacco acreage. And there are a lot more who haven't joined up who are going to grow tobacco regardless. A good deal of the Estill land just north of us, which has never grown a stack of tobacco is going in this summer. It looks like there will be more tobacco acres this year. On hogs, it is likely there will be a reduction because people are sick and tired of raising hogs for less than nothing anyway.

I wish you would tell me the sense of reducing acreage in the country which will produce crops naturally, and increasing acreage where they will have to irrigate, and spend millions of dollars to build a dam to hold the water in reserve. It looks to me like robbing Peter to pay Paul.

Instead of giving the farmers a lot of money on hogs and wheat and corn, why didn't they devise some plan to let the farmer have his land and loan him the money to hold it with, at about 3 percent, say? The land would always stand for the debt. But with all these corn and hog papers, we have people claiming more than they ought to have, and the government has to stand over them with a club to see if they keep sufficient land out of cultivation as they have agreed to do, whether they let their livestock eat off some of the grass that is not intended to be pastured, etc. The greatest benefit of these Federal farm programs goes to the people who need the least help.

Do you know shortly they will begin to work on the reduction of beef cattle, then dairy products, then poultry, and then sheep?

The women clerks in the county office said today, "If we aren't all crazy by the time this is over, it will be a wonder."

But let 'er go! I can hold on as long as anyone, I guess, and whatever happens none will hate it worse than I, if it is bad. I can't see that business is so hot on the upgrade, but I do think the morale of the people is better. They have their faith and hope bolstered up.

CIVILIAN CONSERVATION

Towards the end of the year he wrote to Cousin Lillian:

I have corn-hogged until I am worn to the nub. The three of us committeemen for this township have had the visiting of farms and examining the soil to attend to and it has necessitated so much walking and climbing of hills and hollows I was glad of a day in the office to meet those who had to come in to make changes in their papers. But we had a beautiful warm week in which to work and I was delighted to get first-hand information about the farms all about us, and delighted to find most of them are in such excellent condition so far as soil is concerned, though on many farms, the improvements are in bad condition. Luther Lee told me there were only two good gates in the entire river bottom. Be that as it may, people are not building new fences at a rate which would delight the men who sell wire. I find most of the land promises good yields. That simplified things as we had thought the claims made by the applicants in many cases were exorbitant. I hope we can get the job finished before long and have the papers off to Washington so we can get a little spending money.

Corn is selling high as are most farm products. I paid $1.03 a bushel for a hundred bushels the other day and that is mighty little corn. It is all right about the price when one is the seller but it is terrible when one is on the other end, with hogs to fatten. We gamble on the prospect of having a higher price for our next fat hogs, but my, what a price they would have to have to pay for the high-priced feed. It won't work out on paper. And, I get no satisfaction from the figures in black and white when I put down on one side the benefits to be derived from this AAA government and place against it the costs including the processing tax, which you know the farmer pays. Along with all the others, I am sailing on the ship of state, hoping to come to port, but I feel very much as I did on the old mule boat in the middle of the hurricane when the plates creaked and wondered if we'd make it. As one who knows, I say the money which comes from the government is an incentive to go along with the administration, whether it comes to one on the relief roll, from the triple A, or from the jobs which have been created. Our palms have been warmed with the coin of the realm, and it has a very heavy persuading influence. One gets nowhere saying anything against the New Deal, it is such treason.

Chapter Five

HER BODY IS GONE - HER SPIRIT LIVES ON

January 28, 1933

Dear Ones,

It might be better if I would wait until my brain settles before writing you, but I am sure you are anxious to hear from us.

This Sunday, I am kin to so many more people than I was a week ago, to all those who have lost and miss their mothers.

Back to ten days ago, we were having a revival in town at our church and Father and Mother started going on Thursday. The minister announced he would talk on a "Lost Art in Religion" and test his audience to see if it were so in New Franklin? It was a matter of testimony and Mother and Father made beautiful witnesses to the glory of God. It was no lost art as far as they were concerned. They went in the afternoon, and in the evening that day, and in the afternoon the next day.

That evening, Mother was too tuckered out to go, but Father went with me. Mother said she had "such a funny feeling in the region of her chest." Dad choked up with a severe cold. That ended his church going, and on Sunday, Mother and I put him to bed and kept him there as best as we could. By Tuesday, he was better, and she showed symptoms of her old-fashioned asthma. The case developed rapidly and we burned asthma powder and did everything we could think of, but she had very little relief.

I came back from church Wednesday night and found her up on her knees and elbows, which so often is the only position in which she can be comfortable, saying how much she wished she had something that would enable her to get to sleep, as she was so tired.

I went back to town to see the doctor. He prescribed medicine which was supposed to give her the necessary rest, but she spent a miserable night.

Lillian was with her most of the day. The medicine made her delirious and most of the time, when she talked, she rambled. I sat up until midnight, Thursday night when she seemed to be quieted. She started to cough frequently, and wouldn't keep the cover on and once or twice she was out of bed walking about the room.

You will remember the ways of asthma, how you keep hoping and thinking each paroxysm of coughing will be the last and everything will be all right tomorrow. We were not alarmed. She seemed to be in the same old fagged condition we had seen her in nearly every winter.

Lillian came out with me at noon and Mother seemed so bad Lillian decided to call the doctor. He got here about 4:30 and told us later he was alarmed at her general condition. He asked her if she would mind him hypoderming her. She told him she could stand anything, but added, "But there isn't a thing that hurts me, doctor." He also gave her a heart stimulant in the vein and said he wanted her to have another one the second day following.

Just a few minutes after he left, Lillian said to her, "Mother, you must feel like you're in Heaven, now, so comfortable," and she replied that she did and "she felt so good, it was so nice," and dropped off to sleep.

I came home about six and Lillian called me to her bedside and I noted her breathing was quite labored and Lillian and I were alarmed. Still we attributed it to the medicine she had been given, and while we watched, the breathing became normal. Her hands and face were warm. So far as I could tell, her pulse was strong.

Lillian went to the phone and told Carl she wouldn't come in that night. She cried as she was telling him that we had become alarmed at Mother's effort in breathing. We went in often to watch her. She seemed to be sleeping soundly, and we were thankful she was getting needed sleep and rest.

We read to Father and visited in the dining room until the

phone rang and the doctor was inquiring about Mother. Carl had walked home with him from church and had told him what Lillian had reported. So the doctor called me at once. He said I should give her some medicine he had left. It was a stimulant. I asked him if I should forcibly arouse her and he advised I should.

Julia, Lillian and I tried to awaken her to give her a capsule, but we couldn't do it. I called the doctor to come and give it. None of us had any experience with very sick people. He came and told me afterward he thought at first she was doing very well. She was asleep on her left side and he asked me to help turn her over so he could proceed with the examination. With difficulty we got her turned, and while he worked, her breathing became labored again. He finally injected more medicine in her vein and said he was returning to town for more medicine and would return as quickly as possible.

I was terribly worried, asked him for a frank opinion and he said he was fearful of the outcome and I had better tell the children to come at once. I called Rosie first at Richmond, as she was the furthest away. She told me not 10 minutes before I called she had experienced the strangest feeling, thinking, "What if I never see my Mother again? She is ill and I am going down Sunday to be with her." She and Will started within a half hour. I was able to get in touch with the others quickly.

From the time we turned Mother over, her life began to ebb, and by the time the doctor got back and looked at her, he told me it was too late for medicine to do any good. Father saw us running around and me at the phone and wanted to know what was the matter, and he like the rest of us was just bewildered. Julia, Jere, Lillian, Carl, Taylor, Bob, Margaret, Jean and I were there when she just ceased to breathe about 10 o'clock. She was never conscious after falling into the sleep she said was "so nice."

Mother had so often said she hoped she would never be a care to anyone, and hoped she would just go to sleep like her mother did.

It took me a little bit to realize after the doctor said, "It's all over, she's gone," that there are times when everything is futile.

When we next saw Mother, she looked so carefree, so peaceful. None of us gave a thought to having her taken from the home and we waited here until Mr. Duncan had finished his work. He brought with him a dress of the palest pink, for temporary use while she reclined on a couch of lace. Never had we seen Mother in pink, and we decided the color must be orchid or grey, in the event we did not dress her in some of the clothes she was accustomed to wearing.

While we were debating in the morning about what it should be, we came to the conclusion the dress Mr. Duncan had used was so becoming, we would just use it. As aforesaid, it was of palest pink, with a little lace at the neck and a little jacket effect in the material of just a slight tone deeper.

Rosie, Margaret and I chose a casket in gray, perfectly plain and tufted closely inside with a sort of twilled satin in white. Then we went to the florist and had a huge spray made, dark red roses, with bits of heather woven among them on a foundation of ferns, and tied artistically with lavender ribbon. This was made so when the casket was open, it was draped across the casket; and when it was closed, it was placed lengthwise and covered the entire top. The roses were lovely against the gray of the casket. Margaret ordered a little bouquet of sweet peas in pink and lavender, which was placed on the front of Mother's dress and it was just the little touch which completed the costume. In recent months, Mother had waved her hair so beautifully. Every morning she would get out her little pan of water, her brush and comb and her "wavers," and after combing a while, she would invariably say, "Look here, Lilburn, at the hair that came out this morning. If it keeps coming out, I wont' have a hair left."

I would tell her since this had been happening for months, I felt some of it must be growing back, or she would have been as bald as old Mrs. Tuggle. And I would recommend having a wig made, an idea which got "no house" from her. Then I would see her with the combs stuck in and a string around her head to hold them in place and presto, she looked as if she were leaving the hair dressers. Well, we wanted to have her hair waved like she had been wearing it, and the girls tried, but with little success. They just couldn't get it right, so her hair was combed back from her forehead, and it was so silvery and fluffy. She looked just as if she were asleep and so natural, as is generally said, but I have never looked on the face of the dead yet, to feel deep in my heart they looked natural. But what was left of Mother was so lovely in its way I felt comforted, and I almost wore the carpet out, looking again and again. The body which had housed her spirit, wore its eighty-two plus years lightly. All those to whom I have become kin, know the things we have felt, the things which have come to our mind to puzzle us, and the reproaches we heap on ourselves for omitting to do so many little things and big things which the one who is gone would have appreciated.

The Eastern Star offered to use their ceremony for burial, but I wanted none of that. I shall never forget the time of Aunt Fannie's funeral. The Stars had it and all of the women were so overcome they couldn't do their parts, and the service was prolonged almost indefinitely (it seemed to me). So we had no Eastern Star ceremony.

At two o'clock today, a mixed quartet from my Boonville choir sang a song. I can't tell you what it was, but it was beautifully done. Then Bro. Kimbrell, a pastor of ours some thirty years ago, read impressively the 23rd Psalm and the 90th Psalm. I knew Mother loved the former and Father frequently recites the latter from memory. Then Bro. Pogue, our pastor twenty-odd years ago, made a beautiful prayer, which began with something about "How beautiful are thy mountains" - you probably know which psalm it is from, if any. Then the quartet sang "Sweet Hour of Prayer," which Mother loved. That concluded the service here at the house. I told the ministers they wouldn't have to eulogize Mother; everybody knew about her already. Brother Kimball remarked to me since he has been here at this meeting that he had preached my Mother's Christianity all over the State.

The casket was closed before the service began. There were just stacks of beautiful flowers, red colors predominating. Quite a lot of rose and lavender sprays. They were lovely. You have heard me say that I think it is a shame to spend so much money for flowers, when their purpose is so short-lived, and in these hard times the money spent for them could be used to better advantage. I "contentioned," as our washer woman says, along that line, but others of the family said we should let people do as they please, and we did. Tonight Father said to us, "I have felt it extravagant to have so many flowers at funerals. In this case, I believe every blossom that came was sent as a token of love for Mother." It was a gorgeous expression, and we cried and said, "Mother would have loved them all," and would have wanted a "slip" off of every blooming thing in the lot, to start in sand.

The grandsons were the pallbearers. At first we thought we four sons and two sons-in-law would serve in that capacity, but at the time of decision, I didn't think I would be able to make it. But I could have for when the time came, it didn't seem like Mother on which the casket lid snapped shut, who was being carried out to the family lot. I felt quite reconciled. Nothing has happened to us which we had no reason to expect, and our blessings have been so many, I haven't a breath with which I could complain. I don't know just how I am going to get along without Mother, but people are accustomed to doing that which is necessary, and so shall I somehow.

I won't be able to scold her and fuss at her because she loved me and told me so, and because she would do things which her son disapproved of sometimes. You know that seems insignificant compared with the lot I might have done. Why, I didn't bring her near enough sardines and potato chips and dozens of other things. And now I have heavy lumps in my throat.

Father is wonderful, a brave man. He is terribly shaken by grief, but tells everyone he knows it was for the best, that Mother just slipped into a place better than this and it won't be long until he will be going on to join her. His cold hangs on, and I am doing my best to keep him doctored. But we are recently seeing changes in his vitality. With his broken heart and lonesome days, he won't have much incentive to keep on keeping up. As always he is a wonderful example and like him, we cry bucketsful, straighten up our faces and go on accepting the situation. Crying is no sign you are not submitting to God's will, is it?

Tonight Father was talking and recalled a verse of a song which was sung at his Mother's funeral. It is so flowery I must pass it on to you. Father said it had such a pretty tune:

"Sister, thou was mild and lovely. Gentle as the summer breeze. Pleasant as the air of evening, as it floats among the trees."

My Dear Cousin Lillian,

Two weeks ago tonight Mother went away. I say "went away," which was what happened to her living presence, her physical being, but I have been so hovered over by her beautiful loving spirit that I do not mourn. It is with me all the time and I feel her admonition and advice more strongly than when she gave it to me in words. I was so used to it I sometimes fussed at her for advising me, as it seemed, so needlessly, but the mystery which happened two weeks ago has changed all that and I find myself listening for the guidance of that blessed spirit.

I still have that which animated her body and which made her life so full and beautiful, the spirit of her, and I'll not raise a finger in protest at my lot in losing her. And if I yield to the guidance of her spirit which is so all-present with me, I may be able to become a good old man. In her things left at home were clippings from papers of exalted thoughts which no doubt at the time were clipped because they echoed the deepest emotions of her being. They are lovely thoughts and just little markers to indicate the beautiful thoughts which occupied her time.

The saddest incident pertaining to Mother's death and burial (and to me the most pitiful) was dear Dad's trying to see Mother's features. He did want to see her clearly and several times tried so hard. I got the strongest light I could find and finally told him to "see with his hands" if his eyes couldn't, but that was little satisfaction and he just bent over, kissed her forehead, and said, "Well, she just slipped away into a better land than this," and turned away.

THE KILLER PIANO

October 29, 1933

Dear Cousin Lillian,
Tragedy Stalks Today.
This afternoon Horace left home about 3 p.m. leaving Minnie. She had promised she would go back to bed and to sleep. She had been terribly weak for the last two weeks. At five-thirty the maid came and was unable to arouse Minnie to let her in the house, and finally went to a neighbor's to borrow a key which would fit the back door. Inside the house, she followed the usual instructions not to disturb Minnie until dinner was ready, so went about preparing the meal. Horace came home about a quarter of six, washed up and then went to see if Minnie was all right. She wasn't in the bedroom, nor his bedroom. He went on through the house, not finding her until he stepped inside the door of the front room. There she was on her knees with her head caught under the top of the grand piano. Stunned by the shock, he removed her from this position to the floor, then called the maid, who summoned the doctor and neighbors. Minnie had been dead an hour or two.

The doctor thought it best to call the coroner, and decided it was necessary to comply with the formalities by having an inquest. Horace called Minnie's mother, Mrs. Williams, who lives in Mississippi. She was unable to make any plans and will phone tomorrow on whether she is able to come at this time. Funeral arrangements are dependent upon her plans.

Dear Aunt Rose,
There are no more particulars about Minnie's death. We are wondering just how it happened, but of course, there is no solution to the problem. Mrs. Williams came on Saturday. Carl Jr. met her in St. Louis and drove her here in time for the funeral at three o'clock at the house. Three rooms and the hall were full of people and many were standing outside. A mixed quartet sang,

"My Jesus As Thou Wilt," and "Beautiful Isle of Somewhere." One minister read a passage of scripture; another read a prayer, after which the body was buried in Walnut Grove Cemetery in Boonville.

It was a long-standing request no one should see her after she was dead - that she should not be removed to an undertaking establishment - that she should be buried in a shell pink dress or robe and she should have three pink rose buds in her hand, with the thorns all removed from the stems. Besides Horace, whom I presume viewed the remains which were taken to the undertakers, no one saw the body until the casket was brought to the house on Saturday around noon. The casket was opened for the benefit of Xena, Mrs. Williams, the Bragg children, a neighbor who had seen the body crumpled on the floor and wanted to see it prepared for burial, then the Negro cook, another Negro woman helper and two men who were raking leaves off the lawn.

I was there at the time and Horace, starting in with Mrs. Williams, told me to just make myself at home. Julia happened to pass through the parlor at the wrong time and before she realized it, her eyes were riveted on the form in the casket, and she said she would have given anything if she hadn't passed by at that moment. One of the Negroes, telling me about it afterward, said, "Of course, you could tell who it was, but she looked so worn and 'haggleedy' with her hair unmarcelled, and without the little touches of loved ones which often seem to soften the sight of the departed. The pink dress was nothing like Minnie had ever worn, low V neck with cheap looking lace filled in and the rosebuds were red instead of pink. As she requested, she was buried in a metallic coffin, a handsome thing, which was encased in an underground vault of concrete. When one considers how wasted the body was, what's the use of preserving some skin and bones, but I suppose Minnie always thought of herself as the body she admired and loved pretty much all the time we have known her.

Minnie, I understand, left a will or something, giving a good part of her jewelry to Xena, a number of the handsome pieces to

Delice Bragg, and practically nothing to her second girl, Betty Grant. It reminds me of the way the Darneal family of Richmond take on over Alice Katherine because they think she looks like the Darneal side of the house, and barely give Mary Sue a crumb because she "takes after the Kingsburys." One of the Darneals took Alice to the fair in Chicago this summer and is giving her piano and violin lessons. It looks like the Darneals will put it all over the Kingsburys! I shall never forget the day I brought Mary Sue home from the hospital in K.C. and Mrs. D didn't even look at the baby.

Of course, no one is grieved, for Minnie was so miserable, and must have kept Horace in suspense constantly. She said she had nothing to live for and was always threatening to jump into a cistern that was just outside the house. We are glad she did not make the cistern. We are shocked stiff, even though we expected something to happen. But when one considers the manner of her going, it sounds like a fantastic tale. I have never read of anything more unusual in fiction and I wonder if there is a parallel case? It looks like fate stepped in and prevented something which might have been voluntary.

Chapter Six

AMERICAN HISTORY IN PRESSED GLASS

Earlier Lilburn had written his cousin Lillian he was becoming an "historical dilettante." Dilettante he might be, but his history hobby horse carried him away on a search for the origin of glass and its development in this country. Of this he wrote to Charles van Ravenswaay:

Dear Charles:

I feel like I have come through the wringer, but my buttons are still on. Today was the big works and I shot them. The soiree was at the student center of the Episcopalian Church. Among other displays, I had two tables. On one table I had a full set of pleat panel glass and the half dozen Haviland cup and saucers; on the other, a row of copper lustre pieces and many hobnail specimens. I stood behind this table during the execution.

The talk seemed to go over good - there were about 150 "skirts" packed in and they were all more or less agog. I was pleased. Many of the women were in costumes of the long ago.

Once the festivities were over - such a bedlam set loose - and I was almost torn to shreds by those on all sides who wanted to know such things as "What is the difference between tear glass and hobnail?" "Now my pitcher is black, smooth inside and rough outside and 190 years old." "Do you know where I can get the tail put on the lion on my compote?" "Do you believe this to be Steigel?"

As for the talk, I'm enclosing a copy of what I mostly used:

When we look at the brilliant articles of glass which are unused in our homes today, there is nothing to suggest that they are all descendants of such a common, lowly ancestor as sand, any more than I am reminded by your presence here that the first man was made of clay.

In the human family we find different personalities due to circumstances of birth and environment. In the glass family we also find many different types. While we cannot always account for certain traits of character in people, in the glass family, personality can be explained. We may not be able to tell why Mary is a more colorful personality than Susie but we do know why one piece of glass is blue while another is red.

Plain old sand wedded to potash and soda with a little strain of lime, produces very beautiful glass but it lacks the brilliance, the resonance and weight of the product which bears a strain of lead. If one piece of glass is more colorful than another it is due to the metallic oxides which were used in their manufacture.

All glass has common characteristics. You know to your sorrow how brittle glass is. At a high temperature it becomes fluid so it can be stirred, ladled, poured and cast. It may be rolled like dough. It can be blown into hollow shapes by human breath or compressed air. Under pressure it may be molded. It can be drawn into a solid rod or a hollow tube of indefinite length, spun into a thread so fine it floats on air or woven into cloth which may some day be used for clothing.

Inferior glass was made in Mesopotamia more than 4500 years ago. The industry moved westward through the centuries, into Syria and Egypt. In the Middle Ages, Spain and Southern France and Italy were perfecting the art. Bohemia, Germany, the Low Countries, England and Ireland in turn became glass conscious but the efforts of the last countries were mainly contemporaneous with our own in America.

As early as 1806, the London Co., made up of adventurous spirits, resolved to come to America to establish a colony and to engage in the production of glass. In England there was a future for glass but production costs seemed prohibitive and the London Co., had heard that in America there was an unlimited supply of the basic element of glass, sand, and there was an unbounded supply of timber to fire the glass furnaces. They brought along mechanics, laborers and carpenters since 48 out of the 135 who embarked were gentlemen who looked upon any kind of work as disgraceful. They found the hardships overwhelming. Disillusionment came fast. A crude factory was built but it was a failure. Other expeditions followed to combat disappointing conditions. But eventually the glass industry got under way and was operated successfully at many points along the Atlantic seaboard. Window glass was an early product but bottle glass was the chief commodity until as late as 1860. Our ancestors grew more fruit and grain than they could use on their tables, consequently they conserved it in wines and whiskies.

Much pressed glass was made prior to this date and of this ware and its production, historians find records. But of glass made subsequent to this date, when the production was so plentiful and the patterns changed so often, records have not been preserved to reveal the history of its making. Consequently many people, who are interested in collection sets of pressed glass of the later patterns, are floundering in their efforts to determine definitely who made it, when and where.

While many collectors are discriminating and are interested in only the earliest and consequently rarest pieces of glass, hundreds of collectors enjoy an abiding enthusiasm about pressed glass made during the last half of the 19th century. The fact that there are over 300 patterns of glass which may be collected in sets, attests the ingenuity of designers and manufacturers of those years.

Just as designers and manufacturers keep their fingers upon the pulse of the public to cater to their whims and fancies, those of earlier days watched carefully the trend of the times. They were constantly producing patterns they hoped would appeal to particular groups of people or better still to the public in general. Some of their productions, judging by the amount of glass to be found today, must have gone over with a bang. Some of them were duds. But over the course of the years there were patterns to suit the most fastidious tastes in the nation.

In the bird group, cardinal, owl, parrot, pheasant, eagle, nesting bird and frosted stork, for the women whose minds ran toward the zoo, lion, squirrel, polar bear, opossum, deer, bison and monkey.

Those with a Biblical appeal, Jacob's ladder, Jacob's coat, Rebecca at the well and cathedral.

Floral patterns were popular and afforded a wide choice: fuschia, windflower, wild flower, rose in snow, cabbage rose, forget-me-not, bellflower, ivy, dahlia, tulip, daisy and lily of the valley.

In the fruit patterns were pear, strawberry, blackberry, loganberry, grape, peach, cherry, currant and gooseberry.

In planning patterns which would appeal to the public the factories never lost sight of the cross section of people who buy during periods of emotional excitement. They seldom failed to bring out glass for the market when there was a national crisis or when there was an event, historic or political, of prime importance. Thus we find today many pieces of pressed glass which bring to our minds events in the history of our nation.

Lafayette's visit to America in 1824-25 will always be classed as a major event. It was immortalized in glass, upon cup-plates, vases and bottles. The Cadmus cup-plate recalls to our mind that it was the ship which brought Lafayette from France to America to be the guest of our nation. The *Cadmus* was built in 1816 and fitted out in 1824 at the expense of a patriotic merchant to convey the patriot to our shores. It took 31 days for the old ship to cross the ocean but when she arrived in New York there was a monster demonstration. She was met by other great ships of that day, the Chancellor Livingston and the Robert Fulton and escorted to the battery amid much acclaim. Lafayette was invited to make a tour of the fine glass factories of America and in Pittsburgh, the Bakewell Pears factory presented him a pair of elegant flint vases engraved with his home La Grange on one side and an American eagle on the other.

Another cup-plate memorializes the building of the first railroad in New Jersey, the Camden and Amboy chartered by the state in 1830. The plate bears the imprint of the first engine which was brought from England and christened significantly, "John Bull."

The battleship *Constitution,* launched in 1797, went through a valiant war with the Barbary powers on the north coast of Africa as Edward Preble's flagship. During the war of 1812 it did heroic service under command of Capt. Isaac Hull, against the British. By 1830 it was considered obsolete and ordered destroyed.

When Oliver Wendell Holmes heard of the order he wrote his famous poem "Old Ironsides" with which you are familiar:

> Ay, tear her tattered ensign down!
> Long has it waved on high.
> And many an eye has danced to see
> That banner in the sky;
> Beneath it rung the battle shout,
> And burst the cannon's roar;
> The meteor of the ocean air
> Shall sweep the clouds no more.
> The poet's verdict was:
> Oh better that her shattered hulk
> Should sink beneath the wave.

The sentiment of the people was aroused. The Sandwich glass-works designed and put on sale a "Constitution" cup-plate which helped defray the expense of rehabilitating the old ship in 1833 and it was preserved as a memorial of a proud period in history.

Shortly after the heavenly apparition, Halley's Comet swept across the skies and startled our forebears in 1835, the glass houses struck off cup-plates as souvenirs of this unusual phenomenon which returns every 76 years.

The Ft. Meigs and Tippecanoe and Log Cabin cup plates direct our attention to William Henry Harrison our ninth President. He was long a national hero, having made an enviable reputation in dealings with the Indians, both as a diplomat and as a warrior. He defeated the Shawnee chief Tecumseh in Indiana territory at Tippecanoe and later, at Ft. Meigs successfully defended his fort and his men against the British. A part of Harrison's home was of logs and during his campaign for the presidency his supporters brought out the Log Cabin cup-plate which depicts the cabin with a cider barrel by the door. It was said of him that his table, instead of being covered with exciting wines, was supplied with the best cider.

Major Ringgold was the hero of Palo Alto and cup-plates were issued for sale to those whose imagination the exploits of the Major had captured. The battle of Palo Alto was fought on the Mexican border in 1845 when General Arista with 6000 Mexican soldiers attempted to cut off Gen. Zachary Taylor and 2000 men from Ft. Isabel which was the source of supplies. Just what part the Major played in the battle I do not know. Here we have a great soldier immortalized in glass more than in the histories and encyclopedias to which I have had access.

Fire in Baltimore in 1850 laid in ashes a great portion of the city and to memorialize the spirit of the people who went immediately to work rebuilding their losses, bottles were made bearing the words, "Phoenix-resurgam."

An attractive salt was issued during the administration of Millard Fillmore, the thirteenth President of the U.S.. His political career began with the birth of the Whig party and ended with its disintegration. He became unpopular when he signed the Fugitive Slave Law in 1850. He served a term as Vice President before he became the head of the nation and is said to have been so tactful that neither side in Congress was ever able to know his personal views upon questions at issue. It is said he had little to do with important events of his administration.

Jenny Lind, the delightful Swedish singer, came to America under the management of the great circus man, P. T. Barnum, under a contract which paid her $1000 per night for 150 nights. This was considered a staggering sum and the public calculated that it would bankrupt Mr. Barnum. But her American tour created unprecedented enthusiasm, the nation took her to its heart and the glass industries sold Jenny Lind Bottles. The tour grossed Mr. Barnum $700,000.

Henry Clay, famous American statesman, was a nominee three times for the Presidency of the United States and was considered a fourth time. He was such a friend of the glass houses that they, upon occasion, struck off and sold cup-plates bearing his picture, using the sales to promote his candidacy. These are attractive plates, some of them being peacock blue and very rare.

Niagara Falls' importance as a honeymoon center was recognized very early and every bride took away one or more of the cup-plates which bear within the space of a few square inches, the imprint of the falls, the little boat "Maid of the Mist" riding the turbulent water below and the sun shining forth resplendently. The little boat seems more in danger of the violent rays of the sun than of the water which pours over the falls.

Zachary Taylor, the twelfth President of the U. S. and the second to die in office, when elected had never held public office before but he had a splendid record, surrounding himself by the smartest men of the time, to none of which he owed any allegiance. He had been a soldier for 40 years and it was on this record that he was elected. He was affectionately known as "Old Rough and Ready." Old Rough and Ready whiskey bottles are much prized by collectors.

The Westward Ho pattern of glass commemorates the movement of civilization westward, the trek of the forty-niners across the plains and around Cape Horn, to California. It is one of the most popular patterns. To acquire a set of this requires much patience and some money.

When the Atlantic cable was laid in 1865 by Cryus W. Field, a pattern of tableware with several variations was turned out to mark this momentous event.

A platter bearing the picture of Locomotive No. 350 commemorates the opening of the Union Pacific Railroad in 1869.

A few pieces of glass from earlier days

When Abraham Lincoln was assassinated, a pattern known as the Lincoln Drape was offered to the public. It is said not much was sold south of the Mason-Dixon line. The glass has such heavy folds of drapery impressed upon it that one is depressed at the sight. The Garfield has a much lighter design, rather airy festoons, symbolizing perhaps that times were brighter than when Lincoln died. After the tragic end of President William McKinley a memorial plate bearing a full length likeness of the President was placed upon the market.

The Liberty Bell or Centennial pattern came out in 1876 during the celebration of the signing of the Declaration of Independence at Philadelphia. The chief motif of this glass is the Liberty Bell which was cast in England in 1752, and after breaking, again in America in 1753, broke the last time while tolling the funeral solemnities of Chief Justice John Marshall. The tray in this pattern bears the names of all the signers of the Declaration.

Coin glass, which we find with the impression of dollars, halves, quarters and dimes of our money impressed upon it, was made in 1892 at the time of the Columbian Exposition in Chicago

While, like little orphan Annie's goblins it will git you if you don't watch out, if practiced judiciously, it builds happier and consequently, better citizens.

Lilburn's letters to relatives continued to report on hobby horse rides. On October 22, 1932, he wrote his cousin Lillian Agnew of a galloping ride. Later when his speech-making hobby developed, he drew upon such letters for the interesting incidents he mixed in with his historical research.

My quest for valuable old glass has taken me to Pike County. A week ago, Lillian and I went to Louisiana and Bowling Green, thence to Frankfort and New London where I left Lillian with a school friend and I proceeded to Hannibal to sleep. The next day I roamed afar, picked Lillian up and we came home with about 70 pieces which were all more or less good.

In January 1934 he made one of his first talks to a Woman's Club in Boonville. It was simply titled "Pressed Glass."

As far as my interest in Pressed Glass is concerned, life began at 40. At that time I attended a public auction and saw glass bid in spiritedly at high prices which amazed me. These old things had come from the home of an old lady who had lost interest in them in favor of modern glass. Someone told me there was a great demand for old glass to be used with antique furniture to create the proper atmosphere of early homes. I had a lot of old furniture but no glass and as I had a high regard for atmosphere I resolved to go forth to see what I could discover.

Mindful that a prophet is not without honor save in his own country, I went far afield that first day into a strange land. My gleanings far exceeded my expectations. After that I went again and again. It became an exciting game: finding good things which were of no value to their owners and could be bought for a trifle! Matching wits with men and women to gain admission to their homes and once in, to persuade them to open the doors of their cupboards, cellars, attics and store rooms. Driving bargains for the loot! It was delightful to visit with old people whose years were enriched by long living, to listen to stories and their sound philosophies of life. I learned that a weather beaten cottage with beds of old fashioned perennials was a likely place to stop, that an old lady's love of flowers went hand in hand with an appreciation of fine old things saved from early days. I learned to read clotheslines, apparel for young children being the flag or signal to press on down the road; that everything there had been broken up long ago.

Of particular interest were my experiences with the old darkies. There was old Uncle Gilliam who had driven the carriage for his white folks and Julie, his wife, had cooked on the neighboring farm. Julie swore she didn't have but one piece of old glass to her name but while she retrieved a cake stand from the chicken coop, old Uncle Gilliam gave me the clue which led to dozens of pieces of rag-wrapped glass hidden away in boxes and trunks in the little half story room upstairs. I bless Uncle Gilliam to this day.

I had some disconcerting experiences. During my strange glass interlude I had a door slammed in my face. An old white man to whom I made my politest speech about my mission listened quietly, then spat and said, "You ain't got nothing else to do, I reckon!"

Just at the time that I became interested in glass, at the request of my father, I had assumed the responsibility of the farm and orchard where I was born and reared and where it was expected I should die. My father, concerned about my farming career, said nothing about my glass excursions but I knew he looked upon them with many misgivings and thought I could spend my time to better advantage at home.

I also maintained an insurance business in town and my secretary, a woman older than I who had known me all of my life, looked with silent curiosity at the things I brought in and then struck an attitude which announced to me she thought I would do better to stay in the office and bring home the bacon rather than to gallivant over the state hunting glass. And I knew I was gallivanting too much.

When Mandy Jones lost her husband, she put on such deep mourning that her clothes were black from her skin out. The lady for whom she worked asked if she didn't think she was overdoing things a bit. Mandy replied, "No mam, 'cause when I mourns, I *mourns*." This story illustrates the spirit in which I pursue old glass.

My office which once had been a banking room began to overflow with glass. At first I hid it behind solid doors of cabinets or locked it in the vault. But presently glass adorned tables and desks, the tops of cupboards and even parts of the floor. My insurance customers had never seen anything like it and I knew it. I had too much atmosphere and in self defense, determined to sell some glass before I spent another cent.

One advertisement in the *Antique Magazine*, published in New York, made me a dealer, almost overnight.

The longest, slickest, blackest cars I had ever seen began to nose into the curb in front of my office. Men and women came to my door from Maine to California, from Minnesota to the Gulf just as if I had invented a superior mouse trap. Every time I had an insurance customer in a big deal, a group of glass collectors breezed in.

My glass patrons were, as a rule, interesting personalities, delightful personalities with a few old sour pusses thrown in for contrast. Our chief of police, (chief because he was our only one) had curiosity which would fairly burst at the sight of cars with out-of-state licenses. He used to wreath his face with his hands and press it against the plate glass window of my office, to peer in and see for himself, his badge of office gleaming conspicuously on his vest. My guests never said anything when they noticed him but I hesitated to price anything as long as Bill was peering in, lest they have me run in for profiteering.

So you see that in my glass life there were many inhibitions, but in spite of them I had a swell time. But they determined finally that for me glass should always be an avocation.

I no longer range through strange cupboards. The shelves in my office are bare of glass. I hold insurance conferences to my hearts content but at times feel nostalgia for the old interruptions. I kept a few pieces of glass to maintain the proper atmosphere in my home. Today I am not a collector. I am not a dealer. I think I was so busy enjoying people that I failed to study glass enough to attain the rank of connoisseur. I'm just a dilettante.

Along with his antique furniture, glass and china hobby rides, Lilburn became attracted by Lustre. He regaled many women's clubs with talks based on the following text:

FOLLOWING A WANDERLUST TOWARD LUSTRE

To a casual observer, a collection of lustre-ware may be just a row of things on a shelf. To a person of artistic temperament it may appeal because of graceful lines or decorations. But to one who has sought and found these specimens, buried in dust or sentiment, and has brought them out of retirement from attics, store-rooms and cellars, they have a peculiar charm. Many pieces reflect little stories of human interest incidental to their discovery and acquisition.

Wandering and hunting for early American lustre, on which the season is open the entire year, is great sport. Not alone for the intrinsic value of the "game" brought in, but for the interesting contacts with "old timers" in many communities, who delight in reminiscing and in relating historical and romantic facts.

The contacts are indeed of diverse sorts. Occasionally there is a soul like the aged woman reputed to possess many refinements of early days. In response to my rapping with the elegant brass knocker at her home, she demanded from behind the heavy door what was wanted. The ominous growl of a dog inside added to the discomfiture of making, against a blank door, a plausible request for permission to hunt lustre inside the premises.

"You just wait 'til I open the door," she replied, pleasantly enough, it seemed. While waiting I anticipated with suppressed enthusiasm the purchase of treasures I would presently find inside this early 19th century home, for like all amateur collectors, I possessed an abundance of that quality which is "the substance of things hoped for and the evidence of things unseen."

But after half an hour during which there was no further sound of woman or beast, it dawned clear in my mind that there must have been a peculiar emphasis on that word 'wait' which in my eagerness I had at first failed to detect.

Another elderly woman, six feet tall, raw-boned and clad in a gray woolen dress which had a high collar, mutton-leg sleeves, tight fitting waist and a flaring skirt which swept the floor, came out of the house in response to my knocking. With hair combed straight back from a weathered face and tied in a knot at the crown of her head, this fashion plate of the gay nineties glowered at me over old-fashioned glasses with rectangular lenses, as she crossed a screened-in porch toward the door by which I was standing. She hooked the door, stepped back, placed her arms akimbo and demanded sternly, "Well?"

Her hostile manner inspired me with a feeling of trepidation. If the act of locking the door in my face gave her a sense of security, the knowledge that she was locked in revived my courage which already had been stimulated by the sight of a lustre pitcher of considerable size which was being used with an old metal washpan on a stand inside the porch.

To every appeal for admission to the house and every offer to buy the pitcher, she was adamant. "No sir-ree," she said, "A burnt child don't play with fire. You guys aren't what you are cracked up to be. I wouldn't trust a one of you. Why, there was a nice appearing man here taking orders for specs just last month. He got my ten dollars and that is the last I ever heard of him. He said he was one of the biggest eye doctors in St. Louis, Dr. B." And she added naively, "Maybe you know him."

But generally old people are friendly and hospitable. They enjoy contacts with people outside their sphere and would talk all day. Time and again I have fallen under the spell of their stories until the hunt for lustre itself seemed of secondary interest. An old veteran with souvenir musket across his knee, boasting of his prowess in a Civil War battle during which the enemy shot a cannon ball right through his father's house! Does not the visible scar in the wall still speak for itself? An old lady weaving her story of linsey-woolsey clothing, carding a bit of wool and spinning it into yarn on a wheel just to show me how it was done when she was young and had to accomplish her "daily stint." An old minister relating the details of the schism which occurred in his church when a majority of the elders voted out the spittoons, no less serious than the one when the custom of segregating the sexes was broken and promiscuous sitting was allowed! A gracious widow of a river steamboat captain, seated on the white-columned verandah of an imposing old brick mansion set on a bluff commanding views of the Missouri river, recounting stories of steamboat days when veritable "floating palaces" with gorgeous appointments and gallant captains, plied the river in the 60s and

70s; of boat races, the music of piping calliopes floating across the water, of wrecks and thrilling rescues and concluding with a yearning sigh, "Alas. Will we ever have such fine steamboats on the Missouri again?"

But with attention recalled to lustre, many of the old folks are eager to be helpful in discovering it. Others consider the quest pure nonsense. Some feel that a "loose screw" is responsible for such a complex. A few resent the suggestion that they would part with their heirlooms. Others are glad to turn "old stuff" which they look upon as rubbish, into money.

So, in response to a well applied "line" of talk, elastic enough to fit many different situations, they willingly, reluctantly, or indifferently, as the case may be, lead the way to old cupboards, trunks and boxes in search of something desirable. While I, agog with anticipation and in close pursuit, all but tread upon the heels of my guide. Too often there isn't a rare thing left. But here and there, in the backmost corner of the top shelf of a cupboard, I find a lustre tea-pot, a mug or a plate. Such a discovery always brings me up short like a setter pointing a bird. A great moment for a lustre snooper!

One day a large lustre pitcher with wide pink resist band, arrested my attention. Trying to seem casual, I admired the modern china and the green glassware from the five and ten, then seemed to see for the first time, the object which a little bit before made my heart miss a beat. I ventured to inquire, "What about the rusty old pitcher on the top shelf? Is it of any use to you, or would you like to dispose of it?"

"Land sakes! That old dust catcher up there was John's pappy's grandma's," came the reply. "She was so proud of it as long as she lived because it was all she had left of the things her family brought out of Johnson county when the Federals run them out and burned their home under Order No. 11. But I've been dusting the old thing spring and fall for years and I'd be right glad to get shed of it. John won't care. I reckon I'll ask you seventy five cents for it if you don't think that's too much."

An old man with faltering step led me to a cupboard. When

I offered to buy a coppery brown bowl, he took it in his palsied hands and seemed overcome with sentimental reminiscences. "No indeed," he declared, "Money couldn't buy this bowl. Why it was my Mother's when she was a little girl! Why I ate porridge out of it when I was a baby!" Then his reasoning changed and he continued, "But you're right. What will become of it when I am gone? All my folks are dead and I'm going on ninety, just living on borrowed time. I can't be here long. I believe I'd like for somebody to have this little bowl who will appreciate it. Young fellow, you go down to the store and get me a couple of plugs of chewing tobacco and I'll trade with you."

In the Ozarks a log cabin which looked as old as the hills themselves, with its chimney of native stone, was intriguing, but the barefooted old mother, clad in gray calico with a small remnant of Paisley about her head, who came to the door declared she had no relics of early days. However, when the situation was "lined up", the lid of an old trunk was lifted and out of the depths of musty clothes, she lifted a silver lustre teapot, a beauty. In the negotiations which ensued, dollars wrestled with sentiment. But to the woman of the hills, the rustle of crisp new bills was sweeter music than the whisperings of memories, and she yielded the ware in sale.

But as she packed it up, she fondled it and soliloquized, "Don't reckon I ort to sell it, it's so old. A lot older'n me! It was grandmammy's, some of her fust buyin's back in Pennsylvania when she set up to housekeepin'. My children'll be put out by me asellin' it. But if they ask me whar is it, I just won't tell 'em whar it goed."

Old colored people possess some interesting pieces of lustre, picked up at public sales or given them by their "white folks". The "line" fitted to them generally elicits the question, "Boss, is you gittin' up these things for the Worlds Fair?" Advice to the contrary leaves them in doubt and they ask, "Then what in the name of G— are you going to do with it?"

But they are quite willing to throw open for inspection the kitchen safe, the cubby-hole under the house and the trunk in the coal shed, hopeful of bringing forth something to sell. Or to show with pride, something given them by a well-to-do white friend, 'ole Miss' or 'ole Marse'.

Some desirable things are easily acquired from them, but many long-sought articles are so highly valued through senti-ment, it takes much coaxing and scheming to get them, if indeed they can be had at all. A number of the aged colored people feel superstitious about disposing of anything which has been given them if the donor is dead. One woman said, "Not fo' nothin' would I depart from dese copper cups. They was a present from my dead husband an' they'se goin' right in de coffin wid me!"

Hannah Flint had heard that I bought "old things" and wanted to sell me a small lustre pitcher in order to get some money to buy chances on a quilt being raffled off at her church. Noting an unusual decoration on the side of the pitcher, I remarked, "This looks like it might be etched." Hannah, fearing that this was some defect which would block the sale, inquired anxiously, "Boss, don't you reckon you could fix it?" In high humor I told her it was etched worse than any pitcher I had ever seen, but I might give her a quarter for it anyway. "Bless God," exclaimed the old woman, "Jesus is sho good to me!"

Aunt Cindy Harris, an aged colored woman, was said to have lived long with "rich folks" from whom she had acquired unusual things in old tableware. When I visited her, she opened the door and inquired through the narrowest slit, what was wanted. She declared emphatically, "I've done got shed of all my old junk." Not fully convinced and scheming to gain entrance, I called a few days later with a basket of fruit. She opened the door wide enough to admit the basket, then after an earnest application of the "line", reluctantly admitted me into the kitchen. After much wheedling I was permitted to open the doors of an old corner cupboard. There, amid stacks of nondescript dishes, covered with dust, reposed three pieces of good lustre.

As I stood there with covetous and scheming eyes fixed upon the desired articles, she kept muttering, "Taint no use to look! Ain't nothin' old! Couldn't nobody buy them things nohow."

Finally drawing herself up with a determined air and shaking her bandana clad head, she announced, "My departed husban' done give 'em ever' one to me an' I sho God ain't goin' git exposed of 'em 'til I dies!" With this ultimatum delivered, she settled into obstinate silence. The basket of fruit had worked no subtle charm. The session closed without a doxology.

But as I passed out through her yard, disappointed at the outcome of the visit, flowers peeping up along the walk gave me fresh inspiration. Upon my next visit I took the roots of many perennial flowers for Cindy's border. Cindy may have had many weaknesses, but one of the biggest was flowers. That day I "brought home the bacon," everything I wanted from that cupboard.

At first Mandy Kelsey's old lustre cups and saucers, stuck back in a dark pantry, were too sacred, she said, to sell for any amount of money. 'Ole Miss' had given them to her and she was now dead. In a second effort to obtain them, a bottle of toilet water and a box of bath powder were proffered in exchange. From these, as she considered them, Mandy took deep, frequent sniffs of fragrance which rendered her oblivious to her sentimental feeling about 'ole Miss' and the lustre dishes.

Arriving definitely at a decision, she burst out, "Go on an' take de dishes, white man! I'se got to have dese cosmetics! I sho loves 'em!" But her mood changed suddenly and she continued, "Lawd knows tho' I'se an ole fool not to git money to pay my doctor. I know my looks don't deceive it but I'se suffered death now for goin' on nine years. Nine long years I'se been mighty low, not able to do no washin' and no heavy liftin'."

Mandy was such a picture of health, I felt impelled to find out what ailment could be so devastating and yet leave no visible traces of its ravages, so I asked her if the doctor had discovered what was the matter with her.

"Law Boss, yes!" she replied, "de doctor he done call it de chronical narvous nuralgy ob de intestinal," and with a sigh, added, "An' he say they ain't much hope."

There is hardly more than Mandy Kelsey's hope of recovery for those who have become addicts to wanderlust toward lustre.

The "chronical narvous nuralgy" of the hunt drags the stricken ones far, along the highways and into the byways. But they like it. They find compensation for trials and tribulations in the contacts with the old souls "just living on borrowed time" who relate their fascinating romantic tales of early days, who clothe their antiques with traditions of pathos and humor. And in running down and occasionally bagging a rare piece of lustre, be it for profitable resale or for adding to the treasures of one's private corner cupboard.

Chapter Seven

SADDLING THE HISTORY HOBBY HORSE

Lilburn's interest in history began in 1939, when he was elected president of the Cooper-Howard County Historical Society. The name later became the Boonslick Historical Society.

In December 1937 Lilburn wrote to Lillian:

Dear Cousin Lillian,

I enclose a couple of clippings, one of which will enlighten you in regard to the Historical Society. I got hooked up in it the night after I was in St. Louis, and perhaps while I was "still in my cups" or something. But now I am in, and find every one I ask to serve on various committees so willing, I am encouraged and hopeful we may have an up-and-doing organization. An editor of a paper recently called to ask my opinion about some historical data which he had gathered. He had been informed that at one time my grandfather Horace Kingsbury and Billie Marshall tried to dam up the flow from the old Salt Lick [*where Daniel Boone and his sons made salt*] for a body of salt water in which they expected to plant salt or sea fish and oyster beds. I had not heard of it before, but father said that was Billie Marshall's idea after he bought the land from Grandfather and those who formed the company and put down the well at the spring. Grandfather had nothing to do with that wild dream.

I have a horror of being called on for talk in public meetings and at the banquet I seated myself near an exit and planned to leave as soon as the banquet was served and the guest speaker had made his address. I feared since so few Howard Countians were present, I would be asked to say something for the county. But the order of the meeting was changed and the business session held before Dr. Violette was asked to speak. When it came time to elect a president, my name was put up, the nomination seconded, nominations closed, and I was elected by acclamation. It was done before I could set the coffee cup from which I was drinking at the moment down on the table. Roy Williams had me framed. He didn't want it himself and he was just slick enough to plan to put it on somebody else. Instead of sneaking out the exit as I had planned, I went in response to invitation to the President's chair, utterly dumbfounded and amazed and embarrassed beyond words. They asked Dr. Violette to speak and during that time I was trying to think of something to say for I knew my time had come. There were 60 prominent people and I couldn't just lie down and die.

I scarcely know parliamentary rules and when called on to preside over the balance of the business matters, I had to turn to Roy for help and had a terrible struggle, but it seems the audience thought I had assumed a pose, and they thought me funny and I got by. Mrs. Chilton said she had not realized I was a natural born wit. I wasn't. I was just a darned fool, but the Lord was kind and kept the fact concealed.

On August 22, 1938:

Dear Cousin Lillian,

It is funny how my interests change with the years. There was a time when it was music, then it was genealogy, and now it is history.

But I am terribly interested in a project which is giving me relaxation in a way, and yet I wear myself down to the nub at it, simply because when I am interested in something, I work at it like I was putting out a fire. My project started out as an effort to discover the graves of the pioneers who were the political, economic and social pillars of the Boonslick Country.

I soon discovered no one today knows where the unmarked graves of Boonslick pioneers are. Most of the private cemeteries are wrecks. It was obvious with the passing of another generation, many old graveyards would be obliterated. It occurred to me it would be a good thing if all the marked graves in the county were recorded for the benefit of posterity, and, not having done much for posterity, I decided to undertake that project. I know John Doe of the future will feel impelled by a sudden interest in genealogy, and want to find out something about his Howard County ancestors.

Some of what he found:

HOWARD COUNTY FAMILY GRAVEYARDS

Old graveyards are numerous in Howard County. By the middle of the last century there was a graveyard on nearly every farm. In many instances it was within a stone's throw of the house. More often it was farther from the dwelling, on a high point chosen because it commanded a beautiful landscape as if the spirits of the departed might be accorded the enjoyment of such a view, very lovely in early spring or in the blue haze of Indian summer.

During the past summer and fall I visited every marked grave in Howard County which comprises the heart of the Boonslick Country, seeking traces of the pioneer men and women.

Seventy percent of the private graveyards of which there are more than 200 now extant, are unfenced and overrun by livestock, with many tombstones on the ground. Some ten percent, though fenced, have reverted to wild vegetation. A few are so overgrown with saplings, weeds and briers as to make them almost impenetrable.

The graves of most of the Howard County pioneers who died here are lost forever, having unlettered rock or cedar tree markers, or none at all. No person living now can identify them. Many of the inscribed markers which did grace graves are flat upon the earth, some in fragments, broken off by browsing cows and horses which delight in rubbing their bodies against the sharp edges of the brittle slabs.

The marble monument which stood at the grave of Colonel Benjamin A. Cooper, leader of the first settlers who came to the Boonslick frontier in 1810, courageous protector of his people during the war with the Indians and in later years an outstanding citizen in the county, lies shattered on a hillside.

Lilburn continued adding to his files of grave data cards as new family cemeteries came to his attention.. When he died, his cemetery card files became part of the Lilburn A. Kingsbury collection in the Western Manuscript division of the Missouri State Historical Society in Columbia. There are approximately 1300 cards in these files. In his letters and newspaper columns he writes of some of his graveyard experiences. An example of this is his Boonville Daily News _Column of March 27, 1972. It follows:_

WE JUST PIZENED A BABY

In making records of the tombstones in Howard County, I wondered about the infant mortality which occurred in some families during the 19th century.

Lewis cemetery near Glasgow. Original tombstones for Lewis children

In the endowed, well-groomed Lewis family cemetery two miles east of Glasgow, there are two small rows of tombstones, ten in one and eight in the other. They mark the graves of children fathered by two brothers. Seven of the family of ten died before they were one year old. One lived until its second year, one until its third, and the other one attained the age of four years. The stones which mark their graves are exactly alike and appear modern, as if they might have replaced old-fashioned ones erected a century ago.

Six of the babies in the other family lived but one, five, nine, eleven, and fifteen days and one less than a month. A seventh child survived six months; the eighth, eleven months.

The deaths of the ten children extended over a period of twenty-four years from 1839 to 1863. Those of the eight occurred within twelve years, 1854 through 1866. The graves of the latter are marked by small obelisks alike except one is larger than the others. It marks the grave of the last child to die. Each has a little lamb as an emblem just above the name and the dates.

I was so deeply impressed by and curious about these cases of infant mortality, I went to see an elderly man in Glasgow. I thought he might remember having heard something about it.

He had seen the two rows of tombstones many times and he too had wondered about them until he talked with old Mose, an aged black man who had been a young slave owned by one of the brothers.

Mose was feeble of body but had a clear mind. With emancipation so far behind him he spoke casually of the deaths of the children. He said, "Cose I remembers. Ever time one of the Massas whupped one of us, we just pizened a baby."

Such stories of slaves squaring scores, "gettin even", still persist.

Lilburn's graveyard visits provided many tasty anecdotes to embellish his frequent talks to clubs and societies. A favorite title he used was:

SOME GRAVE REMARKS

One day a woman looked out of our front window toward Mt. Pleasant cemetery and saw something which excited her very much. She called me and explained she had seen no one go over to the graveyard, yet she could see what appeared to be a woman, dressed in black. She seemed to move behind tombstones as if hiding, or, she would appear to stand erect and then stumble after a step or two and fall to the ground. She was sure the woman was either intoxicated or desperately ill. Nothing would suffice but for me to investigate. There was a woman in black, a frail little thing from a distant city. She was not ill. She was not intoxicated except as one gets drunk on genealogy. She was searching for the graves of her ancestors. At times she stood up to read the inscriptions, sometimes in front, sometimes behind the tombstones. Again she would lie almost prone upon the ground to study the time-worn names and date, which accounted for the disappearing act which was visible from the window.

Robert Taylor and Alice Kingsbury's Monument

In Howard County, the D.A.R. and Real Daughters of 1812 have placed bronze plaques on granite stones in the Court House Yard at Fayette, in memory of all of the Soldiers and Real Daughters of the Revolution and all the Soldiers and Real Daughters of 1812, known to have been buried in Howard County. These plaques bear 100 names but only 31 of these citizens have marked graves. The History of Howard and Cooper Counties lists 230 names of men who were in the forts of 1812, but only thirteen of these names appear in my survey of marked graves.

When deaths occurred, the early settler buried his loved ones on his own land, or if some kinsman or good neighbor had already started a God's acre, he opted to use it. Often the plat was close to the flower garden or within a stone's throw of the house. Sometimes a more distant site was chosen because of elevation.

Clark's Chapel, in the south part of the county, commands a magnificent view of the Missouri River valley with the rolling hills of Cooper County in the distance. I once heard a man say he would like to have his last sleep there, so that on the Resurrection, when Gabriel blows his horn, he might arise and enjoy the view the first thing in the morning.

In the family cemeteries, cedar trees were planted, sometimes in lieu of markers at the graves, more often to outline the boundaries of the plot, but always as symbols of memories to be kept green forever. Some of these old cedar trees, as old as the graveyards themselves and nourished by the bones of men buried beneath them, are keeping faith with the dead, but hold their skirts of evergreen boughs high as if to keep them from the desolation underfoot. But they, like rock retaining walls, massive box tombs, marble shafts and iron fences, all designed by men for permanency, are being humbled into the dust by time.

In some cases the condition reflected indifference on the part of surviving relatives, but generally the direct descendants of those buried there have passed on or else removed to parts so far distant that feeling of responsibility has disappeared, or if they do remember, procrastination sees that there is no material manifestation of the thought.

Judge Owen Rawlins was a prominent man of the county and first Commissioner of Schools. He was buried on his farm in one of the more pretentious private graveyards of its day. Hogs from a wallow had lolled against a handsome square marble shaft, flat upon the ground, from which I scraped the mud to read:

"This monument shades the remains of Judge Owen Rawlins, a native of Kentucky, long a resident of Missouri, and State Senator for 20 years."

Upon an impressive shaft, ten feet high, still standing erect in memory of Elder Thomas Fristoe, early and powerful minister of the Gospel in Howard County, who served Chariton Church for 30 years, is inscribed under a victor's wreath:

"In all the relations of life he was faithful and true. He was distinguished by an unaffected humility, unswerving candor and inflexibility of purpose, over all of which was thrown the charm of unquestionable piety, a religious spirit pervades the whole character. Though dead he yet speaks."

But not with such vehemence as one who hacked his way through the thicket of brambles and saplings higher than the monument itself and fell into the vine covered burrow of a groundhog searching to discover the identity of the gentleman who merited such a splendid monument.

The ashes of one of the Daughters of the American Revolution whose name appears on one of the plaques in Fayette, lie under an unusual box tomb of rectangular blocks of sandstone, a massive flat stone for a cover.

There was another tombstone with the inscription turned down doing duty as a doorstep. The tenant farmer said I might examine it but if his wife appeared I should say nothing which would indicate to her what the step really was. We had copied the name and dates and were putting it back in place when his wife stepped out on the porch. Pointing an accusing finger at her husband, and in a voice more severe than I was accustomed to hear, she said: "Abner Jones, you've been lying to me all the time about that doorstep!"

Tombstones had been removed from their places of dignity to be put under down-spouts. Others were used as flagstones, and at one place they propped up the walls of a sagging house.

Not many graveyards, comparatively speaking, have been entirely obliterated. It is probable when the river was washing the Franklin town site away, the bodies interred there were removed to a spot a short distance north. There was such a cemetery there with tombstones until twenty or thirty years ago. At that time, the owner of the land, tired of plowing around the graveyard, dug a hole, buried the tombstones and plowed his furrows straight.

A fine barn covered most of one cemetery and the monuments which had not been in the way of the building were broken off and lay shattered in the mule lot. A lady who lived nearby looked upon this act as desecration and told me with significant emphasis that no sooner had the owner finished his barn than he hung himself.

Another man, tired of a small graveyard in the corner of his pasture, stacked the tombstones neatly under a tree and planted a potato patch. An old Negro woman living near it told me, "He raised a good crop an' the potatoes wuz fine to look at. But when I tried to cook 'em, they wuz such funny doin's in de skillet, I throwed 'em all out."

In one cemetery the entire space was covered with a wilderness of fragrant, blooming honeysuckle which almost concealed the gravestones. On one of them I found the name of a man which recalled to my mind his obituary which I had read in one of the early Fayette newspapers. It had been written by one of his daughters.

There was another cemetery which fairly shone with care. Not a weed or a bramble in sight! A genial farmer sat with me on an old box tomb and talked of it. "The old graveyard looked so bad it was just a disgrace," he said, "and I just had to do something about it. So I cleared off all the brush, built this new fence around it and planted me this watermelon patch. And melons! I bet I've picked a dozen fine ones just between here and Uncle John's tombstone over yonder."

Presently he moved away, thumped and picked a big melon, carried it back to where we were sitting. As he dropped it lightly on the marble slab, it popped open with a sweet sound we all like to hear. As we regaled ourselves with the delectable heart of that melon, I was moved to say, "Mr. Bill, I do believe you have the best kept cemetery in the county." But even so I felt a little melancholic!

In running the files of the *Missouri Intelligencer* of 1822, I came across this unusual notice of a wedding:

"Married, in this county on the 21st day of October, Rev. Thomas Campbell to Mrs. Pembroke Paul. This reverend gentleman in the morning attended the preaching of a funeral sermon on the death of his late beloved wife and in the evening walked over to the dwelling of his intended, and the marriage ceremony being performed, took his lady by the hand and returned together with the invited guests, to his own house, where all parties partook of a supper which had been prepared for this joyfully solemn occasion."

Now I knew Jerusha Campbell's tomb was a short distance from New Franklin and the marker at her grave bore the second earliest date in existence in the county.

It was quite usual to have the burial service and defer the funeral sermon as was done in the case of Jerusha Campbell. If a death occurred during cold weather, or if some favorite preacher could not come at the time to preach the funeral, it was in order to postpone the service until a more propitious time.

Before the present building at Clark's Chapel was built, there was another church on the same site, but it faced east. One of the young daughters of Zion (Sarah Jane) who had been reared to know better, went to a dance in a neighboring community without her flannels, caught cold, contracted consumption and died in 1863. But not before she had talked earnestly with her relatives and friends admonishing them to be less worldly and to turn their minds toward spiritual things. It was her last request that she be buried beneath the big walnut tree by the front door of the church so that all who passed in or out might see her grave and be reminded of her untimely end. There she was buried. Eighty-three years have passed, the church has been turned around, the old walnut tree is dead, only a bit of the stump remains near the marble shaft erected in memory of Sarah Jane, with this epitaph: "Forget not dear friends that it is here I lie. But remember that you too must die."

My presence in private cemeteries naturally excited the curiosity of people who came out to see what I was doing. Sometimes they lingered awhile, telling of the history of the place or of the people buried there. It was often very revealing and interesting. I shall never forget the frail old lady who walked with a cane and followed me around, and said when I was studying one tombstone:

"An old bachelor's buried there, and if ever there was a cranky piece it was him. Why, his dyin' request was to be buried in his overcoat, and in mid-August!" I assured her I never heard of anybody so queer. "If you think he was queer you ought to have knowed his Ma. She must have marked him. Why it was her dyin' request to be buried in nothin' but her nightgown, the one her niece sent her from Kentucky. You see she come from Kentucky herself. It was embroidered nice and looked very pretty, but it seemed to me like something was lackin'."

As for epitaphs, most of them fall into two classes. In one, the sentiment would appear to be expressed by the departed. Here is one: "Affliction sore for a year I bore Physicians were in vain. At length God pleased to give me ease and free me from my pain."

And another: "My heart once heavy is now at rest, My groans are no more heard, my race is run, my grave you see, prepare for death and follow me."

One seems to depict great travail and then sweet peace:

"This languishing head is at rest, It's thinking and aching are o'er. This quiet, immovable breast, is heaved by emotion no more."

The other class included those which express the sentiment of those bereft. There are those which pay tributes such as I have already given. And then this type: "May heaven's most tender lay, fall gently on his ear, and sweetly charm his thoughts away, from all he suffered here."

Or: "Tread lightly o'er these hallowed grounds. A kind lamented one lies here. You who have felt misfortune's frown come pause and drop a tear."

And some are in a class by themselves. Here is one which depicts a contest in which the already departed members of the family are victorious over those still living: "In manhood's prime from promise bright thy spirit fled to endless light. Father, brothers, sisters, babes three cried 'we could not give thee up, no, no.' But Mother, Wife, stronger than we with God prevails. Thou dids't go."

But in what class would you put this one?: "Here lies Eliza Jane, the beloved daughter of Mary and Joseph Brown and Henry Brown."

The Clark's Chapel Cemetery stone with the earliest date— Mark Arnold, 1819. Nancy Snell and Jesse Walker were the only centenarians.

CAPTAIN OF THE FORTS OF 1812

Sarschel Cooper was one of Boonslick's heroes. He was Captain of all of the men of the forts of 1812. You will recall how, one stormy night in 1815, he was shot by an assassin through a chink hole in the wall of his cabin at Cooper's Fort as he sat by the fireplace with his baby on his knee. He was buried in the graveyard near the fort. Years passed, his children prospered, and they planned to erect a fitting monument at his grave. A handsome white marble stone was chosen and inscribed. It was about to be set at his grave when the mighty flood of 1844 covered the Missouri River valley from bluff to bluff. When the water subsided, a deep covering of silt had obliterated every trace of the graveyard. No one could identify the site of Sarschel Cooper's grave. The stone was set in a slave cabin at the Joseph Cooper home, and it remained there for many years, even after the land had passed out of the possession of the family. The late parents of Robert Clarke of Fayette bought the farm. Robert and his sister, Mrs. Henry Black, reminisce of how as little children, they played in the cabin and the strange stone which leaned against the wall filled them with misgivings. One day Nestor Cooper learned of its presence at the Clarke's farm and asked that it be given to him. He took it to his home west of Fayette and set it under a walnut tree in the front yard. Here it remained several years until it passed into the possession of Central College for its museum.

In 1903, another flood, second only to that of 1844, covered the Missouri River valley. Strangely, where the first flood had buried the site of the cemetery of the Fort, the second one swept all of that cover away and even swirled the earth out of the graves, leaving the bones of those buried there exposed to view.

Col. Stephen Cooper, learning of what had happened, visited the scene. He and others noted the spade marks in the gumbo soil on the sides and ends of each grave were as clearly discernible as if they had been made that day.

Now it was tradition in the Cooper family that Sarschel Cooper, though 44 years of age at the time of his death, had a perfect set of teeth. Examination disclosed that one grave contained a skull which complied with this condition. This proved to Col. Cooper conclusively that it was the grave of his great-grandfather.

He removed the bones from the grave and interred them in the Joseph Cooper graveyard on the bluff above the house where his tombstone had set for so many years. From this high point is a sweeping view of all the land which the Coopers possessed. The grave of Sarschel Cooper is still unmarked. His monument stands futilely against a wall in the basement of the Library at Central College, or it did the last time I saw it.

EPITAPHS

Epitaphs have interested me ever since I began to prowl

through cemeteries. Some are so unusual they are beyond belief until one sees them or sees pictures of them.

Some of the earliest were published in the *Missouri Intelligencer* in 1824:

Here lies my wife who killed herself.
All of her own accord,
The Lord that gave have taken away
And blessed be the Lord.

• • •

Here lies, thank God, a woman who
Quarreled and stormed her whole life through.
Tread softly o'er her moldering form
Or else you'll rouse another storm.

• • •

Jane, to her spouse could not bestow
One tear of sorrow when he died
His life had made so many flow
That the briny fount had dried.

• • •

In Dedham, Mass. at the Inn I inquired if any Kingsburys had ever lived there. The hostess replied: "If you had looked out the window of your room you would have seen a graveyard full of them."

Around the corner I found them. I read on Abigail Kingsbury's tombstone, "She lived in the state of single blessedness 18 years, in the married state 20 years and in that of widowhood 25 years during all of which her conduct was amiable and exemplary." I felt proud of her but left the place wondering about my great-great uncle Henry beside whose tombstone there were two others, one for his wife and the other for his consort, both of whom died the same year.

In one of Howard County's cemeteries stand two monuments side by side. One was erected in memory of Lee Cloyd's Right Arm Amputated Aug. 7, 1875. The other in memory of Lee Cloyd who died Nov. 17, 1876, aged 13 years.

One wonders as he reads:

"My Dear Husband, May He Rest In Peace Until We Meet Again."

"My Wife Lies Here, All My Tears Cannot Bring Her Back, Therefore I Weep."

Someone was telling me of Miss Mary Goodblood, a spinster who was concerned about her epitaph. Among her effects was found a memorandum which advised: "Don't put MISS on my tombstone. I haven't missed near as much as you think I have. Mary."

Obituaries of Long Ago

Lilburn's interest in cemeteries and epitaphs led him to search out obituaries. This quest resulted in the following excerpted column.

Today, newspaper obituaries are concise. Generally they give us what an old issue of a newspaper mentioned as "the principal events in chronological order in the life of the deceased. Outside the circle of relatives and friends these facts might suffice but among them they supply but the meager knowledge of the life and character of this truly good and noble man (or woman)."

The editors of newspapers seventy, eighty, ninety years ago undoubtedly wished to please the friends and relatives of the deceased. They published obituaries written at length by preachers, relatives or themselves. And one who reads them today feels that nothing was omitted.

People have changed. Few people today would wish an obituary of a loved one written in the phraseology of those earlier years. Sorrow may be just as keen but he does not wish his personal thoughts or feelings hung out in the newspaper like garments on a clothes line. For instance, of Mrs. Wilsy Buckshire (that was not her real name) it was written:

"Her sun is gone down while it was yet day. She has been summoned to join the inhabitants of another and better world. The appropriate words of the sermon were tender and touching in extreme and were as effective as the cool dew of evening to the drooping flower. After the most touching sermon the pallbearers conveyed the body to the hearse which waited at the door and the sad procession filed slowly and sadly to the cemetery where, with all possible tenderness, the body was laid to rest.

"She faded from our sight like a flower beneath the early frost. She daily grew thinner and weaker, the conviction forced itself upon her that there was no hope of life. Yet there was no repining, no shudder on the verge of the dark valley. She was a patient sufferer, perfectly resigned to her fate and passed away without a struggle.

"It was only when we stood by her coffin and gazed upon her closed eyes and silent lips and forehead so white and cold that we realized we should have her with us no more. We laid her to rest on a sunny hillside, looking to the south, at the home of her childhood, beneath the cedars whose branches seemed to weep for her.

"Possessed of a lovely character she was revered and honored by all who knew her. And when the boatman stood with beckoning hand, bidding her to come, her spirit departed for that haven of rest to meet her loved ones who had gone before."

Perhaps old obituaries enabled the bereaved who read them to relive their grief as long as they lived. In none of them was there a request that flowers be omitted. There were none except in an occasional case as described in a letter written in 1870 about a funeral at Clark's Chapel, "The Porters were over from Boonville and laid a wreath of geranium leaves and white flowers on the coffin. It looked so pretty."

Obituaries in the long ago were usually published on the front page. Today if you are not somebody superspecial, I'll read of your demise on the back page.

There is one more epitaph which I have for you, and I believe when you have heard it, there will not be a man in the audience who would not aspire to have it on his tombstone. It is short, only five words, the tribute of a wife on the modest stone at the grave of John Stapp. Here it is: "He always rendered home happy."

RACEHORSES WERE HIS HOBBY

Lilburn's history hobby horse rides led him to interesting discoveries about his family and the Boonslick Country. These culminated in his two part article "Boonslick Heritage," which appeared in the January and April, 1966 issues of the Bulletin of the Missouri Historical Society. *The following excerpts are about his Grandfather Gearhart and his race track and his Grandfather Smith's distillery.*

Grandfather Isaac Gearhart was renowned for his agility and strength. He was a chunky man, not powerful in appearance, but he could pick up an anvil in each hand, strike them together above his head, and hurl them some distance from him. For that matter, he could lift a whiskey barrel and drink from the bunghole.

Grandfather was a fighter. A scar on his face, clearly discernible in an old photograph, was put there with a corn knife by his neighbor John Yowell Smith, and he bore this mark like a saber-cut with pride. More than once he was hailed into court on charges of assault and battery. On one occasion he pleaded guilty and was fined $5 and costs. On another, he and Thomas Barnes, after two bitter fights, sued each other for damages.

Isaac charged that Barnes "beat, bruised, wounded and ill-treated him with sticks, fists, hands and a certain knife, thereby greatly injuring him until he was weak and distempered for three months." Barnes admitted that he "did necessarily and unavoidably, a little, beat, wound, and ill-treat the said Isaac Gearhart, but in self defense only." The wheels of justice had moved too slowly for Isaac, and on the twelfth day of the three months in which he claimed to have been incapacitated by the first fight, he had sought out Barnes, and "licked the stuffing out of him." Barnes now countercharged that Isaac "with great violence laid hold of him by the nose and greatly pulled the same; plucked and pulled large quantities of hair from and off his head; struck him many violent blows with a stick and gave him many severe cuts with a knife; shook him violently, threw him on the ground and rent and tore his clothing."

In each trial the jury found for the plaintiff, but Barnes got only $25 instead of the $6,000 for which he had sued, and Isaac Gearhart had nothing but the satisfaction of having whipped his opponent, for the jury awarded him one cent damages, though he had sued for $5,000.

Isaac Gearhart bought the Franklin Race Track and the farm on which it was situated in 1829. He gloried in its possession, but it was a source of great distress to his wife. She was one of those women who wept often over "disappointed hopes in her companion," imploring Isaac to give up the track. But Isaac owned White Stockings, a fine sorrel mare for which he had paid the highest price ever known in those parts, and she had earned him a lot of money. He had hopes for at least one more successful season. Touched by his wife's tearful pleas, however, he made her a promise: "Now Sally, if White Stockings loses the next race, I will give up the track. If she wins, I won't."

The season came on, and the first race was called. The odds on White Stockings were large, and from the first she took the lead. Sarah Gearhart listened tearfully as the crowd roared, and then suddenly there was silence. White Stockings had fallen, and was injured so severely that she had to be shot. This was a devastating blow to Grandfather Gearhart. He had lost a beautiful and valuable mare, and he had lost the large sums he had bet on her, but worst of all was the matter of his promise to Sarah.

He had given his word, however, and kept it. When spring came, the Franklin Race Track was plowed and planted to corn.

A Little for the Stomach's Sake

Among Missouri pioneers, the use of whiskey was fairly common. The records of early travelers indicate that with few exceptions the taverns and inns all had bars. Aside from its social uses, whiskey was highly regarded for its medicinal value. Since intermittent fevers were universal in the newly settled areas, it was common practice to administer large doses of whiskey and black pepper to ward off chills. It was noted that those in the habit of drinking large quantities of malt spirits were seldom seized with typhus or other low fevers, whatever other effects such imbibing might have.

Every well-established community in Boonslick Country had its distillery, and it was not unusual for farmers to operate private stills at their homes with their own grain, just as they made sorghum from their cane and lard from the fat of their hogs.

The Franklin Mill and Distillery was established by John Yowell Smith, husband of Grandfather Smith's sister Jincy, and Mark Finks Garr. The mill was powered by an oxen on a tread-mill, for which a man named McCleverty made cogwheels of hickory wood.

In 1850 Grandfather William J. Smith and his brother-in-law Jonas Finks Blankenbaker bought the mill and distillery. They paid $3,000 for the plant and a slave named Alfred, and an additional $600 for a Negro boy named Thorton. Another asset, acquired for $335, was a herd of hogs, considered a necessary adjunct, since they fed on the mash from the distillery and fattened rapidly.

Jonas Blankenbaker died of cholera in 1851, but Grandfather Smith continued to operate the distillery, enlarging the plant and modernizing its facilities. The prices of their whiskey varied. A single gallon retailed at 35 to 40 cents; a single barrel ranged from 20 to 28 cents per gallon. In lots of several barrels, the price might be as low as 15 to 20 cents the gallon. The chief purchasers were local merchants from New Franklin and the neighboring towns of Glasgow, Fayette, and Boonville, who bought from one to thirty gallons at a time, and retailed it mostly in grocery stores.

Selling it by the individual drink was prohibited, but there was no law against dispensing it gratis to a substantial customer as a token of appreciation, or against permitting a customer to buy a quart or a gallon and drink it on the place.

Economically, the mill and distillery were tremendous assets to the community. They bought enormous quantities of grain, rye bringing 35 to 40 cents per bushel, wheat 50 to 60 cents, and corn $1 to $1.25 per barrel. They provided an outlet for thousands of loads of wood to fire their boilers, a boon to settlers who were continually clearing land for cultivation, and equally constantly in need of the $1.25 per load which the mill paid for wood. They employed a group of expert coopers to make whiskey barrels at 50 cents each, and flour barrels at 20 cents. They bought hoop poles for flour barrels at 50 cents the hundred. At times they rented storage space for their whiskey. They hired teams to transport materials to the mill from the steamboat landing at "Old Town." They paid large sums in ferry fees to deliver whiskey and flour to Boonville. They acted as a clearing house where patrons could settle accounts with business concerns in nearby towns. They were willing to barter for wood or supplies, thus obviating any cash outlay. For grinding corn, they charged 10 cents per bushel; a pound of wheat could be traded for a half pound of flour.

Grandmother Elizabeth Gearhart Smith was as vigorously opposed to her husband's connection with the distillery as her mother had been to Grandfather Gearhart's racing activities. In vain he argued that the distillery made money and provided them with everything they wanted. She knew no good would come of it. "A man's hopes can easily be blighted," was her dire prediction. And events proved her correct. On a summer night in 1853, lightning struck the mill, and it burned to the ground, a total loss. There were 300 barrels of whiskey in the storeroom, and the noise of the bursting hoops and exploding barrels was like a cannonade above the roar of the flames. Tradition has it that whiskey ran down the road "clean to 'Old Town.'" Uncle William Wallace Smith was a little boy at the time, but years later he used to tell how Grandfather Smith awoke to see the blazing light of the fire, and silently turned his back; and how Grandmother Smith cried and shouted for joy. The plant was never rebuilt.

Grandmother Smith was not the only one averse to whiskey and its traffic. There were many teetotalers among the settlers. In New Franklin the Sons of Temperance met in the Seminary, a large two-story building used as a school and a meeting place for the Masonic and Odd Fellows lodges. The subject of morality as it applied to liquor was brought into open discussion. Many of the men and women from Clark's Chapel attended regularly. Each member pledged himself against the use of liquor in any form. At each session the Grand Patriarch asked the solemn question, "Who has violated his oath since last we met?" Each faithful member placed his hand over his heart and responded, "Not I." Anyone who had broken his pledge was asked to retire from the meeting until his conduct could be investigated and his status established.

Chapter Eight

Clark's Chapel

Clark's Chapel was an important factor in Lilburn's life. It was a spiritual and social center which built strong bonds of community fellowships. The church was organized in 1822. When Lilburn was gathering his cemetery data, he determined the earliest grave was closed in 1824 and that all of his grandparents, half of his great grandparents and scores of other relatives were buried there. As a child, he attended services and the many social activities; as an adult he played for services, weddings and funerals. He frequently wrote of the Chapel. One such article appeared in the Farmland *magazine in May of 1970:*

Fortress of Religion

Clark's Chapel has been a fortress of religion in the Boonslick Country of Missouri for 146 years. It stands on a hill to which the people who dwell on the rich land surrounding it have lifted their eyes as a symbol which has influenced them "to do justly, to love mercy and walk humbly."

The large graveyard, with many generations sleeping together, extends downhill back of the church and along the ridge to the east.

My mother and father were born and reared within a couple of miles of each other with the site of the old church in between. As children they walked up the hill on weekdays to school taught in the church. On Sundays they rode with their parents to hear the preaching. Later, as husband and wife under the weight of life's responsibilities, it became a sanctuary where they sought inspiration.

In the course of more than four score years, their lives touched others of five generations who came to Clark's Chapel, from the earliest settlers to the last babies sprinkled at the altar.

Nobody knows how many times they came up the hill when relatives and friends were laid to rest in the churchyard.

Until they joined the hosts at rest in the churchyard, it was their gentle pleasure to make a trip here every Memorial Day, to walk around and lay flowers on the graves. I accompanied them carrying the baskets of flowers.

It was as if they were visiting with old friends, not unmindful of their strengths and weaknesses. These were not sad occasions. But there was something sacramental about the manner in which they performed some rites of remembrance.

Especially at Sallie's grave to which they always went first. She was my father's first wife of a year and my mother's sister. Both of them had adored her in life and the passing of sixty years had not diminished their memories. As mother arranged flowers brought from home, father went to his grandmother Chandler's grave nearby.

"I wish I had enough flowers to cover some of the graves completely," my mother would say. "I must bring more next year." Here is Aunt Hannah's grave...she was the sweetest thing to me on our trip to Yellowstone, more like a sister than an aunt...and this is Mrs. Casey's, how I loved her...Grandma Chandler's rose bush is in full bloom as always...when we children used to go to her house, she always made us do what she called "stints" of work before we could go out to play. How ashamed I feel now at having stuck my tongue out at her when she turned her back. It is hard to make amends with flowers. How long ago it seems.

"I'll never forget the last time Sister Fannie and I went to visit her. We rode horseback. We had to ford Sulphur Creek. Right in the middle of it, Fannie's horse reached down to drink, the saddle girth broke and Fannie fell right into the water. And, she had on one of the beautiful silk dresses she bought when she married. I'm saving the big red peonies for Fannie's grave."

"And here is Napoleon Gearhart's grave," my father took the thread of conversation. "He was such a promising young man when he was carried off so untimely. He was Annie Booth's sweetheart and some thought they were engaged......Uncle Noah rests here, nothing new to him for he rested all his life from cradle to grave.

"And Aunt Sukie is buried here beside him. Although she was a powerful church member before, she would never darken the church door after they bought the organ. She was against any musical contraption, even a tuning fork," my mother resumed.

"And her brother Sidney buried here beside her used to plant everything in the sign of the moon and pa used to tell him he would do better to put it in the ground. Look at these three little tombstones all alike put up for the three little children Uncle Noah and Aunt Sukie lost, almost right together during the cholera epidemic of 1851. Do you suppose their great loss had anything to do with them naming the next boy and girl born to them, Sodom and Gomorrah. They used to call him "Soddy" and her "Mote.""

"And here is Mr. Nance's grave and big tombstone with a globe on top of it, the latter an emblem to him of a world to conquer. don't you recall how he defied the Missouri river at flood time? He shook his fist at it and told it if it fooled with him, he would turn it upstream?

"He used to pray so fervently in church. Maybe if he had asked the Lord in the proper spirit he might have helped him do it. But he was always so independent, even when the ladies put spittoons in the church for the convenience of those who chewed tobacco. Why he wouldn't even spit in a spittoon!

"And poor little Sophy Jordan sleeps here. She just laced herself to death, tied her corset string to a bedpost and pulled until her ribs just overlapped. Finally she went into galloping consumption. How silly all of us were trying to have waists like wasps."

Here my father took over. "Didn't you tell me that vanity carried off cousin Sarah Jane Gearhart too? That she took off her flannel underwear in the wintertime to go to a dance, caught a deep cold which took her right into galloping consumption? Here is her grave. Let's drop some flowers on her resting place.

"Poor Richard Kimsey. He was a handsome, misguided youth.

Quantrell shot him off his horse during the Civil War right up the road nearby and he was buried here. I doubt if he has ever had a flower on his grave for none of his folks lived around here. One won't be amiss from us even if his band of so-called bushwhackers did raid our farm and steal my old mare." My mother added, "and he took Miss Guss Gallway's button charm string and rode away with it tied to his horse's tail."

"What a long time since old man Murphy died," continued my father as we went on down hill, the supply of flowers diminishing rapidly. "He made all the coffins for people around here, even made his own and had it ready. Kept it under his bed."

"Dear Cousin John Lee," said my mother, "do you remember the terribly hot day he was buried? The young preacher who loved him like a father was so overcome (by emotion) he couldn't go on with the service. He announced that all should come up for the "last look" before they carried him out to the cemetary for interment, and that next Sunday they should all come back for the funeral.

Now and again they paused to gaze over the bottom farms or toward the rolling hills to remark on the beauty of the landscape. They would point out familiar places, old homes where they visited and played as children. The site of the pioneer town of Franklin, the race track, the distillery. The old forts of 1812, and in the distance the hulk of Mt. Pleasant church of 1812, now moved and used as a farm barn. And nearby, the city of Boonville with its silvery highway bridge.

To them the broad scene was like a stage upon which generations of men, women and children, had enacted dreams of conquest, sport, religion, war and love for more than a hundred years, of remembered tales that were told.

Year after year as I heard them recount the stories of those who had lived and died upon the acres around Clark's Chapel, they made the actors come alive for me. They moved them like puppets in their roles and made them speak their lines.

Dear to the hearts of my parents were the Memorial Days. Truly the stories were their heritage, simple perhaps, but told with deep appreciation.

ROSE BUSH MEMORY

The following "Remembering is an Eloquent Moment" is another example of Lilburn's writings about the Chapel:

My great-grandmother Sarah Gearhart Chandler was buried at Clark's Chapel Cemetery one hundred and one years ago last February. Someone planted a rose bush on her grave.

I first noticed it after Memorial Day was established and I went with my parents, carrying baskets of flowers to lay on the graves of departed relatives and friends. They didn't remember who planted the rose bush. It was of considerable size and full of blossoms with dark red velvety petals. My notice of it might have been casual had I not seen my father go to it, pause as if choosing the prettiest flower then cutting it off with his knife.

My father, Robert Taylor Kingsbury, Sallie Smith and her younger sister, Alice, (my mother), were born on neighboring homesteads in the Clark's Chapel community and grew up together.

They also went to school in New Franklin at the Seminary. He rode a pony about four miles, while the girls walked from Sunnyside, the present home of C.I. and Clara Smith. Each day after school my father would gallantly offer to let Alice ride his pony home which she liked. Then he walked with Sallie.

Even as far back as their Clark's Chapel schooldays, according to old folks who remembered, he and Sallie were recognized as sweethearts.

They were married in 1870. The next year she died tragically during childbirth. Recovering outwardly from shock and grief or perhaps to console each other, Robert Taylor and Alice were married a year later.

In all the years I accompanied them to Clark's Chapel Cemetery on Memorial Day, never was there a time I was not reassured of their devotion to the memory of Sallie. They went directly to her grave where it seemed to me mother was going to lay all the flowers.

As she arranged them carefully, my father would go to the bush on his grandmother Chandler's grave, and select the prettiest rose, bring it back and lay it on Sallie's grave. It was an eloquent moment.

As long as father lived, this was his chief Memorial Day observance. After he died in 1938 it seemed to me he had established a tradition which should not die with him. So for 39 years it has been my pleasure to cut the prettiest rose from my great-grandmother's bush (it has always been in bloom on Memorial Day) and lay it on Sallie Smith Kingsbury's grave.

The rose bush which grew and bloomed so profusely since nobody knows when, appeared frail and bore no more than a dozen blossoms. But one was enough.

Recently I visited the cemetery and the rose bush was gone. Not a vestige of it is left. Evidently the caretaker thought it was old and useless and a hindrance to a clean swath of blue grass. He didn't know anybody revered it. I should have told the story sooner.

Chapter Nine

Robert Taylor Kingsbury's Death

By June of 1938 Robert Taylor Kingsbury's physical condition had deteriorated very badly. Lilburn writes of this to his cousin Lillian:

The Death Watch

Father is not able to sit up any more. His abdomen becomes so distended he threatens to have us get drum sticks. We had the doctor come and we told him father had said if he were a cow the doctor would just stick her and let out the gas. The doctor seriously said he had it on his mind to suggest the only thing that might be beneficial would be to "tap" him. Well, we all felt terribly at the thought, for that does no good except temporarily, and we filed remonstrances. The doctor said he would give me some medicine which might be efficacious, but thought he would have to tap dad for the sake of his comfort. Well, the trouble abated and while his stomach has been distended numerous times, it has not been so tight until today. It looks pretty bad to me. It interferes somewhat with his breathing. He says there is no soreness to speak of, and he never complains, so if there is any inconvenience suffered he says nothing of it. His complexion is rosier than any of ours, and his face isn't so thin, and we think his body has picked up considerably. However we have a hard time finding anything that will agree with him and we think taking so much medicine has upset him and are trying to get along with less of it. We don't always know what is best to do.

Well it has all been very sweet caring for him during this illness, and a privilege to do everything possible for him. Hardly a day goes by that dad's sense of humor does not manifest itself.

We called Dr. van Ravenswaay in and he found dad terribly uncomfortable and badly bloated. He said there were only two things to do: tap or give serum. That night dad was worse than he had ever been, could not get in a comfortable position for his breathing was labored. This serum affects the kidneys so the surplus fluid in the body drains out through the kidneys, and within twelve to fourteen hours, a gallon or more had passed and father was much relieved. He was able to sleep fairly well last night. I was up about every hour and a half to help him change his position, but slept soundly between calls. Today father has an appetite again and enjoyed some stewed chicken and a few little bits of other things.

Several nights later when father seemed so poorly, he said he wanted to talk to Horace and me, as the eldest and youngest sons of the family. He wanted to tell us what he desired at his funeral, etc. and wanted a very simple inexpensive coffin. He preferred to be buried without a steel vault, wanted just the old-fashioned box of wood. He wants his funeral service at Clark's Chapel and for songs: "Abide With Me" and "Nearer My God to Thee;" for scripture, "John 14 will be good for there are many good verses." The Rev. Rutherford, our pastor, is to preside at the service. Wants the seven grandsons to be the pallbearers, but if not enough of them are available, fill in with nephews. Wants a Masonic service. Said he knew there would not be room in the family lot for the service and suggested it be held just outside and west of the church. Because he is the oldest Mason in the County, the Lodges of other towns might wish to be invited, and perhaps the Knights Templars might wish to have part in the service, since he is one of the two surviving charter members. He wants a simple marker on the grave. He concluded his interview saying these were wishes which he would like to see carried out but if we, as a family, thought best to make any changes, we should feel at liberty to do so. Horace assured him his wishes would be carried out as closely as possible.

Father hoped I would carry on the farm which I would not mind doing if I could make it pay for itself, but since I have been fooling with it for eleven or twelve years, it has not paid suffi-ciently to do more than keep two men working for me and put me some in debt. I don't know how I would ever make the farm pay unless times get better. I shall see how things stack up when dad is gone. I might feel more endeared to the old place, or I might not care to keep up such an expensive operation. The household expenses have not come out of the farm earnings because there have been none in recent years. It is sort of a wild thought to think the home will go on as it has during the lives of mother and father.

4 July 1938

Dear Cousin Lillian,

Friday and Saturday nights the doctor "hypodermiced" father. He slept all night Friday and until noon Saturday and in the afternoon he was conscious and shook or nodded his head when we talked with him. He drank about two thirds of a glass of lemonade and wanted a good deal of ice water. He suffered most with his left leg. About nine o'clock last night the doctor put him to sleep again. Mrs. Cartner was with him until about 2 a.m., then I was with him the rest of the night but so worn out I dozed off. But there was little perceptible change in his condition, except for a higher pulse and a little slower breathing.

I went downtown about 9:30 Sunday morning and came very near going elsewhere on an errand, had not gone to Sunday School, but went back home instead and almost immediately learned there was a change for the worse. In just a few minutes it was all over, just a few short breaths, and the sounds were those of a bottle being thrown in the water and making little gurgling sounds as it fills up and sinks. And then everything was quiet. I am so glad to have been at home when he died.

THE MASONIC FUNERAL SERVICE

On July 8, Lilburn wrote his Cousin:

Of course everything was conducted according to plan.

The church was comfortably filled. I have a way of getting in the wrong places in Masonic processions and Lillian, Will

Darneal, Rosie and I followed the coffin down the aisle. I noticed none of the relatives followed us just then, but the Masons and Knights Templar came piling in, then the rest of the family! My face turned a little red, but on the way out I managed to do the right thing. Some family members suggested that in the family procession, the eldest son should come first and the next in line and so on, but it had not been worked out, however I do think the rest of the family other than those mentioned, did line up according to age.

We stood until everyone had entered the church, then were seated and the minister read the 90th Psalm. Then my quartet from the Boonville church sang, "Asleep in Jesus" and the Reverend read from John 14, and followed with prayer. Babe Edmonston says he prayed for twenty minutes. This part of the service displeased me because in my mind, it was not a pretty prayer. I sat and thought "You just would not be done out of preaching a sermon, would you?"

Then the quartet sang "Abide With Me," and the procession filed out to the grave. Under a canopy, chairs had been arranged, but none of us cared to sit, so we stood throughout the Masonic service which was rendered most impressively. Representatives of the Knights Templar were there and at a place in the ritual they crossed swords above the casket as it was in a position to be lowered, and in unison said the Lord's Prayer. When the Masons finished, following was the benediction.

A reception was held for the relatives and friends who came up to condole with us and to visit with us, and this continued for at least thirty to forty minutes with groups all the way from the lot to the front gate. I think I visited a little with everybody who was there. It was just in the good old Clark's Chapel manner and what a fine thing it was. A blessed occasion I called it. Much inviting on the part of Lillian, Ellen and me, we had decided to pool our food and have a pick-up lunch at Ellen's. Many of the family who had come for the funeral were leaving immediately after lunch and this made it the only way we could all be together.

There must have been about forty for lunch at Ellen's and everything went well. Ellen had a baked ham, we took fried chicken. Then there was a relish of vegetables, peach pickles, apple sauce, stuffed tomatoes, iced tea, ice cream and cake.

At Clark's Chapel a few people came up and expressed their opinion that it was "a fine, dignified, impressive funeral." It was, and if there is such a thing as father hearing it, perhaps he liked the reverend's long prayer. Who knows?

I now find myself wishing often I could do some of the chores again which were necessary in taking care of Father. We're busy trying to get our lives adjusted.

Chapter Ten

Farm Life in Boonslick Country

After his father's death in 1938 Lilburn was able to
devote more of his time to Fairview and the orchards. He wrote:

I have recently spent most of my time on the farm, and away
from the office. The chance to work around the house has enabled me to produce for the passing public, a colorful show place.
The iris and peonies along the terrace in front of the house are
simply wonderful to behold. [*He had set them out so they spelled*
out Kingsbury Orchards] Such lovely colors and such a profusion
of them. I have extended my planting about double what it was
last year and as the years go by and I continue to keep this up,
I shall really have something quite showy. This year the spirea
and syringa borders along the highway between the two places
are enough to make quite a display. The whole front, south side
and back yards are hand-mowed and strange to say we have the
best stand of blue grass in years.

Farming gives a sense of health to me. It is refreshing to
watch at dusk while a herd of cattle flows toward the barn and
hogs respond to my calling.

An Apple a Day

Lilburn took active measures to promote his apple sales. To
previous customers he mailed the following letter.

"An apple a day keeps the doctor away. But - don't let anything keep you away if you want good winter apples. Come early
and be SURE.

If you have bought apples from us, you will be back. This is
to remind you come soon. To others we extend a cordial invitation to visit our packing shed and see how WELL the quality of

our fruit matches our PRICES. We have a good many apples but the demand is brisk.

He mailed penny postcards to a list of prospects with this message:

Come to the shed with the sign BIG RED APPLE, on Highway No. 5 (a rain or shine road), 8 miles south of Fayette and 1 1/2 miles north of New Franklin.

-Lilburn Kingsbury

Fairview

TIDBITS

But all life on the farm was not refreshing as these tidbits show.

On March 11, 1946:

Dear folks:

Louis heard us talking about the recent Missouri article in the *National Geographic* and was anxious to read it. After he had done so, he commented at the table, "Fred's a good writer, but it is just such things as what he wrote about you that makes a fellow lose confidence in what's printed. Now they ain't no apple barons in Howard County, none in Missouri though it seems to me I did read of one down in the south part of the state a few years ago. But a man with only 25 or 30 acres of orchard ain't no baron."

I think I mentioned Bettie, the cow, gave birth to a calf without a tail - not even a bob or a stub. I think I have a museum piece. What will the poor thing do when the flies get bad? Someone has just sent me a clipping of "Believe It or Not," showing a picture of such a calf. Sorry I didn't make a dollar by sending mine in first....And, to make you envious of me and my farm life, last week I was trying to drive big sows into the chute to put rings in their noses. I had one headed that way when she turned quick as a flash and darted between my legs. She was so big she just carried me backward for quite a distance. I don't know how I managed to stay on, but it was quite an exciting ride before she stopped in a corner. I am thinking since I did so well, I am taking up rodeo as soon as I have time.

I also got a box of buttons from Bessie Cragle, the widow in Rolla, in exchange for ear bobs which I bought and sent her for her collection, but they were not worth a "Hoot." That last word makes me think of Buck who works with Russell, who is disposed to get drunk. Russell's father is ill and may go at any time. Buck told me he said to Russell, "What is you goin' to do if word comes your Pa has done died and you is half-hooted?"

Buck is the pillar and bolster of the Negro Methodist church here in town and no longer takes a drink. He also quit smoking because he said, "If I smokes, I's got to buy smokes fo' the boys, (Juny and Tommy) an' I just ain't got the money."

The pigging season has been a nightmare. It didn't start according to schedule and for several days and nights I was on alert but nothing happened. Finally I found some pigs on the coldest night of the year and that was Friday night. From that time on, every night until Wednesday morning, I was on the alert, going to the barn every two hours, and on the last night spent most of my time midwifing three separate sows. I got terribly fed up with wiping off slimy things that become pigs with the first gasp. You can have this life; it's too exciting for me.

This morning when dawn came there were three new baby calves as black as crows cavorting around as many proud moms. Their papa was on the other side of the fence looking very nonchalant, I thought, considering these were his first born. At the end of a few days we should have eleven new calves. Last fall ten came to bless our farm - eleven really, but the spirit of one took its flight. We nursed them along and sold them the other day, short yearlings and they averaged $75.00 per head. If expenses were not so great, labor and feed, etc., I could throw a big spree or something, ride a streamliner or fly somewhere with TWA. Instead, I just order more coal for the furnace. I am debating whether I can have a new suit and overcoat out of these deals.

CHANGING TIMES ON A BOONSLICK FARM

In a talk Lilburn gave in 1952, he tells of some of the changes which had come about in farm life since Fairview was first built. In a letter to me, he wrote:

I gave the enclosed talk to the Boonslick Writers' Guild last week, a very appreciative group. This Thursday night I gave the talk before the Boonslick Historical Society here in New Franklin. They seemed to enjoy the changes of farm life as depicted by me.

The talk mentioned above probably presented much of the information in his article, "Changing Times on a Boonslick Farm," which appeared in the July, 1952 issue of the Bulletin of the Missouri Historical Society *(St. Louis). The article follows:*

APPLE ORCHARDS

The house in which I was born, reared and still live, is one hundred and twenty years old. For the last eighty years it has been flanked by apple orchards, gorgeous with bloom in the spring and rich with ripe fruit in the fall. It is in the southern part of historic Howard County, in the Boonslick Country which U.S. Highway No. 40 crosses 150 miles west of St. Louis.

Slaves laid its rock foundation and raised its homemade brick walls to the then skyscraper height of two stories. Within short distances are the sites of the old log forts, Hempstead, Kincaid, and Cole, which the early settlers built during the War of 1812 for protection against the Indians. Within a stone throw of the house stood a log chuch, Mt. Pleasant, the first Baptist outpost in the Boonslick Country. A little farther away was another one, Clark's Chapel, in which the Methodists shouted their praises.

Our old house has withstood the years which have marked the passing of most of the early landmarks in the interest of progress. The old house itself has been changed in the interest of comfortable living. Its parlor was once a duplicate of the Missouri room now in the St. Louis Art Museum, but in the late 70s my father and mother, with a brood of young children, grew tired of reaching up for soothing syrup, paregoric and castor oil, so they lowered the mantel shelf twelve inches. Through later years, other features of the house were altered to accord with the requirements of modern heating, lighting and plumbing.

When Charles van Ravenswaay comes to see us now, we know he silently despises the desecration which he feels has been committed. We try to divert his attention to other attributes of the home which seem to be pleasing to us.

And so the old house has changed. The orchards beside the house are always changing. The general order on the farm is different. But we should not be surprised at anything. One of my grandfathers, who was a close-communing Baptist and an ardent Whig in 1840, was a shouting Methodist and a loyal Democrat when he died in 1882.

Among my first memories are those of my father's first apple orchard he planted in 1872 - the first commercial apple orchard of Howard County. It was then in its decline. There were scattered trees of several varieties, which without the help of a spray program still bore beautiful apples with distinctive flavor: Bellflower, Red Astrakhan, Greening, Rambo, and Jeneton, none of which are grown in Missouri orchards today. Finally, as a succeeding orchard came into bearing, the old one was cleared out and that land was for several years used for general farming before it was, for the second time, set to orchard along with considerable new acreage.

Horticulturists had propagated new varieties, among them, Ben Davis, Gano, Winter May, Clayton, Missouri Pippin, Huntsman Favorite, Roman Beauty, Early Harvest and Maiden's Blush, most of which enjoyed seasons of popularity after they came into bearing some ten or twelve years later. But most of these have faded from the orchard picture of today. Ben Davis and Gano, steady prolific producers and best income providers, long known commercially as the "pie apples" are almost impossible of sale in Missouri now. We must look for a market in states where apples do not grow, and where the public palate is not so conditioned to highly flavored varieties. Golden Delicious and Red Stark are prime favorites while the luscious red Jonathan lords it over all.

I do not remember when the worm first ate of the apple, but the first work I ever did in the orchard to combat one was turning the crank of a little machine with a bellows, mounted on a horse drawn sled, which blew a fog of lime and arsenate of lead through a long tin pipe to cover the fruit on the trees. When we became discouraged with this method, discovering the worms grew fat on the poisoned dust, a liquid spray was recommended. We bought a power sprayer run by a gasoline engine which pumped the liquid poison through a long hose and a nozzle which vaporized it. This method is still in general use. But with the latest invention there is no hose. The "Air Blast" blows the vaporized liquid through the trees with such power and speed that it sounds like a cyclone and does its work almost as quickly.

Here, a tractor and the sprayer, coordinated, are designed to meet the shortage of labor and one man does it all.

The manner of harvesting and marketing apples has changed radically. Buyers used to contract for apples still on the trees in late summer to be packed in the fall under their personal supervision. This pleased the grower, as his responsibility for the quality of the apples ended when the apples graded by hand, rolled into the barrel by which the inspector stood. They were graded and barreled right in the orchard among the trees which were being stripped of fruit.

Today, all grading is done in a central shed and the apples are packed in bushel baskets or in the newer Friday pack cartons, where they are handled in the manner of eggs. While most of the grading is now done mechanically, there are still some phases which tax the mind and hand of the worker, who continually watches the apples roll by and must make instantaneous decisions. It is hard work.

We always reserved apples to supply the home trade within a radius of fifty miles. There were few orchards in the county then. Farmers from a distance used to come in groups, in a string of horse drawn wagons. They would arrive shortly before sundown. After watering and feeding their teams, they set up camp in the lane and cooked their supper over an open fire. The evening air was redolent with the aroma of frying bacon and boiling coffee. It was good to go down after supper to hear them talk about their homes miles away. At bed time, they took their blankets inside the barn and slept on the hay.

Early the next morning, after padding their apple boxes with blankets and straw, they loaded them full of apples. They bought not only for themselves but for neighbors. Loaded, they turned their teams homeward in a procession for the all day journey, waving goodbye and calling, "See you this time next year." What a contrast to the speedy transportation of today!

Everybody used to handle apples very carefully, loading them on old comforts or straw to prevent bruising. Some still do, but many customers are in a great hurry. They dump the fruit into containers or pour it loose in their car and are gone. For customers who now buy in large quantities, we load, with their approval, 700 more bushels into a trailer with a bare floor, and pile them six feet deep. Upon arrival of the truck at its destination, the apples are scooped into pick-ups that move in many directions, and the apples are manhandled again when peddled at the cabins of tenant farmers on cotton plantations. Perhaps they buy them for the bruises.

Most new houses are built without fruit cellars. Burying apples is no longer popular, though some still do it to have apples "with that earthy flavor." Apples are sold at the grocery stores the year around, where many people prefer to buy for their daily needs. Time was when the apple was king of fruits in Missouri and oranges were seldom seen except at Christmas time, but the latter fruit, along with grapefruit and bananas, share the honor now, in spite of the adage which claims for the apple only, that one a day will keep the doctor away.

LABOR PROBLEMS

The labor problem has often plagued us, and with young men going to service and the older ones into defense plants or on old age assistance rolls, the prospect is darker than ever. But each time the problem seems to resolve itself, though some times it means getting on by the skin of our teeth. One year tramps were common. Every one of them who came to our house begging for food was invited to remain to help with the apple harvest. A sufficient number did. Unknown to me, one was a college graduate from New England, bumming around in search of material for a book. When it was published, it gave a splendid picture of the apple harvest activities on the farm. He eulogized my mother's hot biscuits which she, pinch-hitting for the cook who was ill, baked by the dozens three times a day to feed the crew. Today they would get light bread, which in those days had not attained the position it enjoys today. It is a bread described by an old gentleman in my neighborhood as "very popular, but little thought of," an opinion in which many Howard Countians concur.

A few years ago with the biggest crop of apples I had ever grown, we looked forward to the harvest with desperation. No local help was in sight. As a last resort and with many misgivings, we ordered some Jamaican Negroes, thousands of whom had been imported by the Government and were scattered over the United States to relieve the wartime labor shortage. Many preliminaries were involved. Uncle Sam had to be assured everything would be lovely for the Guest Workers. Since living quarters had to conform to definite specifications which would have been expensive to provide elsewhere, we decided with some qualms to house them in a small cottage in the corner of the yard. We need not have felt concern for nothing objectionable occurred.

In the evenings by a hot fire, they lounged and strummed stringed instruments, and sang far into the night. At a distance the serenade was delightful and I used to fall asleep reminded of what I had heard my parents tell of their childhood pleasures in listening to the slaves singing in their cabins.

But there were times when I wished for the prerogatives of Simon Legree. While they were provoking at times, generally they were useful and certainly they helped save the apple crop. Perhaps provocations were the consequences of misunderstandings of speech. Hailing from this British mandated Jamaica, they spoke English but not in the vernacular of Missouri's Little Dixie. Their a's were so broad, the syllables of longer words so elided, and their diction so rapid, that my Missouri ear could not cope with it.

They were such a loquacious group around the grading table I had to ban conversation. Perversely they decided to sing. This was not displeasing as it did not interfere with their manual performance. Rather it seemed to improve it, just as the rhythm of music aids stevedores in loading river steamboats. Their repertoire seemed unlimited, but again and again they repeated that grand old hymn "St. Anne" and "God Save the King." One man with a fine baritone voice carried the air and the words, while the others stimulated a harmonic orchestral accompaniment of wind instruments. The tuba was exceptionally fine.

They also spoke at times, especially after I had reproved one or all of them, a jargon which seemed to have no resemblance to English. With it they shut me out conversationally, as effectively as if they had placed a wall between us. When working in the orchard, they sounded like a pack of monkeys gibbering in the trees. Once I remarked to my only native Negro helper that we should invent an "unknown tongue" and spring it on them, so that they would know how we felt at being excluded from their conversation. With seeming pride and satisfaction, he exclaimed:

"But Mr. Kingsberr, mostly I understands what they says." I knew he did not but I inquired, "Well, what are they talking about?" "Well, boss," he replied, "mostly makin' fun of you."

These Jamaican Negroes in their homeland never dreamed of the prosperity they enjoyed in the States. They bought gay sport clothes, stringed musical instruments, expensive shoes and luggage. They delighted especially in wrist watches, but reserved their wear for Saturday night jaunts to neighboring towns where they walked alone, the native Negroes eying them with suspicion. Being from a hot country, our fall mornings pinched them. Each bought himself a cap with fur-lined ear muffs, which he buttoned down securely whenever the temperature dropped as low as 60 degrees.

Hog Killing

No farm operation has undergone a more complete revolution than "hog killing." Under the old system, plans were made days ahead and care was used to choose a time "when the sign was right." No housewife who fried meat wanted to see a big cake of sausage in the skillet shrink to a mere pat, or a slice of bacon melt away until little was left but the rind. Nothing was allowed to interfere on the day set aside for the butchering. There were many phases of it and everybody in the household had a part. Extra help was hired. Often neighbors came in to trade work and bones.

On the days before the killing, the hogs were penned up for overnight. A ditch was dug and a large vat, later to be filled with water, was set in place over it. Firewood was laid under the vat to bring the water to a boil. A work table was set up close to the vat, and a long heavy beam was trussed up horizontally from which to hang the butchered hogs.

When all hands were assembled and the water in the vat was scalding hot, a rifle shot in the head laid the first hog low. Haste was used to thrust a knife accurately into its jugular vein. After it had bled sufficiently, the hog was lifted into the scalding vat to loosen its hair. Soon it was drawn out on the table, steaming hot, and men with sharp knives worked feverishly to scrape off all dirt and hair. After this close shave, the clean white carcass was suspended by the hind legs from the beam, drawn, rinsed, and left hanging the rest of the day to "cool out." A lighted lantern, suspended from the beam, was left to police these prepared carcasses, warding off dogs and varmints.

The following days were busy ones. The carcasses were cut up, the joints trimmed, the sausage meat made ready and ground. The fat was prepared and rendered over an outdoor fire. The women made link sausage. They fried down some or cool-packed it along with the tenderloin. They boiled the heads to make head-pudding and souse. They pickled the feet. Each year they reached a state of desperation which caused them to declare that they hoped they would never see another piece of pork! Presents of backbone, ribs and sausage were sent to neighbors, some of whom would return the favor when they butchered. The men sugar-cured the hams, shoulders and bacon. The Negro helpers greedily appropriated the small intestines or chitlins, which they fry and enjoy as the greatest delicacy in the world. Livers and ears, given them by the boss, were great boons. They were also thankful for the pigtails, knowing full well the sweetness of these tidbits. You who love chicken neck will never settle for another, after you have tasted pigtail.

When the confusion of butchering was over, everybody, through necessity, entered a pork-eating marathon. We exercised the strength of our combined appetites to keep the pork from going strong. Taking part in the marathon, we had sessions with boiled backbone, baked ribs, cold or fried hog-head pudding, sausage tenderloin, vinegared souse and pigsfeet. If life on the farm had been mounted on ballbearings, it couldn't have rolled smoother. My memories are lubricated forever.

I think most people agree with me that the best part of the hog is ham. I am reminded of Mandy Brown, a Negro woman who was a great leader in her church but a failure in the art of remembering names. Rev. Hamm came to hold a meeting in her church. When she wished to introduce him, she could never remember his name. He prompted her patiently several times, and finally said, "Sistah Brown, maybe I kin hep you remembah mah name. Whenever you wants to remembah mah name, jus think of the best paht of de hog!" "Oh! Sho! Sho!" replied Mandy Brown appreciatively, and turning to her friend said, "Sis Fluke, I wants you to meet Bro. Chitlins."

ICE IN THE HOME

And what a change has come about in serving the home with ice! Father used to watch the deep pond, down the hill from the big barn, for ice thick enough to harvest. That was before we became painfully sanitary. A hard freeze was supposed to purify the water. And it did, so far as our experience with ill effects from pond ice is concerned. Today nobody would use pond water ice without first boiling it. We had as an ice house, a hole in the ground about fourteen feet square and sixteen feet deep, with a roof like an inverted V, walled up originally with logs, but later with brick. When the ice was thick enough, a man went out on the pond with an axe and hacked a small hole. Through this hole, he inserted the end of a crosscut saw. The man with a saw hewed a straight line for thirty or forty feet, then repeated the operation in another line parallel to and about three feet from the first one. Then he sawed across the ends of the lines and with his axe, broke the long slab into large rectangular blocks. Other men with hooks pulled these blocks deftly out of the water and scooted them to the edge of the pond. Usually this process took place during weather so cold even handling the ice was a dry-gloved operation. Men with teams and wagons filled the wagons with blocks of ice, then drove toward the ice house, wheels crunching in the cold snow and frosted breath pouring from the nostrils of men and beasts as if they were propelled by steam.

The ice was slid down a chute into the ice house. When the space was filled, the ice was covered deeply with straw packed closely in the corners. Then it was forgotten until warm weather.

Getting out ice was for many years one of the burdens of my youth. Being the youngest of five sons, when I inherited a chore, I reigned for a long time. The pack of ice had to be uncovered and a supply hacked loose from the mass with the axe, which had a way of getting lost in the straw. The ice had to be hoisted out, loaded on the wheelbarrow, wheeled to the cistern, rinsed off, and then put into the big ice box on the porch without disturbing a single jar of milk or cream. And woe to me if I forgot to empty the drip pan under the box! How simple by comparison, is the modern method of refrigeration.

GIVING OR TAKING MILK?

I was, as I have said, the youngest of five sons. An older brother, realizing I knew the spending value of a nickel, but little else, paid me to "pail the cow" for him until I became adept at it. He then persuaded my father to bestow upon me the Kingdom of Squeeze and Squirt. I reigned for more years than I like to remember. There are two schools of thought about milking. One contends that the cow gives milk. The other holds that you have to take it. I belong to the latter.

It is strange to find something on the farm that has not changed. There are no dairies or milking machines in our community. Milk is taken in the primitive way. It was my good fortune to renounce my kingdom years ago, but I sometimes have to pinch hit. I have often resolved that I would resort to store milk and patches of oleo an inch square and paper thin, before I would again associate with a cow regularly, to milk her twice a day. But fresh golden butter is beautiful, and luscious to the taste. And there is something about skimming from a gallon jar cream a half inch thick to put on your cereal, your sliced fresh peaches, and increase your waistline. It was thick enough to spread like butter on your toast. There is something about putting a lump of cream in your coffee and watching the contents change from black to that subtle shade of brown. It makes you respect and remember the farm cow fondly.

I have highlighted only a few of the changes which have occurred on the farm. I haven't mentioned the synthetic feed which we give the cow in winter which fools her into producing milk as if she were eating the luscious grass of springtime.

Master minds are working constantly to invent machines to save time for men and women. Undoubtedly they succeed. But since there are still certain farm operations which cannot be accomplished mechanically, and the farm labor shortage has become so acute, the farmer has more to do and is busier than ever before in his life. He may wear a white collar, but he has a calloused palm. It used to be commonly said the farmer leads an independent life, that he is his own boss. Today it may be said he is his own hired hand.

Of course we welcome all the labor-saving and pleasant devices which tempt us to spend our money. But changes, improvements in these gadgets come in such rapid succession that they present a problem. The farmer hestitates to buy a garbage disposal unit, a television set, or an electric organ today lest before an installation can be effected tomorrow, the chosen model may have become obsolete. And he is not satisfied with anything except the latest. I think if a theme song were chosen for the farmer, it might be, "You haven't got anything I haven't got."

Meeting oncoming changes in farm life is like facing an incoming tide on the beach. Most of the breakers we take in stride. Sometimes a big one may swamp us a bit. But all in all they are exhilarating, and pleasant.

In his letter he wrote:

> Preparing this talk reminded me I have wanted to do a story on things about which I never hear any more, much less see, buzzards, bedbugs and tumblebugs. I can remember how cautious mother was every time the house was cleaned, in the days when we had the laundry done by some Negro woman in her own home. Mother always examined the clothes when she got them home before she put them away. I don't remember ever seeing a bedbug except once in my life. But each spring the beds were taken apart and the joints were all rubbed with coal oil. Of course we see no buzzards any more because when a farmer loses a head of stock he phones for the "dead wagon" from the fertilizer plant up on the Lamine river and no animal is left to feed the birds. One would never know there had been a livestock death unless he should fall in behind the dead wagon on the highway and be unable to get ahead of it.
>
> As for the the tumblebugs which I used to love to watch rolling their balls of dung in the lane out home, since I no longer have any stock, they have gone elsewhere to work. I tried to get information on that type of scarab from Washington, but was referred to Mexico City and they sent me a 312 page volume about tumblebugs, their love life and everything, printed in English. To think that entomologists would spend all the time they have on the tumblebug's life amazes me. How they push and pull the ball and sometimes the mama rides while papa pushes, how papa walks on his front legs and pushes with his hind ones, etc. I must do more research on buzzards.

No Money – No Beer

Louis Williams was the principal farm hand, taking over the cottage in the yard when the boys left home. He was wonderful to all the grandchildren and we called him Uncle Louis. He was a masterful craftsman, who could do anything which needed to be done on the farm. In later years he became addicted to alcohol and created problems for Lilburn as reported in these letter excerpts.

In early May, 1943:

Louis has been haywire since Saturday, when he went to Columbia. He said he was going over to see if he could rent a cabin to live in, but was advised it would be impossible. I sure wish he could. Anyhow, he got back bad drunk. Monday he went to town and got him a bottle, and people down there had him picked up, put in a taxi and sent him out to me. He could not get in the house and Rosie heard a thud and went in to find him sprawled on the floor. She helped him to the bed, and later went back and found him prostrate on the floor again, and decided she wouldn't strain her guts again. Tuesday, he repented a little, but this morning came down town and got another bottle. I went in just as Louis was hiding the bottle under the cushions of a chair. I took off the cap and enjoyed pouring the whiskey on his head and down his back. I thought maybe it would do him good outside as well as in. Such a problem. I guess I shall have to take over his pension money and dole it out to him. The beer parlor woman cooperates with me by refusing to sell him beer. Guess I shall have to request cooperation from the liquor store.

December 26, 1945:

Dear folks,

Charlie Chipley worked for us so long, and his mother has worked at Rob's apple shed for so many years, and seemingly has been so near death's door so often without having it swing open to let her in, it seemed a somewhat momentous occasion when she actually died. Her funeral was held last Saturday afternoon at the undertaking parlor here in town. Even Louis, who prides himself on never having attended a funeral, felt called upon to go. I suppose it was somewhat of a strain upon his emotions and only natural, when somebody invited him to step into one of the back rooms to have a drink from a bottle, to accept it.

Late that night, a taxi driver accompanied Louis home, through the snow into his room and turned the light on for him.

It was so cold I went out to start the fire, and found him very contrite. He knew he should not have taken that first drink at the funeral - that one drink for him always called for one more. He lamented, "Why is it people drink more at Christmas than any other time...why I never went to a toilet in Franklin or Boonville that it wasn't crowded with people taking a drink - sitch down and viseth a little."

Having eaten more candy that evening than I knew was good for me, I was inclined to be very lenient. I was almost kind. I offered, as I have done frequently before, to get him some liquor to use at home, if he needed it, and he was horrified at the suggestion. I offered to get him some good straight rye whiskey with that rich robust taste of the grain, so highly prized by men of rare discrimination. Its taste always stands out - Old Overholt, or some Old Forester, whose elegance is solely due to original fineness developed with great care - or some Schlitz, brewed with just the kiss of the hops, no harsh bitterness - or Budweiser, which is something more than beer, a tradition! But, did I get anywhere? I was eager that he remain on the waterwagon for he has been so sick I was a little afraid for him to even go to the undertaking parlor. But he seems none the worse for his spreeing in the privies of Howard and Cooper Counties.

Soon afterwards Louis' health failed so badly he had to be placed in the County home for the aged. Lilburn arranged for his care, visited him frequently, and upon his death, had him buried in the Mount Pleasant Cemetery.

Buck took over much of the work Louis once did. Before he got religion, Buck also hit the bottle. Lilburn wrote of this in January 1952:

Dearest folks,

Am still feeling the effects of a shock I had this morning. Buck went away last night and left word he would be back in time to do the morning feeding. But when he was not here by 7 a.m., I went ahead with it. I was about finished when the bus stopped and Buck got off. He seemed to be feeling fine, none the worse for wear except for bloodshot eyes. I thought to myself, this is the first time he has ever stayed all night in Boonville and been able to come back early in the morning. Congratulations! He said he would go down home and get his breakfast before attending to some errands at the barn.

I had been back at the house only a few minutes, when Juny knocked on the door and when I opened it, he said, "Mr. Kingsbury, Daddy's dead." Like Margaret when she asked Mr. Elliott if he was sure he was dying, I asked Juny and he told me how Buck had been in the middle of a sentence and just fell back stiff! It didn't seem possible he could be dead. I didn't know whether to call the doctor or the undertaker but did call the doctor and he said he couldn't come, that if Buck was that sick, the undertaker would have to take him to the hospital, or if dead, the same to his shop.

With that conversation ended, I rushed down to Buck's and Cora met me at the door saying, "I sure thought Buck was dead, but finally I made out he was still alive."

I went in and Buck was sitting on the new davenport, head back and legs stretched out into the room. He was limp as a wet dishrag. I said to Cora, "We've got to get him turned around and lying on the davenport." Cora said, "Wait a minute Mr. Kingsbury till I can get some papers to put under his feet. I don't want him dirtyin' up my new sofa." When we got him squared away, I felt his pulse and then I felt mine, and I couldn't tell much difference. He seemed to be doing all right. I guess he must have had some rot-gut which poisoned him and brought on this spell. He passed out this way in Fayette once, after imbibing something. After two or three days he was able to navigate again, but after that excitement my stomach was upset all week.

KINGSBURY APPLE DYNASTY ENDS

A big change took place at Fairview and in Lilburn's life in 1959. He wrote his niece, Julia Sikes:

I am having the orchards bulldozed out, putting the trees into the hollows where they look utterly crushed. It is quite a break with tradition, or at least with the Kingsbury apple dynasty, established in 1872...and I feel more than if I were having some teeth, a very part of me, drawn. The apple orchards have always been a part of my life. But the expense of putting on a crop, with the old trees bearing small apples, not to mention the wear and tear on me, does not promise income to justify it. Certainly an untended orchard with wild sprouts shooting up is a liability. And so it is goodby to the orchards. The land where cleared looks good though. I shall put the land into corn (rental). Would keep it in pasture were it not for the young trees trying to get established.

So ended Lilburn's Apple Baronetcy.

Chapter Eleven

FOLKLORE HOBBY HORSE RIDES

Lilburn and Charles van Ravenswaay as president and secretary of the Boonslick Historical Society frequently rode hobby horses of the same color. One such was folklore. Charles' remembrance letter to Lilburn on 28 August 1977 says:

Recently you've been generous in sending me copies of your notes on the folk songs and folk stories we collected from elderly blacks in Fayette and New Franklin. What a gold mine they are! Although our sessions were held before tape recorders had been developed, you were able to write down everything we heard, complete with a great many colorful details.

Lilburn's Deep South cultural determination instilled in him the belief that Negroes were a simple race whose intelligence and capabilities were inferior to whites. Much of the prosperity enjoyed by his grandparents was due to slave labor. In his family history research he became aware of superstitions, the belief in ghosts, and the religious practice of Boonslick Negroes - descendants of slaves of the pioneer families. Their fascination for Lilburn and Charles is reflected in the following Buck and Cora paper:

BUCK AND CORA

Buck and Cora Shirley had been married twenty years and had lived on my farm the latter twelve of them when he "got religion." In spite of Baptist heritage, he joined the Methodist church toward which his wife leaned lightly. But he claimed there was "a lack of the Holy Spirit" in this church so he shopped around a bit.

It was at the Church of God and Jesus Christ, Holiness, in

Boonville that he found spiritual cover which warmed him like a blanket. He told me, "I was holdin' back when the Spirit of the Lord which musta weigh 600 pounds jumped on my back an' rid me to the mercy seat."

When Buck applied to me for work, I was reluctant to hire him. I had been told that he never stayed long at any place and that through carelessness he broke a lot of farm machinery. When I told him he would not suit me, he urged, "Just try me, Mr. Kingsbury, just try me. If you let me work for you, you will just love me!" This plea was heard with amused surprise which tipped the scales in his favor, and I hired him. He and Cora and their two young boys soon took over the tenant house.

Buck proved to be a dependable, resourceful, conscientious worker with a disposition generally kind. If he seemed irritable, I attributed it to fits of dissatisfaction engendered by his wife who wanted him to move to town. Often she told him he was a plain fool to keep on working in the country when he could be in town making a lot of money.

Buck was dark brown in color while Cora was light tan. While he was of ordinary size, she was large, weighing about three hundred pounds. Her favorite and usual ensemble was a navy blue dress with red accessories, shoes, bag and a ribbon rosette for her hair, not to mention red cheeks and lips. Buck encouraged her to accent her complexion. He explained Cora wore red before they were married and he wanted her to keep on wearing it. Because of her size, Cora hated to shop for a new dress. She asked Buck to attend to this phase of shopping, too often without success. Once he lamented, "All the biggest outsizes is too little, Mr. Kingsbury; it takes a tent for Cora."

Life appeared to go on reasonably well at the tenant house. When their third and last baby, a boy, was born, she had spent the previous winter months in Fayette so that the young boys might "get better schooling in town." That winter Buck batched in the country. My sister asked Buck what they were going to name the baby. He replied, "Miss Lilyan, when Cora says what she named him I asked her, Cora, is this a God's fact or is this some of your foolishment?" She said, "It ain't no foolishment. It's done put in the record."

"Well, Buck," my sister insisted, "WHAT did she name the baby?"

"Cora says," Buck announced, "she named him Mister Lilburn Junior Shirley."

Buck's many superstitions were a source of delight to me. Once he wished to accompany me to Columbia. As we started across the bridge over Perche Creek, he asked me to stop a minute. As he got out of the car, he informed me, "I broke this lookin' glass an' I've got to throw the pieces in a stream of runn' water."

One day as we worked in the orchard I saw him throw an apple at the little dog to which he was devoted. Surprised, I asked, "Why Buck, what do you mean by throwing that apple at your faithful little friend? He replied, "I never aimed to touch him. I just wanted him to get up. He was rolling over and over measuring off somebody's grave and he was mighty nigh up to me."

Buck became a deeply religious church man. He attended all services. Every pay day he asked me to figure his "ten percent to take to the nestin'". No profane word ever passed his lips. He believed, not without reason, that other people refrained from "cussin'" in his presence out of regard for his feelings. Occasionally I consented for him to work for a neighbor who, when provoked, was careless of his language. Buck told me one day, "Mr. Aycock got all flustered up an' he might nigh let hisself go."

As for liquor, even a soft drink was anathema. He told me of coming suddenly upon two old cronies behind a car, about to drink out of a bottle. When they saw him, one of them pocketed the bottle quickly and said, "Excuse us, Buck." We know you don't indulge no more and we are sorry you saw us like this. Buck told them, "You don't need to apologize for me seein' you, but you sure better watch out for Jesus."

Cora looked upon his religious affiliation with impatience and not a little ridicule. The two older boys, now working and living away from home, shared her feelings. She declined every opportunity to accompany him to "Meetin". She grumbled all the time about him "bein' all the time away from home."

"I can't understand Cora," he lamented. "She used to complain when I smoked and got drunk an' run her off an' didn't have no religion. Now she all the time complain 'cause I got it."

One day Cora went to Fayette, claiming she had been called there to "help take care of my Aunt Prue," an elderly Negro woman friend. A few days later she came back for the rest of her clothes and as much of the household goods as she could load into a car. When Buck discovered this, he was quite disturbed. When he soon heard that she had set up housekeeping in a one-room shack and had a gentleman boarder, he was overwhelmed with misgivings.

"I've got to know if she is really gone for good," he told me. "'Cause if she is, ain't no use in me keepin' the davenport and the rug I am paying Mr. Geiger on, no longer. I've got to get up to Fayette soon and ask Cora herself."

He was too upset to work so I offered to take him immediately. When we arrived at the little shack, Cora, in her fleshy form, was standing in and filling the doorway, one hand up on the jamb, the other on her hip. There was a serious expression on her face, highly rouged as usual. As Buck approached her, they exchanged "good morning" pleasantly. Then Buck plunged right into the matter on his mind.

"Cora," he demanded, "You ain't got no cause to leave me. You know I've been good to you. You had a good home, heap better'n this'n."

Cora shifted her position a bit, lifted her brows and replied, "Well-l-l, I just got tired livin' out in the country so I come up to Fayette to get a little excitement and I'm doin' right well. I work out some, cleaning, and I get $2 an hour. Mr. Jim Boggs is boarding with me. After I get him his breakfast, he goes on 'bout his business and I tend to mine. I'm doin' right well."

Buck tried a new tack. "Cora, you ain't got no right to be living with no man but me as long as you are my wife. And that's a legal law."

"I ain't living with nobody," she replied, with an air of injured innocence. Buck, looking through a crack between her and the door jamb, observed, "Then whose overalls are on that chair?"

Cora ignored the implication and reiterated, "As I said, I got tired living in the country so I come up here and I'm doing real well. My little boy, Sam (erstwhile Mister Lilburn Junior Shirley) is getting along good in school, my church is right up the street. I love to go there. I ain't never coming back!"

As we drove home, Buck observed that it was plain to him now that Cora "has been foolin' around a long time." I tried to assure him that things would be better with Cora gone, he wouldn't have to listen to her constant grumbling, that he would get along all right. He replied, "Mr. Kingsbury, you ain't never had no wife, you're a single man. You don't understand what 'tis for a man who's been married to come home to a cold kitchen with no hot vittles in the stove and the bed all empty and cold."

Elder Teverbaugh of the Fayette church and his wife were pillars of strength to Buck during his tribulation. They encouraged him to "be patient in the Lawd and prayerful." He smiled broadly with anticipation as he repeated that they had assured him, "Brother Shirley, the Lawd will send you a good woman who'll give you delight and make you glad Cora is gone."

Buck said, "I'm seekin' her. 'Course I know that in the sight of God, I've got a right to marry again as long as Cora did this to me. But when I do, I'm gonna marry a woman inside my own belief."

When Buck became interested in the cost of divorces I suspected he had found his Lawd-sent woman. When I asked him about her, he said, "She's older than I am but I've got to marry an ole woman to get one what believes like I do. These young ones don't believe in nothin'." He asked me to find out what a divorce would cost. I thought when I told him the price would be $90, the cost would deter him. He remarked casually, "Don't make no difference how much 'tis. I got to get it. I don't want to keep on being the husband of nobody what's doing like Cora is."

Buck steeled himself to wait until a year had passed. At the end of it the attorney notified him that suit had been filed and if Cora filed no exception within thirty days, the Judge could grant him a divorce at the first session of the court held in Howard County after that time. Buck had the idea that at the end of thirty days (Cora was not expected to file any exceptions) the Judge would be right there to hand him his divorce. He did not know how slowly the wheels of the law grind. He "put out the word" that he and "Sister Catherine," whom he had chosen as his new wife, would be married at the Church of God and Jesus Christ, Holiness, in Fayette on the first Saturday night after the expiration of the thirty days.

But the Judge did not hold court in Fayette in time to free him of his marriage bonds. Buck then set the wedding day for the following Saturday night. Still the Judge had not held court. Finally, on the 29th of July, Bob Kingsbury and I accompanied him, very nervous, into court and testified to his noble character whereupon the Judge dissolved his ties to Cora as simple as melting an Alka Seltzer tablet.

The day before the wedding I asked him about his application for a marriage license. Confidently he assured me, "I'm gonna get the license tomorrow before the weddin'." His features fell when I told of the three-day necessary wait before he could be married."

I never heard of no sech!" he exclaimed. Why, when me and Cora was married, there wasn't no waitin'. We just got the license and stepped across the hall to the justice." He was further frustrated when he learned that both parties had to be present to sign the marriage application. Sister Catherine lived in Boone County. He decided he could go there easier than she could come to Howard County although this would entail the loss of another day's wages. "And I sure need the wages. I am glad I got those pair of rings last Christmas. One of them is on Sister Catherine's hand, the 'gagement ring. And the wedding ring is in my Sunday suit pocket I keep in Elder Taverbaugh's closet at his house so's I can change when I get to Fayette. I'll be glad when this wedding is over. It costs a heap this runnin' back and forth. And on weekends I have to pay for a place to sleep. You know I can't stay at Sister Catherine's house all night. I mean for Elder Taverbaugh to marry me clean."

Sister Catherine knew her way around the Court House at Columbia and they got everything in good shape. Buck returned elated but said, "Sister Catherine says she's too tired of setting Saturdays and Thursdays to get married on. She says we'll just get married on Sunday at two o'clock, when she's all rested up. He asked me to phone Elder Taverbaugh about the latest wedding plan and to be sure and be there at the appointed time and get some attendants for him and the bride.

The plans were changed several times until finally on the appointed evening we drove to the church at eight o'clock. It was ablaze with light but not a soul was there. We sat in our car until nine. Still no one had come. Rather than wait longer, I drove to the house of Elder Taverbaugh to inquire if and when the wedding would be. In undershirt and black trousers with a partly polished shoe in one hand, he assured me enthusiastically, "Yessir, there's gonna be a wedding. I'm dressing for it right now. The wedding bride and her party has arrived and they are next door dressing. Soon we will all get ready and assembled. We'll be down to the church, maybe 'bout ten o'clock." As I departed, he called, "Don't get discouraged, the wedding is sure to come off."

The church building is of considerable size, of concrete blocks with a marked bulge outward of one wall, which was unfinished inside. Entrance was through a roomy foyer with wide stairs on either side of the auditorium. Here were comfortable old upholstered opera chairs with an aisle on either side. A spacious platform extended across the front of the room. On it was a large arch of catalpa branches with leaves hanging limp, with here and there a piece of cedar. Under this the wedding party would stand. Vases of zinnias on either side of the arch added a bit of freshness and color to the scene.

As we entered, "Mother Truitt" (church title) greeted us and graciously conducted us to seats. Immediately I was caught up by the rhythm of the music and tapping my foot on the floor. A man strummed a guitar, one woman beat a tambourine while another played the piano with its bosom exposed. A soprano moaned obbligatos in violin tones while other members of the choir jazzed up "Yield Not to Temptation" and "Just As I Need Him Most," in harmony so close it was poignantly sweet.

Following the song service came the usual testimonial period. As soon as they were concluded, the guitarist laid down his instrument to stand before the collection table. He announced the goal for the evening would be $20, that he was starting the collection with a dollar bill. He held it aloft, waving it from side to side and laid it down as if daring anyone to do less. The members filed up, one by one, quite leisurely, to lay down their money, some going more than once. When finished, the man at the table waited a moment as he looked directly at me. There couldn't have been a more pointed cue to me to bring up the white folks' offering. As I laid it down, there was an exultant "Thank you, Brother Kingsbury. Friends, the King is with us! Praise the Lawd! Let's sing Praise God!"

At the conclusion of the doxology there was a moment of silence, then Elder Teverbaugh appeared, tall and dignified in a black robe which pushed a good expanse of white shirt up on the nape of his neck and with waves of shiny, pomaded hair across the top of his head. In his polished black shoes he strode down an aisle and took a position before the arch. He opened and gazed intently at the pages of a little book. Strains of Lohengrin's wedding march were stillborn as he turned towards the musicians and signaled for silence. The quiet was deadly as the Elder strode out the way he had come. I wondered what else could have happened to wreck the framework of Buck's wedding.

"Mother Truitt" walked to the front and addressed the audience. "Brothers and Sisters, in all walks of life, don't make no difference whether it's in the home or in church, things do not always go according to the plan. So 'tis tonight." Now the wedding party is all downstairs waiting for the ceremony to go on, but a little delay has arose and become necessary. The Elder found out a while ago he couldn't read the fine print in his book under the light above the altar we have, so we sent out to try and find a 100 watt bulb so he can have more light to read the ceremony. Of course I could read it for him (she flashed a winning smile) but he wants to do it hisself. Now as soon as we get the bulb, the wedding will go right on."

I glanced at the light swinging from the rafters by a cord and wondered how they would make the change. Sooner than I had expected, someone brought the bulb. One man pulled a table under it, another lifted the pulpit onto the table and steadied it, while a third climbed up nimbly and changed the bulbs. The hot bulb was like a hotcake passed from his hand to that of "Mother Truitt" who laid it on the table in no tardy fashion.

With more light on the scene and the furniture back in place, the Elder made his second grand entry and stood before the arch. At his signal, the bosom of the piano heaved again with "Here comes the Bride," as nimble fingers trimmed up the melody with magic runs and arpeggios. Guitar and tambourine emphasized the syncopation. To my right, I beheld Buck in all his dark brown glory, coming down the aisle on the arm of the bridesmaid. I glanced to the left for my first glimpse of "Sister Catherine" on the arm of the husky best man, tripping along and swaying her shoulders to the music. Buck was swaying too but in a more modest arc. "Sister Catherine," light in color with graying hair in little plaits pinned close to her head was attired in a dark brown dress. It had a white rolled collar and it, plus a slip that showed a little, came just below her knees. A white knitted throw topped her ensemble.

Elder Taverbaugh declared we were assembled to witness the marriage "of this man and this woman in holy matrimony, but what right has we got to unite this man and this woman? Has anybody got anything to show?"

"Mother Truitt" rose from her seat and went forward with a scroll in her hand. Taking a position by the side of the Elder, she unrolled it and started to read aloud. She seemed to have difficulty with her glasses. She took them off, laid them on a table and without a word, reached up and took the Elder's glasses off of him and put them on herself. Now she peered closely again and read aloud, "This is a license for Albert Shirley, age 48, to marry Catherine Gray, age 67." As the Elder retrieved his glasses, he announced, "This is all the evidence needed and we will now proceed with the ceremony."

Addressing the bride and groom, she with head tilted to one side and a slack expression on her face, he with animated face with head turned to cock an ear toward the Elder who asked: "Does either of you know any reason why you should not be united in holy matrimony?" Buck shook his head vigorously. Sister Catherine might as well have been made of wax. She didn't bat an eye. Elder then turned to the audience and asked, "Is there anybody here knows any reason why this man and this woman should not be united in matrimony? ANYBODY? ANYTHING? After a moment's pause he continued, "If you does, speak NOW or fo'ever keep your mouth shut."

Now join right hands! You all knows which is your right hands, don't you?" Buck looked at his outstretched hands as if to be certain which to extend toward the bride. She made no move so the best man lifted hers and laid it in Buck's. A little later, he asked them to join their left hands. When she made no move to comply, the best man again came to the rescue.

"Now as I goes along, I'm gonna explain this ceremony so you will know what you is doing," he continued, "I want to marry you so you will live a long, happy married life and be as faithful as a pair of old wild geese." As for keeping each other in sickness and health, he advised them, "Always be faithful. Most folks get along smooth and sweet when they is young and well and strong, but let one get old, or sick, they slack up. Now take ME" and he spoke with self-pride and admiration, "My wife was sickly for five years before she die and I never left her side."

Admonishing them concerning chastity, he recounted the instance when a man took another man's wife out in the country and lived with her "outside of matrimony." "Now," he said, "she loved him and she thought he loved her but he didn't care nothin' for her. Now that man wasn't worth a dime and that woman wasn't worth a dime, and that man who let 'em live like that on his place wasn't worth ten cents neither." The whole crowd including the Elder indulged in mirth.

After the Elder had announced "What God has joined together, let no man put asunder," he declared that this man and this woman were man and wife. Addressing Buck, he said, "Now Brother Shirley, you can show your appreciation. You can kiss her." The bridesmaid and the best man both put a hand up before her face as if to prevent him. The bride's face had come to life a little. Buck was visibly disconcerted. When I asked him later why they did it, he said he didn't know, "but you see I barely touched her lips." Then the Elder said, "Now you can sit down and receive the congratulations."

Suddenly the musicians rendered Mendelssohn's recessional. They tore it to pieces. It stirred the marrow in the bones of all the Negroes present and all their bodies became supple. Elder Taverbaugh led the procession out of the church ahead of the bride and groom and Sister Truitt, with the attendants and audience falling in behind, all of them stepping along, swinging their arms and swaying their shoulders to the rhythm of the music. They all smiled and waved to us, still seated, as they passed down the aisle.

In a moment aside I said to Buck, "I thought you had a wedding ring. What became of it?" He replied, "I left it in my Sunday suit coat pocket hangin' in Elder Taverbaugh's closet, but when I look for it, it was gone. I guess someone stole it."

During a two weeks honeymoon spent on my farm, I asked Buck if his bride was going to stay with him indefinitely or was she going to her own home and job in Columbia. He replied, "I expect we is both going to Columbia before long. I've got a chance to go to the University to do cleanin'." Soon they were both gone. The other day he phoned me and I asked him how he was getting along. "I'm doin' pretty good, plenty to eat and a place to sleep. The vittles and the bed ain't cold like they was when I was single up there."

"Are you going to the University now?"

"Nossir, I got here a little late for that but I'm with the garbage collection."

In the meantime Cora had gone on her way with her "boarder." On Decoration Day I had the pleasure of entertaining both of my namesakes. Lilburn Kingsbury Edmonston with his mother and maternal grandparents were our guests for dinner. There was a knock at the kitchen door. Who should be there but Cora and Mr. Lilburn Junior Shirley. My sister invited them in. Cora said they had been over to the cemetery to lay some flowers on Mama and Papa's graves and would just drop by to see us. Cora insisted they were not hungry, but the little boy, now nine, looked so longingly at some food on the kitchen table, my sister fixed places for them. As they ate, Cora said, "Miss Lillian does you ever see Albert? Do his wife look very old?" Lillian said she had seen her the other day and that she didn't have a tooth in her head. Cora's face lit up until Lillian added, "She had her dentures out."

When they were leaving, Cora in her airy manner said, "Miss Lillian, I do wish you could meet my husband."

"Oh Cora, then you are married? "Cora raised her hand in front of her face as if ashamed and replied, "No mam."

CORA'S FUNERAL

I went to Cora Shirley's funeral and during the sermon, there were "Amens," and "Yes! Yes!" and other expressions popping all over the house.

Cora's funeral was almost as good a show as Buck's wedding. Before the services started, the preacher, one of five participating, said to the undertaker, "Now I better tell you we is conforming to the modern trend, shorter funerals, and from the time I begins, till the time I quits, it will be exactly one hour."

Each of the five preachers had his chore. The main discourser told us he was preachin' to Sister Shirley. "I's preachin' to you befo' yo' blood gets cold." And it was very picturesque when he told of the angel of the Lord coming to the hospital and going right into Sister Shirley's room and telling her, "Sister, it's time to go." He didn't give her time to get anything together to take with her. He "jes put his arms right under her and lifted her up and carried her down to de river Jordan. Sister Shirley put her foot in to go 'cross but drawed it back quick, for de watah was cold, but a voice come from the other side, 'Come on ovah, Sister Shirley, you've come a long way,' and she waded right in and went on crost." Over there, the Lord said, "You've come a long way, Sister, sit yo' se'f down and rest yo' se'f awhile!" And this was the cue for the choir to sing "You've Come a Long Way, Sit Down Awhile," as every bench of Negroes in turn filed out and went up for the last, sad look.

It was the largest Negro funeral, the Negroes say, that was ever held in New Franklin. (Lillian and I were so crowded in, we felt completely integrated.) Since Cora had been cohabiting with Joe Boggs ever since she left the farm and Buck, it would seem that adultery was commendable. Something besides virtue has its reward!

Cora looked quite natural except she was wearing a pink carnation corsage instead of red on her black shroud. She filled the coffin to capacity. The preacher said, "You all gonna miss Sister Shirley's sweet smile, her warm handshake and her pleasant howdye!"

Lilburn Jr. Shirley, now eighteen or nineteen, was discarded when he got in the way of his mother and Joe Boggs and was adopted by a worthy Negro couple who have a little farm east of Boonville. He added a dramatic touch when, as the crowd was filing past the coffin, he cried out in distress, "Oh Mama, Oh Mama," over and over until his mother of adoption left her post as leader of the choir and went down to quiet him.

I asked Ralph Reed how come Cora had such a big funeral and he said, "She was very pop'lar."

Ozark Folklore

*Lilburn's and Charles' interest was not confined to the blacks of
Howard County, but through May McCord, the "Hillbilly
Queen," also in the Ozark hillbillies of Missouri and Arkansas.
Lilburn wrote:*

My dear folks,

I left Tuesday afternoon and drove to Springfield and the
next morning joined May Kennedy McCord at her home at 4:30
a.m. and after a hasty cup of coffee we drove to Stone County,
Arkansas for the Folk Festival which lasted all day. The setting
was wonderful, a level area surrounded by high bluffs, some
twenty acres or so, and at one side a 200 foot cliff at the foot of
which there was an opening to Mitchell's Cave. In front of the
cave there was an immense stage and in front of that a "bresh"
arbor which seated 1000 people. The paper said 2500 were there.
They sang old songs, danced old dances, and played old games.
They had a singin' school at which shaped note music was taught.
Then they put on a hard-shell Baptist meeting with singing sermon and all.

There were all kinds of contests mixed in. The prize fiddler
was a woman and I wish you "could a heard 'er." She got a
double bit axe as the prize. I talked with old women and old men
right from deep down in the hills and listened in on interesting
conversations among the natives. Vance Randolph ate with us -
the lunch May had brought along.

May was to go on the program but when they called her up
she was struggling to get into the one privy 3 x 4, a single holer,
the only accommodation for all of the female element until many
in desperation tore up the cliffs. The men resorted to the pine
trees like dogs, on the other side of the bowl. So May didn't do
her stuff down there. She was impromptu anyway. We drove on
some 40 miles before tying up for the night, and after supper
went to a Holy Roller meeting and sat outside and listened. The
preacher was warning that some there might be on beds of pain

before the next night and then and there I was cramping and wondering what woods would be best to run for in case. But in spite of the griping I suffered no embarrassing situations and the next morning we turned homeward. The scenery south of Harrison, Arkansas, is lovely.

Later...

Saturday morning I had a letter from May McCord urging Charles and me to come to the Festival of the Painted Leaves at Branson. I immediately called Charles, found him free and eager to drive to Branson. We were anxious to get there for the initiation into the Hillcrofters which was to be at midnight. We kept going at a good clip and at ten of twelve drove into the Sammy Lane Camp. We parked the car and went up to the ballroom where the dance was in session, and others were playing party games and having a fine time in general. By the time I danced with May it was time to go down on the plaza before the swimming pool for the initiation which was to be around a big bonfire of logs. First the swimming pool had been made attractive by little paper plates being set afloat, each with a lighted red candle.

These little plates floated away from where they were launched and collected in a group at the far end. Around the fire, speeches were said by numerous characters, "The Spirit of Unborn Generations," "The Prehistoric Man," "Spirit of the Flame," "The Pioneer Mother," "The Bones of the Pioneers," "The Indian."

These people were in funny costumes. Each person had on a false face mask and when he or she read, the face of course was immobile. The Pioneer Mother, while reading her speech, set it afire with her candle and burned it up before she could deliver it, but her memory sufficed. Townsend Godsy, one of the best photographers in the state, was there taking pictures, one of them being the group assembled for the initiation before and around the fire. Then the candidates were asked to go up to the ballroom again for the initiation - to ride the goat, some said.

The candidates were lined up in two rows facing each other and the master of ceremonies, Otis Macey, told us to bend over and lay our hands on the floor and to bend our knees if we found it necessary. We all bent over and repeated after him a serious verse, and presently found ourselves bringing it to an end with: "I know my heart; I know my mind; I know I am stuck up behind."

When all the crowd haw-hawed, it made me feel silly but I could take it. Then we were full-fledged members. May had us play an old game called "The Miller's Boy" and it was fun. I was sorry I was not there for the evening basket dinner and for the frolicking until midnight.

The next morning Charles and I bummed around until noon, visiting in the camp with a lot of people who were interesting. A couple of weeks ago one whole page of the Kansas City Star and the St. Louis Globe Democrat showed pictures Townsend Godsey had taken of a camp meeting of the Holiness people, some of them rolling at the altar and some being baptized. He said these people were so enraptured with or by the spirit they didn't even know he was taking pictures, though they must have stumbled right over him. He took a picture of the "Crown of Feathers" which was on exhibit. In fact, there were two. These were taken from the feather pillows of people who had long illnesses and had died, and if you ever find one, or your folks do, it is a sign you were a saintly person. Honestly these things just knocked me with wonderment. One was about the size of a sausage patty like we make in the country and about as thick. The feathers are very compact and each had the quill end in and fitted as closely to the others as you would find them on a goose. I think no hand could make one.

Before the lady from whose pillow the perfect crown was taken died, somebody started to shake up the pillow and felt a lump and mentioned it and someone else said, "O don't shake it up. Maybe a crown is formin'." Lillian has examined my pillow and has found a lump and I told her for heaven's sake not to shake it up, "Maybe a crown is formin'." Those people down there were so wholesome and I was so delighted to meet many whose names were familiar to me since I have been taking the

Springfield paper. May is always telling something they say or do and publishing the poetry they write.

Sunday morning before May got up, some people came to ask her to attend a funeral of their relative whose service was to be at two in the afternoon. They said, "Charlie (one who had frequently contributed to her column) would just love it if he knew you were sitting in the room at his funeral." I think she promised to go but was persuaded to go over ahead of time and look at him and then get back in time for dinner and the speech afterwards.

The after-dinner address was held in the ballroom. For music, Jimmy Demoon, of the Forestry Service in the Mark Twain Park sang ballads and picked a guitar like no one's business. He was six feet six inches tall, 18 years of age and if he had been raised in affluent surroundings, he would have been a knockout. Charles recognized the name Demoon as being of French origin and Jimmy agreed it was. Charles had visions of the family coming in through St. Genevieve. He asked Jimmy from where his family had come into the Ozarks. (There have been four generations of them singing ballads.) Shy Jimmy said, "North Missouri." When pressed further, he said, "Kirksville" and romance was all out for Charles.

Daisy Maxey, who took the part of Moon of the Painted Leaves in the pageant at the initiation was just as good in the daytime as she was at midnight. She told me in a whisper, "He was raised in direst poverty" and when a young woman joined him to play the "gittar" while he played the fiddle, Daisy whispered, "She was a guide in the Marvel Cave for eight years." Otis Maxey's nose was so strange that I have loved mine ever since I saw him. The Lord must have bit a hunk of bologna off and stuck it right above his upper lip. Honestly, it looks exactly like a big weenie, even to the color. Somebody whispered to me that Daisy Maxey had had cancer two years ago but still lived. I have heard May speak of Daisy as the loveliest character extant in the Ozarks. Vance Randolph, arming some widow, was at the night meeting but didn't stay long. Judge Moore of Ozark had a good time speaking to the crowd and ended with such flowery stuff I wanted to say "Phooey, poetical beyond comprehension."

May as Chairman of the Entertainment Committee was a whiz. Nobody old or young calls her anything but May. They all seem crazy about her and she seems to reciprocate every regard.

There were not many Painted Leaves in the Ozarks yet but there are some beautiful trees, sugar maples, in Springfield. But at Branson they were green as grass.

Chapter Twelve

Boonslick Country And The War

The occupation of the German Reichstag by Hitler and his development of the Nazi military power at first aroused little interest in the Boonslick Country. But the Nazi takeover of the Rhineland in violation of the Versailles Treaty, followed by the absorption of Austria and Czechoslovakia, began to penetrate the consciousness of the Boonslickians. The Nazi blitzkrieg of Poland, France and the Netherlands, leading to England's declaration of war against Germany, generated sympathy and support for England and its allies. Enactment of the Selective Service Act and implementation of the Lend Lease Program to supply England with needed war materials met with general approval.

Patriotic fervor was so intense most people disapproved of conscientious objectors. One such Negro member of the Jehovah's Witnesses was on trial for having failed to report for induction into the Army. The trial took place in Jefferson City. Lilburn was selected for the jury to hear the case and was elected foreman. He writes of this:

Jury Foreman: No Hung Jury Here

Dear folks,

It was quite an experience down in Jefferson City. I had thought of coming home each night but while the jury was being chosen the judge stated that 12 chosen disciples would be locked up for the duration of the trial. In my last free moment I rushed out and bought me a pocket comb feeling it would get me by somehow.

I was one of the chosen, being one of those who said he had no prejudice against Jehovah's Witnesses (that I would get up and declare).

And then for thirty-six hours I never visited a toilet without a detective looking in first to see if there was another person who might violate me as a juror. I found myself spending the night with three utter strangers and sleeping with one of them. My bedmate was from Bunceton but I never heard of him before nor do I recall his name. But he was closer to me by ties than any of others - ties of distance. Of the four in my room, three other than myself, the two from Osage Co., and from Camden County, slept together and fussed all night about how hot they were and slept on the blanket and under the bedspread. I spent a very good night with the electric fan on continuously. We had our meals in a private dining room. A detective accompanied the waitress on the rounds to keep her from contaminating us as jurors.

Yesterday morning when we got up my three companions were all worried because they didn't have a comb so I came to the rescue as graciously as I could and I have not seen three more appreciative persons. The man from Camden County lives near Montreal, S.E. of Camdenton and told me that just north of Decaturville, south of Camdenton, there are some Kingsburys at the third house this side of Decaturville, on the east side of the road. (I think loaning my comb created the favor which brought me the foremanship of the jury.)

The trial itself was interesting but we were marched a lot from the court room to the jury room while the attorneys settled their differences before the judge. Things got hot at times.

Mr. Johnson, Negro, aged 27, conscientious objector, Jehovah's Witness, was on trial for not having reported for induction. Most of the audience was made up of Negroes and white people who seemed to sit together just as if Missouri was Kansas. Well-dressed Negroes and well-dressed white people and I wondered if they were there because they were Jehovah's Witnesses. When the defendant was called to the stand he came with his record playing outfit and all the Bibles he could carry and a brief case bulging with tracts. But never was the Jehovah's Witnesses side of the story allowed to be told in court. Johnson had for his attorneys a man from New York and one from Jefferson City, a wonderful looking man, handsome and impressive in his bearing. It was a pleasure to watch him handle his part of the case. The

New York man who must have been the regular representative of the Jehovah society, turned out to be a disgruntled personage when the Judge ruled against his pleadings and testimony adduced from witnesses, time after time. He turned out to be a regular old sourpuss. But when smooth talking Richard K. Phelps, Asst. District Attorney worked, he was smooth. After watching him I swore to behave myself hereafter.

It didn't take the jury long to arrive at a verdict. On the first ballot, it was 10 to 2 for conviction. One gentleman then told what point was doubtful in his mind, so we wrote to the judge about it. We were then herded back into the court room as court opened so the judge could reinstruct us on that point. Another ballot in the jury room and Mr. Johnson's fate was "writ."

Johnson claimed he should have been classified so he would not have to enter the regular fighting forces. He should have, but he had not, according to testimony, made the appeals which are necessary in such cases, although he testified he had come to two members of the Service Board, its Clerk and to see the District Attorney in Kansas City. The defendant testified he went to Kansas City and that he was told by Mr. Phelps to return to Jefferson City and to see Col. Carver. Mr. Phelps elicited this information about Johnson's visit to Kansas City and the time of the visit. Then Mr. Phelps in an exciting court moment making the final argument, and amid a noisy protest from opposing attorneys, said that the party had never been to see him in Kansas City on that date, that it was impossible for him to have been there because he had testified he was in Jefferson City on that date. But the whole decision hinged on whether the Negro received from the Board a reclassification card which the board proved by its testimony was mailed to him. The law says the Board must mail the card but it does not say the registrant must receive it. In other words if the registrant doesn't get it, it is just too bad for him. Johnson, most of us thought, was just bluffing himself along, thinking his religious claims would cut the ice, and just waited too long.

Left: *Captain Barto, USMC. Squadron Executive Officer, VMF-218. Right: Major Kingsbury, USMC. Commanding Officer, VMF-218. Green Island, South Pacific, 1944.*

FLY BOYS

Two of Lilburn's young nephews, his namesake Lilburn Edmonston (Babe) and Bobbie Kingsbury aspired to fly military aircraft, but had difficulty being accepted for flight training because their teeth "did not bite properly." Costly dental work and their Congressman's intervention finally cleared the way. Bobbie went to Pensacola for Marine flight training, Babe to Corpus Christi for the Navy. Both received their wings and were furloughed home at the same time. Lilburn writes of this in a family letter in 1942. It follows:

I think Lillian was a bit disappointed when Babe came home in uniforms which were not adorned with as many bars, buttons, and stripes as Bobbie had. There was much to be explained, why he didn't have as many of these ornaments. And to make matters worse, Margaret said quite openly that Bobbie's uniforms were much more attractive than Babe's. Moreover, Bobbie was a lieutenant where Babe was just an ensign. Babe went over to try and straighten this out, explaining that in the Navy, the rank, "ensign" was the same as second lieutenant in the Marines and the Marines prided themselves on the elaborateness of their uniforms whereas the Navy swung the other way toward simplicity. Life was terribly complicated. Margaret liked the way the Marine dress uniform fits up tight about the neck and almost chokes the Marine, as we saw it do at Hancock's the big Sunday night we were up there. And then there is the matter of photographs.

Margaret said she had no assurance she would ever see Bobbie again, and she wanted the best picture available, and therefore one of the Columbia photographers was visited and he made fourteen sittings and finished off a picture of each one. Babe, like nobody's business, went over to Rehmeier's and as a photographer he don't rate a damn with Bob and Margaret. Imagine Lillian having to admit that Rehmeier only took five or six sittings (crushed to earth like truth!) Margaret had wanted a "very military" picture of Bobbie and one with a sword, but he didn't have any sword. Bobbie thought maybe he would have one sometime and he could get her a picture with a sword then.

We in the Midwest come in for so much public criticism for "complacency" for "not doing more." I wonder what in the name of common sense we can do until called on, and if it would do any good to get out and wave coattails in great excitement. It seems to me it is a blessed thing to have calmness. I have no doubt about this part of the country putting its hand to whatever needs to be done when the time comes. Perhaps I should have gone to the vegetable meeting last week to which I was invited, which was to show people how to cook and eat vegetables. I read where one man who attended ate some spinach prepared there and declared that never before had he tasted spinach which was offered.

WE AREN'T COMPLACENT

I was able to go to Fayette today. I just felt old and let down, had no energy and regretted the time had come for me to sit on the shelf. But I had a busy day in spite of it. In the morning I went to the Gas Rationing Registration School to be prepared for taking registrations on the ninth, tenth, and eleventh. Then I bought myself two pair of work shoes, a pair to work in, and the other to wear to town, as I can't change from high top to low with impunity, being an old man. But I did get me a good looking pair of low shoes and a pair of high overshoes. Couldn't get any for church or anything like that. That made four pair in all. I am hoarding shoes instead of coffee. The shoe men say they may not have any to offer after their present stocks are exhausted. Long drawers are getting scarce too, the ankle length type which I like to break the wind off my old shanks. (First year I have bowed to the need.)

Two other nephews were drafted into service and Lilburn's protege, Charles van Ravenswaay was applying for a Naval commission.
Lilburn saddled up his letter writing hobby horse to report on war-related activities. In January 1942, he wrote:

BABE'S ESCAPE

On Monday morning Babe Edmonston was flying in formation and a plane flew over him too close, was sucked down by the propeller wash on top of Babe's plane and knocked off Babe's tail. That made his plane go straight up and the propeller of the other plane sheared off the left wing of Babe's. Then they both went into a spiral and started toward the ground. Babe tried to level off but couldn't. He yelled to the boy with him to jump and tried to get out himself. The cockpits are so small he is always cramped. He got one leg out but couldn't get the other, so pulled the cord of his chute, and when it filled, it jerked him out. He fell into the water which "thank God" was shallow - about five feet deep. In about half an hour, a fishing boat came along and took him to shore. He is bruised and sore but is full of thankfulness for an escape. He baled out, watchers told him, at less than 500 feet which does not give one clearance as a rule, so he feels especially favored. The boy with him escaped safely, as did the boy with the pilot whose plane fell on Babe's. The other pilot lost his life. He was "Andy," Babe's best friend and they had planned to room together. Bad, foggy weather still interferes with flying at Corpus and Babe thinks it will be February, around the sixth when he will graduate. Bobbie graduates at Pensacola tomorrow, Friday, and is expected home shortly.

A niece of Lilburn, Alice Kathryn Darneal, had gone to work at the Marine Base. She was home for a week. Lilburn reported November 1941:

Dear Homefolks,

Alice Kathryn Darneal is home for a week. Her Bud is up for fleet duty and has the jitters and they don't know whether to marry or not, but are still very much in love.

Alice paints a very lurid picture of free love as it flows around the Navy base, and says it is very difficult for a nice gal because the men seem to take it for granted that none of that kind are around. Bobbie looks terribly dissipated and says he just can't take care of all the women who want to sleep with him.

Mr. Tert Looks Us Over

Bobbie apparently decided it was time to wed. The father of the woman he fancied decided he should visit Bobbie's family to see if they would be fitting in-laws. Lilburn writes of his visit May 1942:

We have just been through an ordeal. For some weeks this had been hanging over us, the visit of Mr. Tert, the father of Bobbie's intended, to inspect the family. Finally, the time of arrival was to be 5:15, Saturday afternoon. Margaret arranged for the family parade at 7:00, to be followed by a buffet supper. Ellen was in Louisville and Horace, Ernest, Hazel, Lillian, the Hancocks and I were there. We arrived on time to be informed Mr. Tert had called from St. Louis to say his train had been delayed three "hou's. Three Pullman ca's had been tu'ned ovah but nobody was hu't." He would arrive in Boonville at 8:47.

The parade was called off, not having any reviewers and we fell to Margaret's old ham and fried chicken, pineapple-cheese salad, peas and carrots, creamed potatoes with Roquefort cheese on 'em, pickles, jelly, hot biscuits and coffee with two slices of angel food cake, strawberries and whipped cream for desert.

Time came to meet Mr. Tert at the bus and Robert started out but Margaret, all of a swivet, decided she was afraid for him to drive alone in the rain and she canvassed the crowd for four seaters but there was none except Hancock's and it was dirty they said, and all the other cars were dirty, so Bob got out on his own, but at Margaret's insistence Ernest got in to accompany him. Time passed. All this time it was just pouring like the Bagnell floodgates outside. Margaret got out Kodak pictures to show us the Florida scene and when we all looked at one of Mr. Tert we knew he and Rob and Ernest would never be able to travel three abreast. So after a family conference, Horace, the head, thought I had better go over to the bus station and get the overflow, which I did and three of us were there to meet the guest.

We got him to Rob's in time for all of us to listen to him for awhile before breaking up for the night. He did not prove to be as large as he appeared in the picture, and from the conversation I learned he is 68, is married a second time, has a son 24, and the daughter, Mildred is younger. His second wife is younger than he. He has a granddaughter "thuty months old." First he took from his billfold a Kodak picture showing the kid loading barrels of marmalade into a box-car. He put it back and replaced his billfold. Frequently he took it out again to show us another snap of the same child with his dog. It was put away and the third time he took it out and showed us a picture of the baby watching a fish at the age of eight months. Fond Grandpa was holding the line with the fish on it and the baby looked as elated as if he had really done it himself. Fond Grandpa Rob reached over and showed him a picture of Kenny, and he looked at it casually but it wasn't as good as his own.

He told us some delightful stories. And a tendency to stammer added spice to the conversation rather than distraction. And I don't know from his speech whether he is part Italian, or whether it is all South Carolinian with some of the gullah dialect thrown in. I do not know whether he is a native born South Carolinian but he went from there to Jacksonville, Florida, and thence to Pensacola. He talks so softly it is a little difficult to understand him at times and Saturday night after he came, Horace was seated on one side of him with an ear cocked over and Bob on the other, cocking his at another angle. We all like "Doc." (he said his son calls him that) mighty well.

Lillian invited them to dinner Sunday. We got down an old ham, sliced it and Lillian fried it beautifully, then we had fruit salad, creamed asparagus and corn, hot biscuits and butter, water melon pickle, raspberry jelly, hot butter cake (un-iced) with ice-cream and hot fudge sauce. We continued to like Mr. Tert and found much to interest him about the place. He looked at the trees, the garden, and my hogs and cattle were at the opposite end of the field, but a call or two from me brought them running and he thought that was wonderful. At the close of the meal we were all touched when he said, speaking of families, "Ah have 'neve' seen anything like this whe' you all get togethe' and even when you all saw each othe' last night, you greet each othe' like you hadn't met fu' a long time. It seems so sweet to me."

Horace took Margaret, Rob, and Mr. Tert on the Glasgow-Marshall tour soon after we finished dinner. I wanted to take him to the Clark's Chapel this morning but it rained almost constantly so that seems definitely to be out. But I know he would appreciate the "setting" of the family I could show him there. Well, he is a personage, a delightful character, and we don't care much what he thinks of Bobbie's folks, but we all like him very much.

He has fo'ty acres no'th of Pensacola, twenty of it in flowe's, and devotes much of his time to the propagation of azaleas. Probably hopes to have a show place some day. He has oil interests, handling oils I think, and making barrels just now for marmalade which is being sent to England in barrels which contain 20 gallons of grapefruit and oranges ground up with something to make it sweet. When received in England, it will be made up into seven times that much jelly with sugar added there. Mr. Tert is leaving sometime today. From his conversation, it seems to me he travels most of the time. He gives the general impression of being older than 68. He is good looking with nice dark eyes and white hair.

Margaret seems to feel that Mr. Tert left with a favorable impression. She said he talked so much about his girl and said it would just break his heart if anyone married his little girl for her money. I think Margaret was so affected she wrote to Bob at once not to marry her for the money. I don't know whether he has that much but evidently he thought he has. He said he thought the people and the country so delightful up here that he wanted Mildred and Bob to drive up here just as soon as they were married so she could have the pleasant experiences he had enjoyed. Margaret said, "But Bobbie doesn't have a car." Tert's response was... "Well, he can have one of mine."

Bobbie decided against marriage when he spoke to his commanding officer about arranging a military wedding. His C.O. told him, "Don't you know old man Tert is as crazy as a coot?" Bobbie subsequently married a nurse. Babe married a girl he had met in college. Both flyers served with Pacific fleet carriers shooting down a number of Japanese planes. Babe decided to become a career officer, but several years after the Japanese surrendered, he was killed in a training flight in Washington.

CHARLES VAN RAVENSWAAY'S FAREWELL DINNER

Dear Family,

We are still having spring-like showers and the whole country is just beautiful, more so than in spring for vegetation is so luxuriant. I had a chance to observe much scenery on the way to and from St. Louis when I fathered Charles to his plane departure and for a business trip to the city to see the world. Charles had asked me to take him down when his time came to leave for service. I had four good tires and had been itching to get to some old newspaper files in the library down there, too. So we got going around six a.m. and arrived at the Jefferson Hotel Air Station around 10:30. I left Charles to have lunch with friends and promised to join him for dinner. I spent my time in the library, joining Charles at the Missouri Athletic Club where his brother, Arie was living. Arie had arranged a farewell dinner party for Charles and it was a swell affair. There was champagne for all and then with the dinner those who had taken dark meat were served sparkling Burgundy, while those with fish had only more champagne. I gathered if you are eating fish, you do not do the reverse of drinking with Burgundy any more than Lillian approves of drinking milk with salmon. Courtney Werner, who was eating fish the same as I, insisted that it was steak until they gave him Burgundy and then he hated it because he didn't have any more champagne. I was glad the rich Van Ravenswaays were paying for the party.

The following day Lilburn did historical research at a library and that evening took Margaret Odom, the daughter of ministerial friends for a ride on the Mississippi Riverboat Admiral. His letter continues:

So Much To Do - So Little Time

All evening the town had been filling up with soldiers. They just poured into the hotels, and the streets downtown were full. I believe the Admiral can accommodate five thousand passengers and there must have been at least four thousand soldiers and sailors aboard. I hadn't ever seen so many people moving about in such a small space, although in fact the space is immense. As we explored the boat I witnessed the amazing spectacle of 3500 of these people throwing all restraint but a little (which saved many of them maybe) overboard and running wild, drinkin', and lovin' like nobody's business.

On the top deck with only the starlight above, the deck chairs, all of which were reclining like cots, had occupants who presented scenes which would have inspired me if I were an artist to do frescoes and murals the rest of my life, which would do justice to those unearthed in Pompeii. I may not be young, but I am terribly impressionable. Those who were not in love clutches and kiss holds that lasted longer than I could time were saying in emotion-cracked voices, "O my love. so much to do and so little time to do it in." Others were gettin' up their drunks as fast as they could to let it be wearing off a little by twelve o'clock when the boat docked. I got a bellyfull of bleary-eyed men and women, going and coming from the dance floor which was as crowded as a cattle truck on the way to market. They danced the rumba, but in St. Louis the wiggle has been eliminated. But even with that off, I did not essay it. We watched. Some did not know they were in St. Louis and certainly they wiggled beautifully and amazingly to me. My Sunday School class has always been against the rumba so I had never seen it danced before. Some of the people danced with so much feeling, if you know what I mean, and those who did not feel, patted it.

I was interested in how eager the crowd was to get off the boat. One bleary-eyed soldier said to Margaret as we were sitting in some comfortable chairs fronting the dance floor, "Lady, will you please get up. You are sitting on my bottle." We thought he was drunk and fresh but he persisted that she was in spite of her feeling under and insisting she was not. Finally she got up and from behind the cushion in the seat, he recovered his pint bottle of whiskey.

It is no place for Winter and Springtime to visit together when there is no disposition to drink something to reconcile the differences in ages. The orangeade was good.

One feels sorry for the soldiers of the Army, of the Navy, the Marines, and may I add, the Cross. If all over the U.S. it is like the Admiral was on Saturday night, the world is in a terrible mess. Aunt Margaret has heard someone say that after the war the people will wear no clothes.

I thought I might get home in time for Church Sunday morning, but I overslept. Lillian held down the fort alone while I was gone. She will not mind taking a job as some lonely housekeeper, if the necessity arises.

I have to go now, since the last shower has about dried off, and throw up hay. I am thankful to pitch hay instead of liquor.

REPORTED MISSING IN ACTION

In 1944 Major Robert Kingsbury was reported "Missing in Action." I presumed he had been shot down but this proved not the case. According to Lilburn, Bobbie's explanation was:

Before the forces in 1944 began a full scale invasion of the large Phillipine Island of Mindanao, the Army, Navy and Marine Air Forces decided they must have an emergency airstrip somewhere on this balmy island on which disabled U.S. aircraft could land during the initial stages of providing cover for the landing forces.

The job of establishing the airstrip was assigned to the Marines and Bobbie was asked to "volunteer." So - he volunteered and was ordered to build an airstrip long enough for freighter planes to land and take off. It had to be about 2000 feet long.

Bobbie and his team, a lieutenant and three sergeants, were

dropped into the area, and with native labor began work on the runway.

In about three days the Japanese discovered the task force. Bobbie, his team, and the natives with their oxcarts, took to the hills. He radioed his Command about 300 miles away. "We are heading for the hills but cannot guess what the outcome will be." He informed them that if they really wished to hold the spot, they had better send some paratroopers in, "lots of them and now!"

The Command, to cover itself, sent a telegram to Bobbie's wife that "Major Robert Kingsbury is missing."

The paratroopers did come in and defended the strip, but failed to send a telegram that Major Kingsbury and his men had escaped the Japs and rejoined the Command.

In all, Bobbie had 500 flying hours in combat against the Japanese.

For his distinguished military service he was awarded the Distinguished Flying Cross, five Air Medals and a Bronze Star Decoration. He continued in government service for the next ten years serving as a Liaison Officer for the Defense Department around the world.

All Lilburn's nephews in the service and his good friend Charles van Ravenswaay came through the war safely. The increased prices of Fairview Orchard/Farm products increased his income, enabling Lilburn to devote more time to his hobbies. The sections which follow reflect this.

Chapter Thirteen

HORACE KINGSBURY'S DEATH

Lilburn regularly rode his letter-writing hobby horse - keeping his family and friends informed. The following excerpts are from a letter telling of his older brother Horace's death, the funeral services and the growing friction between Xena, Horace's daughter by his first wife, and Ellen, his widow.

IN THE RACE TO THE RAILROAD CROSSING - THE TRAIN WON

December 10, 1954

Dear Folks,

Six weeks ago today since Horace had his accident. He either failed to see the approaching train or thought he had time to cross the track ahead of it. His car was demolished and he was badly injured and rushed to the hospital. He made a valiant fight and if ever he thought he might not come through to recovery, he gave no mention or indication of it. He had said the doctors thought he might get home for Christmas. I last saw him Saturday night looking tired, having taken seventy steps with help that day. He laughed and joked with Lillian and me. Sunday Xena talked with Dr. Winn who told her he was not doing well, so she came at noon Monday to see him. She offered to relieve the nurse who replied she could not leave the room even for a moment. Xena went to the head nurse and asked if orders had been given for the nurse not to leave the room and was told there had not been. So the head nurse told the one on duty she could be excused while Mrs. Bragg enjoyed a visit with her father. Later the duty nurse apologized to Xena and told her she had no choice, for Mrs. Kingsbury had ordered her not to leave the room. After the happy visit Xena went to town and bought a beautiful bouquet of red roses and white mums for her father's room, but found when she got back that he had died. Ellen had come and was there when the end came. Horace had walked into the bathroom to the toilet alone but called for the nurse to come. She found him blue in the face. Another nurse was called but by the time they carried him to his bed, he was dead. They tried artificial respiration and oxygen but to no avail.

All through his illness Ellen and Xena have been at cross purposes. Ellen damned Xena for what she did and what she didn't do. She would wave Xena away from her father, whispering she tired him. To me she would say, "I wish I could get it across to Xena not to try to tell her father jokes to make him laugh. It saps his strength." Xena would say, "Dad needs something to cheer him up. He likes funny stories."

Xena said Ellen never left the room so she could have a visit alone with her father, so she planned her visits to arrive when Ellen was at home. And managed some very successful visits.

The doctor wanted to hold an autopsy to find out where the clot was which caused his death and Ellen felt it could do no harm and was willing, but the thought was repugnant to Xena so there was none. Goodman and Boller (Boonville undertakers) were called. Xena said in Huntsville someone or more of the family stays at the undertaking parlor all of the time to receive those who come and to conduct them up to the casket. Ellen thought that unnecessary. She said the man in charge was a good friend of hers and a good Presbyterian and she thought it quite unnecessary to have someone there all the time. In any case there was no one there when the body was on display. The room in which the casket was placed was a bower of beautiful flowers. Great quantities had also been sent to the house. Rosie came home distressed by Horace's appearance Tuesday night. She said he did not look like himself at all. The next day Xena came in the afternoon and she was not satisfied either, so she asked Gus Boller if he could not do something about the mouth and eyes, and comb the little strand of hair in front as he was accustomed to wear it.

When I saw him, I thought he looked fine. Gus told me how he had worked to improve the appearance, some touching up, and Lillian thought a little rouge had been put on his lips. I felt quite satisfied. He certainly did not look his eighty-one years, more like a man of sixty.

In the meantime Xena had ordered flowers for her family, Ellen having taken over the order for the casket, and Gus Boller persuaded Xena to let him order them rather than order and pay Schnell directly. Xena mentioned to Schnell what Gus had suggested and that firm blew its top. Schnell told her they were tired of Gus doing that to get a ten percent commission. They called Gus up and told him so, told Xena she might as well have $12.50 worth of flowers as to get only $10.00 worth so Gus could get a commission.

Ellen, it looked to me, was a little too frugal in buying the casket flowers of red roses and chrysanthemums. But anyway she ordered them. Xena went to the florist and had him put letters in gold on the bouquet streamers, "Husband and Father." When the casket came home with this decorated bouquet on it and Ellen saw it, she was for going to get the scissors to cut the legend off but Anna Rose persuaded her to just turn them into the bouquet so they would not show.

The casket was brought home at 10:30 a.m. Thursday. Ellen had talked with Gus and told him she wanted him to close the casket an hour before the service began as she felt anybody who wanted to see him (Horace), if there was interest enough would go to the funeral home or come early to the house. Gus said, "Well, Mrs. Kingsbury, I am afraid I will be criticized for closing the casket so early." She replied, "If so, you may tell them you were complying with Mrs. Kingsbury's wishes."

Ellen had decided by then she would have the service at home. Gus had assured her the speaking system could be set up, and chairs could be put in all four rooms, the room and hall upstairs and the little side porch so as many could be accommodated there as at the churches. Gus then wanted to know what should go in the paper? When he asked when Mr. Kingsbury was married, Ellen told him 1935 in Louisville to her. She said he had lived in Howard County all his life, and when I mentioned

Florida she said that part of his life was so unsuccessful, it was hardly worth mentioning. The daughter and grandchildren were named. I was watching Xena who was crying, I knew, because her mother was not mentioned. I thought fast as to whether I should put in or not and putting my hand over my face as if I might have anticipated a blow, I said, "It seems to me for the sake of the daughter and grandchildren who may want to keep a copy of the story of their father's death, that his first marriage should be mentioned." Gus said he thought that would be nice. I think with that comment I made myself unpopular with Ellen. Xena straightened up and thanked me several times for putting in. Ellen asked me to call the district superintendent to hold the service. When he called personally, he said he presumed the local pastor would conduct the service and Ellen told him no - she was afraid he might bobble it. (A fear not unjustified.) But the local pastor was asked to say a prayer.

Gus Boller had the house hooked up so there was a speaker in every room. The sound system worked fine and everyone who had good ears could hear distinctly. Finally, time came to bring the casket into the house and Gus Boller was at the front door. Ruby and Anna Rose had been overwhelmed by the odor of catshit around the fireplace in the parlor. They hunted around the flower stands to no avail. Then one of them spied it on the carpet a short distance in front of the fireplace. Gus was held off at the door while Rosie bulked it up and Ruby took it up with a wet rag. Ella, the cook, came bringing the atomizer which was used to purify and sweeten the air. It was right where Gus Boller's handsome catafalque had to be placed. Over that hurdle, the casket was brought and the flowers arranged. All the red rose bouquets were banked on the mantel in the front room and immediately around the casket. A magnificent white bouquet was on the floor and I commented about it being so lovely, and Ellen said, "But you see we have put all the red ones, his favorite color, close to the casket."

As we stood there she took my hand and said, "You haven't been around lately." I said "No," I had assured her she should call me whenever there was anything I could do, and not having been called, I presumed nothing was needed so I kept myself from being in the way. She assured me I would never be in the way in her house.

People began coming in early and for some time I opened the door for them. Men were carrying chairs and placing them in the east living room, the dining room, the middle parlor, the west porch and upstairs in the bedroom and in the hall upstairs where the family was to sit. Ellen had wanted everyone to register. Some did and some didn't. At half after one I saw Gus start to close the casket, but Ellen had just told me she wanted it closed at two o'clock, so I called it to Gus's attention and promptly at two the lid was on, just as Bertha Hitch came and she wanted to see but it was too late. Orders were orders. Gus had asked me how I was going to the cemetery and I told him I was driving my own car, taking Will, Anna Rose and Lillian. When I got settled down with the family, Anna Rose came over and said Ellen wanted me to walk with her at the cemetery and from the house. I went over and told Ellen I would be glad to escort her if she wished, but thought I should inform Gus Boller. She said "Yes" we could all go in the funeral cars.

So I made my way through all the people to the front of the house to tell Gus. I thought it would be easier not to try to return through the crowded lanes of the rooms, and went around to the side door of the room where the family was. I knocked on the door and heard someone move as if to open it. Then everything was silent. So I returned and retraced my steps through the crowded rooms. In the meantime Ellen was put out because someone was trying to get in that door and Lillian overheard Ellen say to her sister-in-law, "Sometimes I wonder if this is my house." Whereupon Lillian turned to her and said, "It was Lib trying to get in." Before the service started, Ellen decided to put on her hat and coat and did so, wearing them through the service. Hats and coats belonging to the rest of us were stacked on the bed in Ellen's room.

Everything was perfectly still for minutes before the service started. One could have heard a pin drop. Martha Hobrecht played a number on the piano, the "death piano" Ellen hates so much. Then Rev. Morgan read the 90th Psalm and Rev. Burton acquitted himself nobly with a beautiful prayer. Then Lawrence White sang "The Lord's Prayer." Following this Rev. Morgan gave an impressive talk. Ellen had told him there was to be no eulogy or obituary. I can't begin to tell you how and what he said, but it really was a beautiful exposition with nothing about it to tear the emotions. Finally he said, as if addressing him, "And so Horace, bon voyage," and wished him beautiful things beyond compare when he arrived at his destination. This little bon voyage bit was sort of a shock to me. Then Rev. Morgan announced, "The song which is about to be sung is one of special interest to Mrs. Kingsbury as it was written in the front room of her home." Lawrence White then sang "Asleep in Jesus." (Ellen told me she was having it sung because she did not believe there had been a funeral in her family at which it had not been used, that her great grandfather helped to write it in the ancestral home in Virginia.

When the service was over and the family had started to go to the waiting cars I was delayed a little getting my hat and coat and involved in the excitement of Margaret Kingsbury saying to Anna Rose, "I know I handed my coat to you when I came in and you laid it on the bed. It's not there. Somebody has taken it. I want my coat."

Everybody was looking everywhere and presently all the coats were accounted for but Margaret's. She had none to put on, and it was her good sealskin coat. Everybody was leaving because of necessity, leaving Margaret to her loss. I caught up with Ellen who said, "I've changed my mind. I'm going to walk with Bernard. I hope it won't make you mad." And so I rushed away to tell Gus Boller Mrs. Kingsbury had changed her mind and I would drive my own car after all. But Ellen wanted Anna Rose to walk with her and took her along. When the Converses, Ellen and Anna Rose were in the car ready to drive off, Anna Rose mentioned Margaret's plight. Ellen looked at the coat she had on and said, "I wonder if I have her coat? Heaven's sake, I have!" In the meantime, someone had looked in Ellen's closet and found Ellen's coat and rushed out with it. Gus Boller took it and asked "What shall I do with this one?" Anna Rose said, "For Heaven's sake take it to that woman over there who must be frozen without a coat." Margaret's face got so red she looked as if she were having a stroke when she thought somebody had stolen her coat. We drove to Walnut Grove and left Horace there beside his first love, Minnie.

It would be inhuman if Xena were not interested in the estate, will, etc. She told us she went to see Roy Williams and asked him what was the usual procedure and if he knew anything about Horace's affairs? Roy said he did not write the will and loaned Xena a book on wills. Xena thought Ellen might want her to stop at the house after the funeral to read the will as Roy had told her that it was done soon after the funeral. If a member of the family lived at a distance, it would save an extra trip.

From bits gathered here and there, the St. Louis Union Trust Company will be involved with everything except the farms. I have an idea trusts will be set up. Everything in the house will go to Ellen because she did not wish any arrangement or controversy with Xena over anything she might wish. Xena is to be reimbursed in cash to the value of the household goods. Everything else is to be divided 50-50. I don't think Ellen had anything to do with it.

Ellen said she would continue to live at the big house and that if she ever decided to make a change she would probably go to Boonville.

Ellen is alone. By hokey she preferred to stay alone every night except for having Ella sleep in the house, and she told Rosie she hoped nobody would come to the house following the burial as she wanted to be alone. Anna Rose said whenever Ellen and Xena were in the house together Ellen was quivering and Xena did not know which way to turn and she herself was tense to the breaking point.

Well, you now know what kind of people you have for relatives out in Missouri. My relation of these things would make anyone think there was no deep sadness, no bereavement, but you know better.

At noon after we had given Gus Boller the information to be sent to the Boonville papers and the A.P., Xena called from Boonville wanting me to write an obituary for Horace to put with what we had already given to Gus. She said she thought a man of the worth and prominence of her father should have some sort of tribute paid him, and would I do it right away so she could drive over and get it in time for Gene Davis to get it in the paper. I just wasn't in the proper frame of mind. I told her I thought his life spoke for itself, etc. But she wanted something his great grandchildren could read, that all his ancestors were written up in the county histories, etc. I had to let her down. But later the Fayette paper wanted information and feeling for Xena I jotted down some things I thought would be appropriate and sent them along. All who have read the story in the Fayette paper liked it and hoped Xena would too. I am sending her some copies.

Appraisers have been busy this week on the various properties of the estate with more than 1700 acres of land. The Fayette paper announced his gift of $25,000 to the Endowment Fund of Central College. And I heard he left Clark's Chapel Cemetery $500. He gave Anna Rose $3000 but I believe it is to be held by me which I do not relish, and I am to pay it to her when she needs it. Each of the grandchildren received $1000.

Xena wrote and told Ellen she would like to be on terms with her, and hoped she might be a mother to her. This was a good joke to Ellen who told of it. To one she told she had not heard a word from Xena since the funeral. To another she said she was going to write Xena and tell her she was a grown woman now and didn't need a mother.

Chapter Fourteen

COLLECTOR OF CHARACTERS

Lilburn never listed collecting interesting characters as a hobby but his letters and columns describe many he came upon in his hobby horse rides. A few interesting examples:

I knew a man out at Pilot Grove who had bad health and the doctor told him he must diet or he would not live long. The man said he just loved to eat and that he would just go on and enjoy food. And after he died, they say he had the most peaceful satisfied look on his face.

From a letter written in 1932:

Dear Cousin Lillian,

I drove to Bunceton yesterday morning and picked up some more glass. And I found a table that is just rare in the possession of an old bachelor who lives alone. I aim to cultivate him. Money is no object to him. He has 55 walnut trees which he won't sell. He showed me one for which he has been offered $200 for the main log, twelve feet long. He met me with a rifle and I wondered if he were more eccentric than I had heard. He talks way up high like a lady. He could hardly speak at first and I didn't understand his predicament until he later explained he had been in the woods hunting and had run all the way to the house when he heard the car. He finally decided to show me his collection of arrowheads and then he showed me some furniture and we looked for glassware of which I found nothing. But he had the rare table I believe is a Duncan-Phyfe. He had a fiddle and a guitar and I coaxed him to play for me, he played a lot of things quite well. He said he "guessed he knowed 500 tunes." He really was good and I bragged on him so much he took me down to the barn and showed me some rare old furniture. As we went, he asked me if there was anything in there I wanted and being modest I said I would like an old kettle he had, which he gave me. And then I was sorry I hadn't chosen the day bed or the wide-bed, though he had told me his brother was half interested in these.

In South Missouri towns there are some interesting characters. At one crossroads where we asked an old man for directions to the next town he said very crisply, "turn to the left and drive like hell." At Mount Vernon, we went to call on the principal of the high school and found her with no stockings on, old worn house shoes and a dirty dress, crying hard times due to the closing of both banks. She said times were so close around there that the school could not get anything in cash for their school activities, and at a recent debate, they passed the plate to get a silver offering for the judges for their trouble in coming and they got just fifty cents.

For Land's Sake

Sometime in 1958 he wrote his sister Anna Rose:

Rosie,

Last Tuesday a handsome gentleman with a shock of white hair came into the office, and said someone told him to come to see me, that we would have much in common: music, collection and what not. He gave me his name, said he hailed from Yonkers, N.Y., and I having recently seen Yonkers from the Hudson River boat, soon had him identifying sights I had seen there. He said his name was Mr. Land and wanted to see my house and I asked what his business was around here. He said he had married Mary Lou Carson's daughter, the one who has aspired to become famous as an opera singer. I was busy every night but Friday, so we arranged he should come then, bringing Mary Lou and Mary if they cared to come. It turned out they didn't so he turned up alone in the last word Ford convertible, and I took him around the country to Clark's Chapel and past the Grandpa houses, etc., before we settled down for the evening at home. He told me secretly of trouble he had had with his wife, how she had done

him last winter after she persuaded him to take her to Europe for
special voice coaching. She made him hire an extra room for her
because she said he snored too loud, left him one night and he
had to put the police on her trail to find her in Milano.

In Yonkers, in his seventeen room house, the Land's having
lived there 120 years, Mary did not like many things he loved
and one day she paid $80 to have what she did not like carted
away to the Salvation Army - a whole collection of books, curtains, drapes and what have you! She used his mother's fine linen
every day, had it laundered until it was wearing out...and why?
Out here in Missouri at Mary Lou's he had been using the same
napkin for ten days! Mary battered the sterling ware around his
house. Out here they had nothing but old 1847 Rogers, which
was good enough, and at home his mother always used that for
everyday. And Mary insisted on this bright new convertible,
making him sell his two cars, and why couldn't she take the train
to go into the city, only a twenty minute ride, but no, she must
drive it and pay five or six dollars to park, and $15 to get prettied
up, and then ride around bareheaded so she could be seen. This
is a strain for me to keep secret.

I asked him to sing at church, and after due consideration,
he consented, asking to rehearse "Tenderly and Softly, Jesus is
Calling" and "The Old Rugged Cross." He had been baritone
soloist at St. Thomas on Fifth Avenue in N.Y. for 17 years. He
had a voice like a horn on a harbor boat and I asked him to mute
it a little for Sunday morning lest the back wall of the church
collapse from the vibration.

All the time he was keeping it from Mary Lou and Mary
where he was visiting, and he reported that his reception when
he went home was anything but cordial. He sang Sunday morning and I think was generally received with pleasure. Lillian invited him to dinner. He said he would like to come but he would
have to go home first. If any dinner were in sight, he had better
eat there; if not, he would come out. He came out later and
reported the girls were playing some game when he came home
and paid no attention to him.

For the next three hours we listened to a mixture of his marital troubles and a recital of his relationships with the high and mighty in the social world of New York, especially the great in the field of music - all the famous singers. Great names rolled from his tongue like water from a roof in a rain storm. How tired we got of it. At 4:30 he thought he had better report to the Marys and left. At 8 p.m. he came yoo-hooing at the side door, wanting to know if we would put him up overnight. He had gone home; the girls were still playing their game (God knows what?) and he waited until 7:00 thinking they would move and get supper. They didn't, so he went to the barbecue down on the highway and got his supper. By the time he got back, they were gone and the door was locked. And so could he spend the night with us?

I told him he should go back and sleep all night in the car if necessary and not give them any reason to say he had left home as they might charge him with desertion or something. He thought that good advice and at 10 o'clock he left us tired and worn out.

We had just got to sleep when there was a rap on the door - a vigorous one. I opened up and stepped out and met someone who said he was Delgar and had Mr. Land in his car. Mr. Land wanted to know if we would put him up the rest of the night. There had been trouble, a row down at Mary Lou's and they had phoned Delgar to come get the "old gentleman" and he didn't want to take him to jail, and if I didn't take him in, he would take him over to the Hotel Frederick. Then I realized it was the Sheriff of Howard County, Delgar Wells. I told him I did not want to get embroiled in this family affair, so he said he would take him to Boonville.

Next day he told me what happened. Before he left Sunday night I asked him why he had not told Mary Lou he was coming to my house, there was nothing criminal about it. Next day, he said he was jackass enough to do what I said, and the girls must have said plenty when he told them where he had been. Words must have been flung and finally his wife threw something at him. They grabbed all his clothes and threw them out in the yard and phoned the Sheriff to come and get him for he was disturbing the peace.

Ensconced at the Frederick after midnight, he walked the streets and went to Holt's restaurant for something to eat several times, then hired a taxi and drove to Mary Lou's farm, had the taxi stop out by the barn, then he walked to the yard "down the the dark highway, and it was God's blessing that he wasn't killed by those enormous trucks." He got in the sports car and drove it without lights to the highway, then with the lights on to Boonville and parked it in front of the hotel. The next morning he looked out and there were the two Marys climbing into the car and driving off. "What a jackass I was to park it there," said Arthur Harold Land. He engaged John Stegner to look after his interests although admitting he had let Mary put the car in her name, so he soon found out he had no claim there. He called New York and stopped payment on all checks, lest Mary draw all his money out.

Monday night I was downtown and Lillian was out in the garden when a car drove up and she saw Land go to the door and then right on in, "yoo-hooing." She first thought of hiding out but feared the car might go off leaving him so she went in. The Rev. and Mrs. Viggers of Boonville were headed for Fayette to a meeting and Mr. Land wanted to be dropped off to wait their return. Lillian told him I was downtown and he said what difference does that make? Can't I stay here with you until he returns? And so he did. She took him in and he sat in our new soft chair that revolves, but before it revolved once he was sound asleep snoring like nobody on earth had ever snored. He had had no sleep for two days and nights. He was still sleeping when I arrived. I sat on the swing in the dark and wondered if the Viggers had let us down and gone home without picking him up. They came back after ten and Mr. Land insisted they must be shown all over the house. I was dead on my feet and thoroughly disgusted by the time they had seen the first floor.

Next day he called to know if we could come to dinner on Wednesday evening at the hotel. By now he had established contact with his banker and seemed to have his wallet refurbished with cash, and he had bought a secondhand station wagon and ordered it repainted white and delivered on Friday afternoon. I made excuses about the dinner hour and then he wanted us to come for lunch. I said there was not time between 12:00 and 1:00. Then yesterday noon he drove over and insisted we come to a dinner party he was having last night...and if we couldn't come to dinner, could we come to a musical he was giving later. But we had had all we could take and lied until my tongue will be sore about prior engagements. Finally he asked me if I would give or sell him the unfinished portrait which Mary Lou's grandmother had left. Lord knows how it came into my possession but I showed it to him the first day I saw him...but I told him I didn't think he had any business with anything that had to do with the woman who had thrown him into the highway. I hope he drives off without contacting me again.

The following summer on an eight-day trip to New York, Lilburn visited Arthur Land in Yonkers. He wrote of this visit to his niece Julia.

I went up to Yonkers for a little visit with Arthur Harold Land, the man who visited here in 1958 and was thrown out in the street by his wife and her mother. I was eager to see him in his home setting, to see if it was as he had said. We arrived at 2:30 and he showed me the twenty-two room mansion filled to the brim with lovely paintings, silver, marble, china, crystal, but everything was old and sort of shut off and dismal.

When I awoke in the morning, fountains were playing in the yard (in my honor he said) and down below was the mighty Hudson with the Palisades across the river covered with beautiful autumn foilage. He took me over Westchester County in his sports car with the top back at the push of a button. It was a beautiful trip and as he has lived there all his life he knew who was everybody's first, second, and third wife, who had lost money, who had spent it there, who was interesting. But he drove with such nonchalance, a lot of the time he was over the line between two lanes so that oncoming traffic was always honking for him to get over. He seemed to pay no attention and the retarded vehicles behind would wait until there was a break and then whiz by with dirty looks from the drivers. Once we stopped for a red light and a big truck pulled along side and the driver said, "Why don't you get your a— back in line and quit your weaving. I'm going to have you arrested for blocking the traffic." To which he replied, "I'll have you arrested for being a damn nuisance." And instead of allowing the truck driver to go on ahead, he pulled quickly forward and kept in the way, with the honking behind getting louder and louder. Arthur Harold appeared oblivious to it all. It rained hard toward the close of day and I begged him to put me on the bus or a train for my return to the city. But, "No," he said. "Your hospitality to me deserves only that I take you back to your hotel." And he did and I never shall forget his carefree driving down Riverside Drive and my anxiety when horns were always honking because he was over the line. He would say, "Well, I'll have you there by 7:15," and I wondered if it would be to a hospital or the morgue. But we made it OK. The next morning when I looked in the mirror there was a curl in my hair.

Chapter Fifteen

BOTTLING

After Mothers Day in 1973 Lilburn wrote:

Jean Edmonston was down to bring Mothers Day gifts to Lillian and wanted to take a drive on the beautiful afternoon. She took us to see Don Kintner. We had a nice visit with him and his wife and this time I climbed the stairs thinking he had arranged his apothecary's shop, but he only has all the plunder for it in an upstairs room, not yet in order but an amazing collection. I do not blame anybody for collecting but how I would hate to have what some folks' fancies do get together.

This triggered the following columns:

COLLECTING MISSOURI BOTTLES

June 16, 1975

There is hardly any article under the sun which some person has not started to collect: coins, stamps, buttons, salt and peppers, toothpick holders, lamps, tin boxes, buttermolds, paperweights, old Valentines, pressed glass in dozens of patterns, napkin rings, and so on ad infinitum.

I know a woman whose hobby is collecting china with hand-painted designs of daisies.

I have met some collectors who have cupboard shelves lined with toothpick holders. I know an office which has one wall covered with antique clocks, all refinished and keeping time. Another man needs little room to hold his collection of thimbles.

I have never thought of myself as a bottle collector though there are about a hundred of them in my office. They just "happened" to get in with many other things I was collecting years ago.

My interest in bottles was massaged and stimulated recently when, upon invitation of a member, I attended the monthly meeting of "The Antique and Relics Club of Central Missouri," in Columbia. Most of the men were from Columbia but others were there from Jefferson City, Mexico, Lebanon, Fayette, Benton City, Rocheport and Boonville. Some of them brought their wives and children. Some of the wives were members of the club.

Lilburn in his office with some of his bottle collection shown on top shelf

The evening program was on "Missouri Bottles." It was presented by a gentleman from Jefferson City who exhibited about fifty containers most of which were imprinted with the name of the commodity which it had originally contained and or the name and address of the Missouri dealer who had retailed it. There were some early, crudely blown soda water bottles which researchers have said were made as early as 1840. Each bottle was marked with its current value. The soda bottles were marked $200 each.

Another feature of the meeting was the showing of antique ink wells which had been sold. It was an interesting display.

There was a bottle auction. Each member, if he desires, is allowed to bring up to ten bottles for the sale. He marks each bottle with the price he must have to let it go. The auctioneer announces the minimum bid and if anyone wishes to buy it he must pay more, even as little as a dime or quarter. If there are no bids the bottle is returned to the owner.

I was interested in observing that among all the bottles shown there was not one like any of mine.

These men of different professions had left business cares and the problems of making a family living on the shelf as it were and were seriously discussing the merits of bottles, their shape, color, size, age, and manner of making, whether blown or molded. They were as enthusiastic as farmers at a meeting discussing cattle, hogs, sheep and crops.

GRANDMOTHER SCHERMER'S HEALTH RESTORER

D. Kintner of Columbia is enjoying an interesting phase of bottle collecting. I was surprised to learn it is possible to find bottles filled with medicines with original labels which interested people three score years and ten ago. He says that in six months he has been able to collect about 400 of them. Many of them are contained in the light cardboard boxes in which they were packed with a brochure of testimonials around the bottle.

One of them of local interest was "Grandmother Schermer's Health Restorer" manufactured by the Eureka Medicine Co., of Bunceton, Mo. Testimonials about its great benefits were dated 1901, 1902 and 1903.

Grandma Schermer, a native of Germany, came to Speed, Mo., to live in 1867. She brought with her a home remedy which she used for family ailments. Finally there were so many requests for it, she and her son, C.J. Walje, decided to form a company to manufacture it commercially in Bunceton.

It was purely herbal, made wholly from leaves, bark, roots, flowers and seeds. It was claimed "to prepare the body for resistance to disease, to purify the blood, promote digestion, regulate the bowels, act upon the kidneys, induce healthy respiration, quiet the nerves and induce sound restful sleep.

In Bunceton Rev. B. Marson, Pastor of the C.P. church used it and praised it for "doing what it claimed to do." Harvey B. Moore was completely cured of indigestion by taking it. W.E. Coleman claimed it did more good than anything he had ever taken for "indigestion and that tired feeling." Mrs. W.F. Howard had tried many remedies but five bottles of the Health Restorer "almost completely cured her." Mrs. Wm. Lusk took it for two months and it did her more good than all other medicines combined which she had tried.

Mrs. Margaret E. Stegner of Speed had been afflicted with catarrh of the stomach for over 15 years, the doctors had declared it chronic. She had tried five or six doctors and patent medicines which had cost her several hundred dollars resulting in little relief. Five bottles of Grandma Schermer's Health Restorer had done her more good than everything else put together. And John J. Blank was sick of indigestion and had a tired feeling until he feared he would take down with fever but after taking one bottle he was entirely relieved.

P.H. Kirby of Bunceton wanted it known that he had chronic malaria, a liver trouble and impure blood about 15 years, even a trip to Eldorado Springs did not keep him from feeling weak and worn out all the time. After using two bottles, he felt as though he had never been sick.

Wm. D. Woods of Tipton after suffering 18 years with malaria and impure blood and "trying several noted doctors," was persuaded to try GSHR and claimed he would not take $500 for the benefit he derived from it.

Miss Jessie Rudolph of Boonville found it very beneficial for stomach trouble which had bothered her for three years.

Herman Kramer of Boonville had suffered indigestion for 10 years, more or less severe, had employed the best medical aid in the city but obtained only temporary relief through dieting. As soon as he began eating again he would bloat up and have cramping pains. He reduced in flesh to 128 pounds. After taking four bottles of Grandma Schermer's medicine, the bloating and cramping disappeared and he weighed 166 pounds.

J.H. Haller wanted the world to know that for 7 or 8 years he got no relief from doctors, but four bottles of this wonderful medicine had cured him entirely.

Mrs. M.J. Goode of Syracuse suffered for three months with a disease the doctors diagnosed differently. One said she was in the last stage of consumption, another that she had catarrh of the stomach and enlargement of the liver. Many remedies were tried without relief. She was almost dead when Grandma's Health Restorer saved her from an early grave. She took only four bottles before she began to feel like a new woman and her friends told her she did not look like the same person.

We wonder, after 70 years, if there are any descendants of any of these people who felt so benefitted by Grandma Schermer's Health Restorer living now in Cooper County.

PILL BOXES

Mrs. Pete Christus of Boonville invited me to drop by to see her collection of pill boxes. She added that she had never thought of making a collection of anything herself but at one time she had a serious ear infection which required several kinds of medicine in the form of pills. Her son-in-law, Robert Preston, observing the assortment, remarked that she had so many she should have some pill boxes.

However, she gave no further thought to it until he began sending them from the foreign country where he was stationed in government service. Subsequently he served in many foreign lands, and visited in others. From each he sent pill boxes to her. It was as if he had acquired a gracious habit. Relatives and friends seeing or hearing about the fruits of his kindness followed suit and whenever they traveled abroad or in the United States they did not forget pill boxes for Mrs. Christus. Thus the pill boxes assumed the proportions of a collection.

Pill boxes! Somehow I couldn't understand the desire of collecting boxes or bottles, reminders of illnesses of life from childhood on up.

And all of the pill boxes I had seen were of plain cardboard, round at first, then came the rectangular ones with a part that was pulled out like a drawer, then finally plastic containers.

One day I mentioned my feelings about collecting pill boxes to a well-informed person. He kindly and gently dispelled my ignorance by informing me that pill boxes may be very elegant; that ladies in foreign lands and even in our own who are obliged to take pills regularly, frequently carry tiny boxes, often quite elegant, containing what they may need when away from home for short periods.

Shortly after that, a lady was dining with me. When she finished her dinner, she brought out a dainty gold box, chased on its sides with a hinged top of red onyx. It was beautiful! When I asked about it she said it was a little something very old which she had inherited, the pill box.

Now, having seen an aristocrat of the pill box family, I was full-steam-ahead to see as soon as possible Mrs. Christus' collection. I did before the end of that day.

At first sight of it, an old quotation flashed over my mind, "A thing of beauty is a joy forever."

Mrs. Christus opened the lid of the clear-topped table. It contained the display, the gift of her daughter and son-in-law. Mrs. Christus had it lined with red velvet and invited me to take up each tiny, rare item to examine the fine work of skilled artisans from many parts of the world. Most of the little boxes are an inch and a quarter in size overall. They are of gold, silver, brass, pewter, with sides delicately chased. But their tops, some fit on but mostly they are hinged, are the spots where we see real artistry in tiny floral embroidery on silk or velvet, hand painted designs on porcelain and ivory, artistic arrangements of colored jewels and tiny sea shells, some all jeweled, others are of enamel, mosaic and damascene.

Lilburn had begun selling off the antiques kept in his office. On 24 August 1977 he wrote Charles:

I had a buyer of bottles and stone jars and jugs. He came in and pointing to an old jug, said "Will you take $35 for it?" I sold him $115 worth of jugs and my two pineapple bottles for $150 each, and $19 worth of old buttons. He left me several offers on bottles and plates which seemed mighty good until Warman's new price book came out last week and listed the pineapple bitters bottle at $275.

The double steeple clock I thought I did well with when I let it go for $550 is now priced at $2500. That is as crazy as the price of hill land in Howard County.

Writers' Conference

In March of 1959 Lilburn attended a writers' conference at which aspiring writers could have a manuscript evaluated. He writes of this to his niece, Julia Sikes:

Dear Julia,

I had a fine time in Springfield at the Writers' Conference.

On my manuscript I got a right good report and everything criticized was right proper. As for style, it was checked for good, easy and smooth characterization: "The people are perfectly delightful." Strong qualities:

"The easy sure way each incident is told. The realness of the people." As to plot: "It doesn't seem to have a plot. It is a series of incidents with one thread, the church music, to hold it together." As for marketing, or a market: "As it stands, I can't think of any. Shame too, for it is delightful."

At lunch I sat by the critic, Loula Grace Erdman, and we talked of everything except manuscripts, and at 1:30 she was quite professional during the interview, when she said some more nice things about the paper. Said she did hope I would go on with it and if I wished her to, she would write to an editor she knew well that I was going to send him a manuscript, not to consider in its entirety, but to determine if there were parts which would be suitable for his magazine.

After the meeting, I was asked out to Adelaide Jone's little house for a coffee in the evening. Adelaide is Director of the Conference, whom I have known ever since she struggled and succeeded in getting me into the State Writers' Guild.

Considering manuscripts as babies, this was a clinic on child care, for the help of crippled children, or the retarded, and I read the "case history" of all who would let me have a copy. Never have I seen so many expectant mothers and fathers. This meeting was a sort of clinic for the hopefully expectant, and those who had given forth successful births were there to advise those who had not. The latter were advised how to care for the child, what to do for its betterment, and were advised in no case was birth ever as simple as made to look in the story the papers carried last week of the woman who wouldn't quit looking at her TV program and had her real baby while looking on. Loula Erdman advised me not to stand on the diving board but to jump in, and never to say, "Now this is how it happened" in telling of it.

One woman's child is 600 pages about Alcibiades. Of him she said, "I have loved him for seventeen years." Another's was the illegitimate child of Wordsworth, another looked like a heathen idol, and one child of a poetic nature was born with its uppers.

The meeting at Adelaide's was sort of an autopsy at which Erdman and some college professors who had acted as judges on a contest, told of manuscripts they "just couldn't read through." They made light of others, and I wondered if put to it, they could show as much ingenuity in writing a story as some of those whose work they ridiculed?

I had wondered if my paper had really been read, but at Adelaide's party, Erdman asked me to tell certain bits of it, so I knew she must have read it. And as I went out the door, she called, "Be sure and do something with that lovely material."

Chapter Sixteen

Music, Music, Music

Lilburn's organ at Fairview

So far as I know, Lilburn never attempted to market his "child," "A Good Part of My Life Was Music." The manuscript, however, became the basis of a talk given to several clubs and organizations during the years that followed. It pictures some of the paces he put his Music Hobby Horse through and in part is reproduced below:

A Good Part of My Life was Music

After our conference assigned Rev. Victor White, a young bachelor, to the pastorate in New Franklin and she had consented to play the church organ, Miss Delia Barton had been as punctual as the striking hammer of a well-regulated clock. On any fair Sunday, you could set your time at a quarter of eleven when she came up Missouri Avenue, riding sidewise on her horse in an easy running walk and dismounted at the stile at the side of the Methodist Episcopal Church, South.

There were always several men, early arrivals, bound for preaching but loitering in front of the church to chew and smoke, and hash over the news until the service would be two songs gone. One of them would hurry to hitch her horse. Before leading it away he watched admiringly while Miss Delia, on the stile, hurriedly unbuttoned her riding over-skirt and let it drop to the floor. Stepping out of it she picked it up, folded it neatly, laid it against the saddle and secured it there with a loop made by lifting the stirrup and hooking it over the saddle horn. With the preliminaries out of the way, she thanked the gentleman, straightened her shirtwaist and skirt, dabbed at her hair and hastened past the other men, toward the church door.

Miss Delia was too comely to pass any group of men unappreciated. As she nodded and smiled, they all greeted her cordially, quids momentarily quiescent in cheek, pipes unsmoked in hand. But as she passed out of earshot, Squire Doolin, wizened and hollow-mouthed except for his quid, commented to those within hearing of his high-pitched voice, "Purty as a partridge, ain't she!" Then with a twinkle in his beady, blue eyes and a little chuckle, he continued, "Wonder how she's makin' out with the preacher? My old lady says Delia's got her eyes on him a heap more'n on the notes in the song book." He then cupped his hand to his ear and strained to catch the words of Lige Cooter who ran the poultry house, "Well, she ain't takin' her ducks to no poor market!"

Miss Delia never seemed the least disturbed by the men but some of the women, more timid, complained among themselves of having to pass, every Sabbath day, before these glimpse-stealers on the way into the church. However, they let it go for none wanted to alienate the men. "After all," reasoned Miss Priscilla Watson, "they are the backbone of the church and we cannot suffer discomfort of a single misplaced vertebra." To which practical Seena Hobbs interposed, "Maybe so Priscilla, but the church would soon be humpbacked if the women didn't brace up the backbone like the stays in a corset."

The older women still talked about the time when the Missionary Society had surprised some of the men addicted to Battle Axe plug tobacco by putting spittoons in the church by the seats where they spat and worshipped. This move toward sanitation in the guise of consideration backfired. Three of them with top seniority of membership felt insulted, walked out and never of their own volition darkened the door of the church again. But each one, when he died, was brought back for his funeral.

Miss Delia's arrival at church usually coincided with that of my parents and me. I always wished I could loiter outside like the men to hear what they talked about. But I had long felt the parental urge to go right in. But there was compensation in not missing a note of Miss Delia's music.

Promptly at 11 o'clock, as the last clang of the church bell warned stragglers to hurry, Miss Delia seated herself at the organ, ready and eager. Rev. White glanced at her with a smile and announced the first hymn. There was a platform for the organ choir and from our family bench, second from the front, I had a clear view as she played.

How busy she appeared! Pulling out and pushing in the eleven round, small-lettered stops: working the treadles smoothly, forcing air into the bellows to make tones, blending those tones into melodies with deft fingers as her hands glided over the keyboard, pressing her legs outward against the knee-swells to give more volume to the music. When she played the pastor's favorite gospel song, "Life Is Like A Mountain Railway," she reminded me of a speeding locomotive with wheels and pistons in graceful motion.

Music was such a part of my life, anything she played fitted my soul and gave it an uplift like a tailored, made-to-order suit of clothes.

My first introduction to and intimate association with music occurred at the home of an aunt who had several children with whom I loved to play. She also had a little music box with a dozen wax cylinder records. My cousins enjoyed my visits as long as I played croquet with them. But I became so enamored of music, the croquet court lost its charm. I laid down my ball and mallet and wanted nothing but to be with the little music box forever. My cousins, decades later, recall this with amusement and remind me of my musical assignation. I confess to a nostalgia for that first mistress, the little music box with her waxen charm, now long dead and buried in the dust of an attic.

I was eight years old when my father gave my mother a piano. With a family of seven children and a large house, she had little time to enjoy it. But occasionally she displayed souvenirs of her college days, a snappy schottishe and part of another piece, "The Maiden's Prayer." In playing the latter she crossed one hand over the other, forming an "X" which intrigued me more than any I ever encountered later in algebra.

One of my brothers filled me with envy when he played chop sticks. I thought he did it well and resolved to do it too. Persistent efforts burst into bloom but until they set some fruit, they sounded like a peckerwood drilling, haltingly, a hole in a tree.

I used to wonder why talented ladies who visited in our home, with so much to give musically, always seemed reluctant and had to be begged to share it. One would offer as an excuse, "Oh, I forgot to bring my music." Another, "I am so out of practice." But usually the dam of pretense would give way to insistent persuasion and the performance would belie all excuses. Then in wonder and delight, I would stand close behind the performer, breathing down her neck, watching and listening.

Visitors commented on the mahogany complexion of our piano, its graceful upsweep, its pretty carved face, soft yellow scarf silk-embroidered-in-silver draped over one of its right shoulders on which was balanced a handsome pink vase decorated with birds and butterflies.

It was pleasing to have these characteristics recognized and appreciated but to me, there was something finer about it, a tonal personality, locked inside. This greatest charm was only for those who could find the keys to release it. The desire to find them spurred me into action like an unscratched itch.

To distinguish at sight the value of notes, I was introduced to the family of clefs and helped with my problem of relating a music score on a staff of five lines and four spaces to octaves on the keyboard. After the "middle C" was spotted and anchored, I could count notes which followed, so many lines and space, up or down, then put them into position on the keyboard, relying upon my ear to lace them into harmony.

After my discovery of the key of "C" I nearly wore it out. But eventually I found others, two of sharps and five of flats. To this day I can release by note only such melodies as are locked under these keys.

Some years passed and I was spending my teens at work, earning small wages. I still wanted to know more about music. This desire inspired self-denial of odds and ends that I might pay for some lessons from an attractive young woman, who, while having no record as a brilliant performer herself, was proficient in teaching others to play. Her pupils advanced rapidly and when they appeared in recitals afforded joy to doting parents.

She too would have me stuff cotton in my musical ear. And first I must master the technique of the scales! At the first session she held and manipulated my hand to show me how, beginning on middle "C", after running the first three notes with the thumb under, and starting with it again, give all of my fingers a chance to finish the scale. She must have thought me very backward when I did not master this technique quickly, and she had to show me again and again. After several lessons she graduated me from the class without praise, saying I could already play by ear better than she could teach me by note.

While I had not learned enough to merit a piece of parchment with a ribbon and seal to confirm me worthy of a Bachelor of Music degree, I had learned that scales might be run up and down one's spine and for that matter, fantasies played without a piano, and very well by ear.

Thus chiefly by my eyes picking up notes on the score and sending them down to my fingers on the keyboard, I learned to express myself musically.

By now I was able to contribute something to the pleasure of social groups, playing two-steps and waltzes for dancing, and accompaniments for any who liked to sing. For the delectation of any young lady who would listen, I tried to play "Believe Me If All Those Endearing Young Charms," or "Just a 'Wearying For You" with great depth of feeling. To me, music was a joy continuously.

She Played Her Heart Out

March 1950

Sunday Lillian and I went to Fayette for the 4 p.m. two piano recital by Nannie Louise Wright and Opal Louise Hays. This time they were dedicating a new concert grand piano, the gift of an old Howard Payne College girl, now Mrs. Chase of Hardin, Missouri. The new piano was beautiful in looks and tone and the recital was the nicest I had ever heard played. The gals played fourteen numbers without a stop and then two encores. I had to sit back in a corner in one of the studios and did not see the performance and I did not hear Miss Wright when she announced that the first encore was a favorite of Mr. Kingsbury and they would play it for him. I noticed people around me looking at me and later Miss Wright said, "Why didn't you come out when I made the announcement?" But even if I had heard it, it wouldn't have occurred to me to push my way to the front and bow or something. I wouldn't have known enough to do it, if that is the proper thing. But I felt so honored when those around me said, "They're playing it for you." It was Miss Wright's composition, "Evening." I never heard it played more beautifully nor on two pianos. The recital was followed by a reception and we stayed until six o'clock visiting with Fayette and Central people.

March 1951

Sunday we did the usual church routing and in the afternoon went to Fayette to attend the Wright-Hayes perennial duo-piano recital, and it was better this year than ever before. Within recent years, Nannie Lou has had a broken leg and Miss Hayes a broken arm but no one would suspect it. From the time they had Bach's sheep grazing safely to begin with until Chopin's "Polonaise" horses ran us down at the close, it was wonderful. They played a number of their own compositions. All of them were very melodious. After the program the girls entertained at a tea and we had a fine opportunity to visit with people we do not see very often. The auditorium was packed as it always is for this recital. Last year I had to sit in a room out of sight of the auditorium and did not know until afterward they dedicated a number to me. This time I was in the front row and they rededicated the number with an account of the circumstances of last year's incident. When they finished, I did two years of bowing and wringing their hands to congratulate them on their work and to show my appreciation.

Undated - Probably March 1952

Dear Folks,

Sunday was a busy day. Lillian's old school mate, Evelyn Botdorf Morris, who lives in Jefferson City, came Friday afternoon. She is a button neophyte, and that evening she spent looking at my button collection with great enthusiasm and satisfaction to herself down at my office. The next day she was occupied with boxes and books of buttons which we could transport to the farm, and I told her she could have any duplicates which she found. What a field day for her! She wanted nothing better than that. And then came Sunday after Saturday night's choir practice. We have a better group now, and they are doing very nice work for a change. There was Sunday School and Church, then a delicious baked chicken dinner at Mrs. Solomon's. Then home to rest after the food marathon until time to go to Fayette to hear Nannie Lou Wright and Opal Hayes in their annual duo piano recital.

Miss Wright is retiring as Dean of the Conservatory in June. A big crowd was present to do her honor. She had written me a card warning me that if I wished them to, they would play Miss Hayes' "Music Box" especially for me. And finally it was time for some encores and Miss Wright announced they were playing "Music Box" for Mr. Kingsbury. This is the third time in four years that they have played a piece for me (and so far as I know during the decades they have been playing, I am the only one so honored). I felt the buttons popping off my clothes all over because of pride.

I didn't hear much of "Music Box," being so busy thinking what I would say when they concluded, but I wondered if there were enough buttons left to hold my pants up when I arose to speak. Fortunately, I held together. Dr. Baskett in introducing (unnecessarily) the artists had made some comparison (which he admitted was odious), saying if it had not been for Dean Wright the college would not have the beautiful piano she would play, and for that matter, the college would not have had the auditorium in which we were sitting. He added that he had brought a pencil sharpener into the school at the cost of a dollar recently and if it hadn't been for him the college would not have had it. So, following that thought, I said I appreciated all Dr. Baskett had said about Dean Wright and personally I appreciated "the girls" because if it were not for them, I would be absolutely destitute of anyone to play "The Music Box" for me.

The "girls" should have felt greatly honored and satisfied for the crowd gave them applause such as I have not heard before, and especially after they played their own compositions. As usual a reception followed the recital and I always like it for I rub elbows with the college crowd whom I do not see very often, but whom I like so much. It was nearly six when we rushed over to Boonville for a visit with Jean, King, and the Turleys. There we enjoyed a stacked dessert, a luscious meringue piled with ice cream and fresh peaches and coffee. Afterward we hurried to church for the evening service, came home and fell into bed.

13 March 1958

Lillian and I are wrung out since we saw Nannie Louise Wright die right in the middle of "The Old Dutch Clock." She and Miss Opal Hayes were playing at their 33rd annual recital. Lillian and I both have had recurring visions of her, in her pretty blue dress, going backward, with her hands still in playing position. She must have been stricken dead while on a last chord (not of the music but hers). Her body balanced on the bench an instant and then fell to the floor of the stage.

Yesterday we went to her funeral, which I would better call a memorial, a beautiful service. She was given so much to red and it was the prevailing color of the flowers on the casket. The a capello choir was in red (not for this occasion especially but habitually) and the pulpit and choir railing were laden with flowers. Professor Spayde, a fine organist, played four of Miss Wright's lovely pieces, among them "Quietude" "Chapel Bells" and "From the Organ Loft" as the casket was rolled in and the family entered, and for a short time after all were settled down. Beautiful tributes were paid her, beautiful scripture was read, and President Woodward concluded with a prayer of Thanksgiving for all of us having known Miss Wright. Dean Meyer read a poem which might have been written especially for Miss Wright, titled "Keyboard."

We had all wondered if in the natural course of events this would not have been their last recital? We were told Miss Wright's fingers were bleeding from constant practice for this recital and she put adhesive tape on the ends of them for protection. We did not go so much for enjoyment of the music, but out of respect and admiration for Miss Wright who accomplished such things at 80 plus.

Sunday afternoon as they played "Sheep May Safely Graze," by Bach, I thought to myself, it was poor grazing with it snowing outside as it was ... and when they played variations by Brahms on a theme by Hadyn ... bombastic, I thought I would be willing for it to be the last recital that I should hear such pounding of the ivories!!! But believe me, when she fell back, we were sorry for such thoughts. Lillian and I have not felt like touching a piano or organ since it happened. Lillian was thinking of having a rebuilt piano from Jenkins in Kansas City, but says the idea of doing it is dead.

MUSIC IN THE CHURCH

The Kingsburys were good Methodists and tried to attend all services - including the "Revival Meetings" held at least once a year. Lilburn had begun playing at the church. He was expected to play at all three services. In an early letter to an aunt he wrote:

I have gone to church until I am callused. The sermon, I mean sermons, not services, are from 75 to 110 minutes long. Last night was the longest one and after it was all over and the people were going out, I just sat there until Brother Allison came over and I asked him to please help me up. Brother Crowe "praught" on "Modern Phases of Disbelief" last night and held the "aujuence" (as Brother Dillon calls it because he can't say it right). Crowe really is a splendid preacher, only he has been preaching "it is wrong to play *tiddle-de-winks* and do the *cake-walk*." Gospel truth. He hollered long and loud about these horrors. Well, you won't catch me sinning in those two ways. As far as tiddle-de-winks and cakewalks go I am just as good as sanctified.

An oh! How he licks his chops with that word "tango." That kind of dancing is the quintessence of magnified sin. But not once has he referred to pinochle or cards when I've been there, so I have one amusement left. But if I keep on going to his meetings, I know he is going to snatch that away from me. Some of the people told me of a little incident. Anna Rose went to church late one night after the preacher had started on the home stretch. She was going to the choir which sits upon a platform to the left of the pulpit. They said just as Anna Rose was ready to step up on the platform, the preacher shouted out something about tango, and Anna Rose hesitated just an instant and looked at him as if she had been electrocuted on the spot.

September 1974

Dear Warren and Madeleine,
One Sunday, the Boonville old people's organization which has decided to visit a different church the first Sunday in each month were at our Methodist church. Dr. Moser, who will be a hundred years old in March sang a solo. You would be amazed how well he did it. Whoever heard of anybody that age singing without voice cracking! His didn't crack once. As organist I played accompaniment. I didn't think of it myself but after church a man came up and said he had never expected to hear a 90-year-old man play an accompaniment for a hundred-year-old man to sing.

Dr. Moser says we must do it again if he lives to be 100, which will be March 7th, 1975. He looks like he might run a race with our Maggie Watkins in a convalescent home here who had her 106th birthday in August.

Two Years Later:

Last night I attended a church covered-dish-dinner given by the women in connection with a wedding reception for their common minister, and his new bride. Dr. Moser was asked to sing and he asked me to play his accompaniment which I was glad to do. Before singing his song, he announced it as a memorable occasion such as many may never have seen or may not see again, a ninety-two-year-old man playing accompaniment for a 102-year-old man to sing a solo. I must admit I had never seen anything like it myself except two years ago when it also happened, only we were much younger then! I had always thought the Methodist women excelled everybody else as cooks but I must be more charitable toward the ladies of the Christian church. Every bite of everything on my plate was worthy of comment.

October 15, 1977, the day following his 93rd birthday party, Lilburn played his Ragtime Composition "Djalna" for my family and me on the organ at the Methodist church in New Franklin. He had been honored earlier for 70 years of service as church pianist and organist.

7 February 1949 he wrote:

Dearest Folks,

I've just received such an interesting clipping from the New York Journal-Post on the inaugural [*Truman*] which the writer, Bill Corum [*who grew up in Boonville*] did not attend, but had much to say about Missouri mules and notables otherwise. He closed with a long paragraph on the origin of "The Missouri Waltz." He tells most interestingly the story of how Jelly Settles of New Franklin composed it and used to play it around here and elsewhere for the dances until one time he was at a hotel in Moberly and a couple of travelling men got interested in it. Jelly called it "The Grave Yard Waltz." One of those men had him play it until he got the tune in his head or in his notes and he later copyrighted and published it. Jelly died Saturday morning, in his mid-sixties, nearly blind, totally deaf, and terribly alone as he lived in a corner of the printing office.

The next fall:

I played at a wedding yesterday afternoon. It was at the Baptist Church of which the groom is a member. The bride is a Methodist but would that Baptist be married in a Methodist

Church? The "modrun" weddings are strange in their arrangements. I had to play a long time until the mothers were seated and then the soloist sang "I Love You Truly." Then I played for the preacher, the groom, and his best man to walk down to the altar. They stood there while the song, "Because" was sung for no particular reason so far as I could see. Then Heaven forbid I should play Lohengrin for the maid of honor to come in by. No indeed, that must be reserved for the moment when the bride took her first step into the aisle. To bring in the maid of honor, I played "Indian Love Call" which I hoohooed as much as I could on the pianner. The preacher married them part way, then stopped for the song, "The Lord's Prayer." Then he finished, benedicted, and I laid down the strains of Mendelssohn.

Have worked with some of the Eastern Star people lately on a barber shop quartet, and a piano presentation of "The Missouri Waltz." With it I gave a little history of the piece and its composer, Edgar "Jelly" Settles. There were about 250 women from the seven chapters of this district.

FUNERAL MUSIC – A FEW NOTES

I believe I have written you that Cousin Bee has left us. There were enough flowers for several funerals and as Miss Jessie McLachlan said, "She was put away so nice." The night before the funeral Lillian and I herded together what would-be singers and emergency singers we could muster and practiced. We had a good alto and finally we had our program nicely assembled, we thought. But as we left the church, Mrs. Wilson, our contralto, missed a step and fell down six or seven concrete steps breaking her glasses, rubbing her face on the stone, bruising a shoulder and a leg. We thought the choir was ruined but that plucky soul doctored all morning and came that afternoon with a hat pulled down over her black eye and did her part. She was pretty game. I played the "Largo" as they rolled Bee in. The songs were "Jesus Savior," "Pilot Me," "Face to Face," and "The End of the Road." After the interment we had open house as Mother always expected somebody to stop in on the way home from Mount Pleasant. At least a dozen of the relatives did.

A contemporary of mine died in Fayette a month ago and when I asked about the funeral service, was told that the music sounded like the things Spade [*Chair of the Music Department at Central Methodist College*] plays out of the ordinary though he was not at the organ this time. A later inquiry revealed the piece in question was "Swing Low, Sweet Chariot," which is not inappropriate, though I had never thought of it being played at a funeral. But when I play themes I hear on the TV serials as offertories at church seldom does anyone acknowledge recognition - for that matter seldom does anyone admit recognition of anything. I believe I could play "Hot Time in the Old Town Tonight," and nobody would know it.

July 1941

Sunday night we ended the day by sweating some at the evening service and then rode up "the bottom" to Ed Watts' because his son had died and I like Ed and I liked the son. We got there about half past eight and there must have been 35 or 40 cars there and the house was full of people and more were in the yard and out on the porch. On Monday afternoon the funeral was in New Franklin and they asked me to play the piano. It took terribly long to open him up in the vestibule and force everybody inside to pass by and look at him after the sermon and the poor little widow couldn't get by and had to come back inside and sit down and compose herself. I played all I knew and made up a lot. It is always a good chance to practice improvising. The crowd is always so busy watching the mourners that they don't know what about music, but it seems to me the music drowns out some of the sound of weeping. At least I can't hear it so well.

Our minister, who came last October, has held eight funerals and tomorrow is to have another. Lillian and I get so tired of being asked to arrange the music. I think I shall charge for my services and then I am sure I won't have such frequent calls. All of these funerals were church members who had paid their dues, so my old rule of not playing at the funerals of members in arrears has not helped me financially at all.

FUNERAL SONGS

There have been many changes in songs for funerals in the Boonslick Country.

I have a little hymnal 2 1/2 x 4 inches and 2 inches thick, published in 1842. It has marks of elegance, leather bound with gold etching and letters "Methodist Hymns." It contains the words of 697 songs with no music.

There were no musical instruments used in churches then. One wonders why they were considered instruments of the devil. The preacher was usually the song leader. After announcing the hymn he would read aloud a couple of lines (it was called "lining it") and the congregation would join him in singing them. Not everyone had a hymn book.

Funeral songs in the 1840s suggested unpleasant problems for the body and soul of one who departed from this world such as:

"And must this body die, the well wrought form decay and must these active limbs of mine, lie moldering in the clay?

In the funeral hymns of the 1870s there were no reminders of "moldering in the clay," corruption, or a choice between Heaven and Hell. The delights of Heaven were stressed.

Those present at Clark's Chapel in the 80s never forgot the funeral at which Rev. W.F. Bell, as if speaking for the departed gentleman, sang a song in a voice that could be heard a mile away, "I'm going home to die no more."

For a decade after I began playing for funerals three score and more years ago, the standard funeral hymns were "Rock of Ages;" "Jesus, Lover of My Soul," "Abide with Me," "How Firm a Foundation," and "Lead Kindly Light." The last had been sung at the funeral of assassinated President Will McKinley and to this day is still a favorite.

In more recent years, the most popular song sung as a solo was "Beyond the Sunset." Its words were a rainbow of poems and its melody so lifting, one could picture angels doing a ballet in the sky on their way to a picnic in Heaven in honor of the spirit of the departed.

Today it is difficult in small towns to find anyone to play or sing at funerals. A stereo takes over effectively. We listen to hymn music played softly and an artistic rendition of Malotte's, "The Lord's Prayer." It is satisfying.

In thumbing through a book of funeral hymns at a mortuary some time ago, I came across one with the unusual title, "Who Will Sing For Me?" I didn't know then, but now I would answer, "the stereo."

Chapter Seventeen

BUTTONING UP — BUTTONING DOWN

For some time Lilburn had been riding his Genealogical and History Hobby Horses. His correspondence frequently reported on the interesting rides he was taking. But, while he never permanently turned these hobby horses out to pasture, in the fall of 1944 he found a challenging new one to gallop off on. It was characteristic of the man that, as a bystander observing respected people enjoying an avocation, he frequently yielded to the temptation to explore its pleasures himself.

Part of what follows is taken from an undated Lilburn manuscript which must have been the basis of a talk given to the Missouri State Button Society at its annual meeting. Later, this presentation, somewhat condensed, was published in the Bulletin of the National Button Society *under the title, "A Missouri Collector Speaks."*

About four years ago I went by Madge Walker's place to see her collection of old glass and found she had become more interested in antique buttons. I am in deep sympathy with all collectors regardless of what they collect, be it coffee grinders, baby shoes, mid-Victorian bustles or mustache cups.

Having run after something all my life, the objects they seek do not always rouse my interest to a boil. To me, buttons were something that popped off at inopportune times or confronted me with embarrassment when I failed to fasten them.

Occasionally I was exposed to cases of button fever, but I remained immune until last fall. Infection then set in, mildly at first, after a traveling saleswoman collector, with button temperature high, came into my office with a card of old buttons and showed me their good points. The result was as if she had loaned me glasses to improve my vision. And Madge Walker, still battling for buttons like a seasoned evangelist, kept calling on me to be converted to buttons, to join the National Button Society band and to collect some buttons while the field was white unto the harvest. My button infection spread and soon I found myself a victim of a creeping activity which progressed until it is all over me now, and I have little hope or desire for a cure! So, in the spirit of adventurous conquest, yet with some trepidation, I set forth to inspect the button boxes of the county.

The faces of the sweet ladies who came to their doors to greet me registered surprise, sometimes shock, when I asked them to open up their sewing machine drawers and their button boxes for inspection. For those who do not know of my family name, it is one which has been around here since Howard County, the Mother of Missouri Counties, the heart of the Boonslick Country, was settled in 1816. More than one lady thought aloud, "Well! This is the first time I ever heard of a man hunting buttons!...."

Always they declared they had nothing at all. Too often they were right. More often they watched me lay aside their more desirable items, enthused by surprise and pleasure that the old box contained anything anyone might want. There was a running revelation of stories connected with the persons who had worn the buttons. Only a few white people were sentimental enough about buttons that they wished to retain them. They gave them away, or sold them for a nominal sum.

Old Negro women — not many of them are left — who have saved things given them by their "white folks," sometimes had beautiful buttons. As a rule they declared they were "glad to be shet of them." Occasionally one would say she did not wish "to depart from 'em," or "to git exposed of 'em." A little financial finesse was in order.

The urge to buy all of the button books and to subscribe for the magazines and state bulletins has been strong and effective. They are all interesting and helpful.

The number and variety of buttons described and pictured in these publications can be overwhelming to a beginner. However, he soon learns that many specimens are to be found in this area. The prospect of discovering rarities is good enough to keep this button hound's nose to the ground all the time — there being no closed season on button game.

I have found coveys of calicoes, stencils, ringers, large and small picture buttons, lithographs, militaries, gilts, handsome lustre — both picture and conventional types — pearls and enamels. Then there have been charm strings made up entirely of small glass buttons — all shapes and colors. Others with paperweights, kaleidoscopes, jewels, puddings, glories have afforded me great pleasure. A Red Riding Hood is the best picture button I have discovered to date.

The possession, arrangement and display of buttons is a lot of fun but friends to whom I tell my button stories raise the question as to whether the people I meet are not more interesting to me than the buttons I acquire.

I well remember when Miss Katie West came hustling into the room with several boxes and in handing one to me, dropped it, spilling the contents all over the floor. She was a stout woman but got down on her hands and knees to pick up the buttons. Being a gentleman, I could do no less. As we worked, conversation a bit breathless at times, shot back and forth. I had never seen Miss Katie until that day but after we had picked up all the buttons and sat down to inspect them, I was impelled to tell her I felt like I had known her all my life! Over buttons, one feels as free and easy as over a cup of tea.

One afternoon just as I stepped up on the porch of the little cottage of Misses Amy and Jennie Bird, lusty feminine voices within were raised in the hymn, "Just As I Need Him Most". My first thought was this was a good omen. Then something told me the Aid Society was in session and I had indeed chosen an inopportune time for my button call. But in these days of gasoline and tire rationing, one can't be daunted by anything else. In response to my knock, and my whispered inquiry about buttons for sale, Miss Jennie said they had none. But Miss Amy appeared at that moment and replied, "Yes! Come right in."

She invited me to be seated in the circle of ladies whose mouths were wide open, singing. Miss Amy whispered she would bring her charm string in. I knew the meeting, which proved to be the Bible Study Class, was no place to haggle for buttons, so I followed Miss Amy into the other room, closed the door and proposed that we hold our tryst in there alone. She consented willingly and produced her charm string. She could not sell it to me, she said, because she had promised it to her dear niece. But she would sell me twelve buttons of my choice. We dickered over the dozen until she stated a price per button and said if I would pay that much I might have twenty-five. But not another one! She wanted only enough to buy herself a dress and a pair of shoes.

She asked me to remain until after the class was over. It was a pleasure to visit as her four-score-years had been full of rich experiences which she related well. In leaving I expressed regret at having deprived her of attendance at her Bible Class. I shall long remember with a smile the twinkle in her eye and her reply in a soft voice confiding tone, "You were a Godsend for I was to lead the class today and I got out of it."

Another day Miss Amy took me to see a charm string which she said "was a rival of mine when I was a girl." The old lady who had this charm string of about five hundred buttons also refused to sell it intact but said I might choose buttons I desired and cut them off until she thought I had enough and stopped me. I got one hundred that day. I have been back for a hundred more. She has not stopped me yet. The remnants of both of these strings will eventually find their way into my collection.

Later, in other homes in this little town, when I inquired about buttons several ladies told me of the two strings I had already discovered and devastated, but in each case I was assured, "They'll let you look at them but you can't get them for love nor money." The old charm string ladies hold well their secret in this little village where everyone usually knows everybody else's business to such an extent that when I was in one home a phone call was relayed to me. "Tell the Button Man to come up to Miller's." Besides myself, there are five or six button collectors in this county.

One of these collectors, after a period of sixty years, has resumed collecting and adding to her forty-years-old charm string. She would not price it to me. I did not encourage her to do so after she told me she had read that an old lady had nothing to fear in old age if she possessed a charm string and a silk crazy quilt as they would bring enough to take care of her the rest of her life.

My chief trouble in button collecting is one of balance. The lure of buttons, the excitement of discovery and acquisition, plus the delight of homey visiting with folks over their button boxes have proven so attractive that I find myself wearying unduly of office, farm and orchard duties in order to indulge in the sport of collecting buttons. Was ever recreation more strenuous and yet more relaxing?

WHAT KEEPS YOUR INTEREST IN THE BUTTON HOBBY?

Another undated manuscript was apparently written for a talk given in Kansas City at a Convention of the National Button Association. The following excerpts from it provide additional insights into his button hobby horse riding:

"What," you ask me, "keeps up your interest in the button hobby when you spend only a limited time on it, don't get to many shows, and are sort of off to yourself?"

My time for the hobby has always been limited because of an insurance business which requires a watchful eye; musical activity in which a record of 48 years of continuous service as organist at my church is involved; the maintenance of a fruit farm, a project begun by my father in 1872 and continued for the sake of tradition and financial reward; and minor avocations. So, life for me is like a tossed salad of interests with the button hobby for a savory dressing.

Geographically, I am "sort of set off by myself," but distances between kindred spirits can be lessened with a typewriter or annihilated with a tankful of gas, so occasionally I do it.

What keeps up my interest? The same phases which involved me in the beginning. They are as numerous and pleasant as harmonious tonal combinations on a Hammond organ. Among them are: love of beauty, appreciation of the artistic, a dash of curiosity, the lure of the hunt, delight of acquisition, keen competition and the communion of kindred spirits. All these are deeply rooted in rich, fertilizing experiences which make fruitful my present lush interest in the hobby.

I was curious to know if people in my part of the country had ever worn beautiful buttons and if so, were any such still extant. Investigation proved they had...and that there were. Back in the 1870s and 80s most young ladies made charm strings inspired by visions of romance. For some the charm worked. Others were not spared from chronic spinsterhood. Some of the latter, still living, I had known all my life. But never by word or deed had they given me cause to suspect they had been involved with charm strings and button boxes in their gay young courting days.

My interest in button collecting always bubbles up when I recall some of the obstacles I had to overcome to acquire certain highly prized buttons. A treasured example is the one Salome showed me, a beautiful carved pearl button displaying a woman's head with her ermine cape. She said it had been photographed by the author of a book on classic buttons for a forthcoming publication. This added distinction to its charm and I coveted it openly. I explained how I needed the button to crown as queen of my collection. Salome said others felt the same way and she, herself, meant to keep her enthroned forever. But little drops of persuasion wore down her rocky resistance. For once a woman changed her mind! I offered her "unto half of my kingdom," and she handed me the head on a tray.

It was an eventful day when I stalked down my first charm string. Strung together were more than a hundred little glass buttons — the first of them I had ever seen — bits of beauty reflecting color and light. Thinking this might be an opportunity which might never knock again, I opened my billfold and without a cheapening word, laid down the amount she said a national dealer had offered her. (I am still interested in seeing that dealer to ask, "Did you?" Another charm string turned up the very next day.)

As with all novices, every button that came to my notice and into my possession was of paramount interest. I have cherished them carefully which accounts for thousands which now take up space. But I recall no keener delight than that afforded by those early and often simple acquisitions. Those little treasures of the first years seem like humble steps up which we climbed to higher levels of discernment. They are as much out of the general picture now as our early school primers. We may not appreciate their charm but it is not lost any more than the morals to the simple stories we first learned to read.

Bombarding me periodically from Paris and London are buttons from my scouts there. Even their written reports of their hunting compounds my interest. How I should like to go back and do some scouting on my own.

From the time Lilburn became excited by Madge Walker's button collection in 1944 his letters to relatives and friends frequently reported on rides he took on this hobby horse. Some excerpts follow from a March 1945 letter:

BUTTON MOSAIC PICTURES

Lillian and I picked up Floye [*wife of a Marine aviator nephew*] and took her with us to Columbia. Some time ago in the Minnesota Bulletin for button collectors there was an interesting illustration of a picture, Star of the East, made of buttons by one Mr. Engler who had just moved from Minnesota to Columbia, Mo. I wrote to the gentleman in Columbia and asked him to stop by and see me. I took him to dinner at the Frederick Hotel and we had a fine visit. I liked him very much. We had much in common besides buttons, but he had much more than I have, a wife and five children, ages eighteeen down to seven, twins among them. He invited me to Columbia to see his button mosaics. We did that yesterday.

I don't suppose anyone has ever made button mosaics before. Engler says so far as he knows, his work is unique. Hung in three of the rooms of the large home he occupies on West Broadway are fourteen large pictures. Among them are *The Minute Men, The Pilgrims Going to Church, Hiawatha, Rock of Ages,* and *The Church in the Wildwood.*

We found that to see the pictures, one must have distance to enhance, just as with oil paintings. At a proper distance, they were wonderful. The Pilgrims Going to Church is very large and the characters in it must be fifteen inches high. It is made of 60,000 buttons. One picture is of a caravan on the Santa Fe Trail and it is eight feet long and about four feet high. Engler mounts them on taut velvet or other cloth, then stretches them on wall board before putting them in heavy gold frames. Some work! He is going to transform a brick poultry house on the premises for his pictures, with each lighted to the best advantage. In the past two years before he came to Columbia — despite the rationing of gas and tires — 1500 people called to see the pictures. I would charge admission, but he says he has no intention of doing such.

CHARM STRINGS CHARM

Charm strings fascinated Lilburn and when he heard of one, he would mount his button hobby horse and gallop off in pursuit. His diligence and persuasive personality enabled him to acquire more than twenty such and to learn much about the fad taken up by the young women of the era. He shares some of the experiences of his hobby rides in excerpts from an article he wrote for the American Antique Journal:

Back in the 1870s and 80s the busiest button collectors may well have been the young women who made charm strings which button collectors seek so avidly today.

These charm strings were made primarily of buttons but the young ladies generally strung upon them a few amulets, steeped in sentiment. Some tokens were from the boys who made their hearts beat faster; others were precious because of childhood or school days associations. Among the most popular charms were dimes, gold dollars, tiny baskets whittled from pecan, hazelnut and almond shells or peach pits, little sea shells, tiny doll arms and legs, miniature merrythoughts, dolls, jugs, keys, horseshoes and religious medals.

Some of the older ladies who still have their charm strings were little girls when they began to collect buttons. They tell us they did it because it was a popular fad of the day, and there was no romantic tradition connected with the hobby. On the other hand, one lady admitted that she added buttons to her string as fast as she could. She believed as soon as it became as long as she was tall, she would get married. Others say they reveled in the tradition that as soon as the 999th button was added to the string, Prince Charming would come riding up the road on a prancing steed, with the 1000th button on his "weskit" and a wedding ring in his pocket — both for her. Wedding bells would ring and life would be happy ever after.

The young girls contrived a sly game to get more buttons for their charm strings. Each secretly selected one on her string as the "touch button." Usually it was the most conspicuous one. As soon as the visitor in her home had enjoyed the stereopticon views and the family pictures in the plush-backed album, the charm string was produced for his delectation. As the guest fingered it, he would be startled by a sharp exclamation of seeming surprise from the young hostess, "Oh dear! You have touched the charm button. Now you will have to give me a button for my string." It was a game which must have paid off well.

It was quite usual for young men to purchase buttons at the dry goods emporiums to bestow upon these fair collectors. Certainly there was no gesture then which would ingratiate them more, or establish their reputations as charming gentlemen. When women and girls had dresses made and got buttons, they bought a few extra ones to give to their charm string friends. The code precluded young women from buying buttons for their own charm strings. They must be acquired from others through grace. Each string was regarded as evidence of its owner's charm. It is easy to understand why it was suspected some young ladies "fudged" a little to bolster their prestige.

LETTERS TELL OF BUTTON RIDES

I wonder why I collect buttons!

Buttons. We all use them. Modern civilized man is a slave to them for he has to handle two dozen or more of them every time he dresses and undresses himself. They are the mainstay of man's raiment. They are its sole adornment. They are a part of man's burden and our wives, no matter how they may fasten their own garments, will have to help men bear this burden, or at least until the old idea of wifely duty is abandoned.

There are (or were before the War) at least fifty million men in the U.S. who are slaves to buttons and it is safe to say that in their dressing and undressing operations, at least twenty buttons are handled by or for each one on the average. That makes one billion buttons which at least twice a day have to be dealt with. Aside from these, there are buttons on all reserve garments, many of them purely ornamental. Then there are the well-stocked button boxes and bags maintained by all good housewives. The number of buttons in existence is stupendous. I have thousands. The other day I acquired a so-called "charm string" of buttons seventeen feet long from an old gentleman who claimed it contained seven hundred items. There were not more than fifty in the lot which were like those I had already. The number of types and styles and designs of buttons is as broad as the fancy of the artists who have designed them.

If we admit that button collecting may seem unimportant to some, I am reminded of Gilbert White, the naturalist who was something of a philosopher as well. He claimed to have discovered a formula for complete happiness. It was short and simple and I give it to you for what it is worth: "Keep interested in the unimportant." Perhaps he means for us to see that nothing is completely unimportant. Happiness lies in the discovery of the relative importance of seemingly unimportant things.

Charles Walker has sent me a button which one of his lady friends let him have to show me. She wants to know its worth and how she can go about selling three of them to best advantage. They appear to be tortoise shell with a dragon or wild horse in gold with silver wings. It is a right smart button and I have offered $5 for one or $13.50 for three. Somebody who did not know any better sent me a set of six large buttons which have on them Lohengrin saying farewell to Elsa. Two or three years ago they were worth $1.75 each. They were on the trousseau of the young woman married in the Burkhartt parlor in 1881 and I shall display them as such when I talk to the Revolutionary Girls (*the DAR*) on May 1st.

May 1945

At Concordia where I recently stopped for gas after a day on the hunt, I was so tired I went into the station and talked to an elderly man as I rested enjoying a coke. There was a showcase full of dogs — china, plaster and whatnot. On it was a label, "MY HOBBY."

I asked the man if they were his and he replied "yes, that he was a dog lover, a dog trainer; that is, he used to train them to be housebroken. He got a few of these little figures and people have sent him others from all over the world. He said he had more than two hundred. After he had expatiated long on his dogs, I told him I had many hobbies but now I was collecting old buttons. He looked at me quizzically and rather incredulously over his glasses and said, "Well, that shore is a strange hobby. I never heard of anything like that."

And then, in a very casual tone, he continued, "Years ago, my hobby was taking pictures of women with long hair before a full length mirror. I reckon I had about nineteen hundred before hair bobbin' come in style. It was afore my wife died.

...whenever I seen a woman with a lot of hair on her head, I could hardly wait to meet her to ask her to let me take a picture of her and my wife would ask her to come to dinner and after we ate I would tell her what I wanted. Didn't but one ever refuse ... she said hasn't no man but her husband ever seen her with her hair down ... and I said of course that was all right if that was the way she felt about it. I reckon if hair bobbin' hadn't come in I'd had a hundred thousand pictures by now. Once there was a woman had the biggest head of hair and I asked her to let me photograph her before the full length mirror. Her skirt came to her shoe tops, and when she took out the hair pins and let her hair fall down, it fell clean to the hem of the skirt, and with her back turned she was completely hid by her hair. I never seen anything like it. ..."

November 1945

A couple of days ago, when the strain of disposing of my apples was easing, I remembered buttons and asked two old ladies who were buying apples if they had any. They went home and told a neighbor who came down with a charm string, wanting to trade it for apples. So for buttons, I just about gave her the pick of the crop. Anyway, we were both satisfied.

Another old lady buyer looked like she might never have had a button, or never knew what a good one looked like. It seemed a waste of time to ask her about buttons, but I did. She didn't have any herself, but she told me her friend across the river in the Glasgow bottoms, near old Cambridge, had a charm string. So I was soon off to Glasgow bottoms and old Cambridge. It was once a thriving city on the Missouri river. Now only a few houses are still standing. I found Mrs. John Wilkes, the lady who told me about her neighbor's charm string. She had learned the charm string had been sold. My disappointment was eased somewhat when she told me she had discovered she had some buttons. There were only a few but one was very interesting. It had been picked up around her place after plowing or after rains had washed the land. Her little girl used to say after a hard rain,

"Mummy, let's go hunt treasures." She had picked up many old coins and a couple of very interesting Catholic medals, one dated 1830. She graciously gave me all her buttons.

I heard that Miss Emma Volrath of Sedalia, aged 83, born and reared in Boonville, had a charm string. That afternoon, when I could resist temptation no longer, I called her to learn she would sell it. I found her an interesting person who had lovely old things from the old Volrath place in Boonville, built in 1845 and still standing. She laid the button string before me and told me the offer made her by a dealer. But she would let me have it at that price. I ended my visit by bringing it home with me and mounting it that night. They are "jewels." You would be surprised to see what unusual buttons I have mounted and what an attractive display they make.

I had to scheme a little and exercise patience with Rose Middein, an old Negro woman. When I approached her about her charm string she shook her head vigorously and proclaimed that she would never depart from the charm string that "ole Missy done gib me." This particular charm string was discarded and given to Rose by a daughter of one of our pioneer families. It contained an array of buttons from waistcoats and dresses of many men and women of prominence in the county. It was long and elegant. It contained jewels, beads in various materials and sizes, many small and medium picture buttons of people, fruit, birds and flowers, a few militaries and gilts, lithographs of many types and hues, paperweights, glories, reflectors, dewdrops, kaleidoscopes, birds' eggs and pudding molds. Such a diversity on one string I had never seen before. It was enough to make one heedless of covetous sin.

Rose's health was failing. Hoping to ingratiate myself in a manner to influence her to sell me the charm string, I asked her what I might bring her that she craved most? "Boss," she replied, "Hamhock an' salt fish is the mostest cravin' I got."

It was some time before a hamhock was available on the farm, but eventually I set out to bait my trap, the hamhock in one hand and the salt fish in the other. Gaily, I went up the flower-bordered walk to the cabin and knocked briskly on Rose's door. A strange, sober face looked out from the crack of the slightly opened door. "Where's Rose?" I asked. "I've come with her hamhock and fish."

Ohh Boss," the stranger said in a hushed voice as tears came into her eyes. "Rose, she's sleepin' in the parlor. She done died last night."

But old Rose could not have received my gift more gratefully than the surviving members of her family. After all, it worked like bread cast upon the waters. After a respectful period of waiting I returned and bought the charm string from Rose's husband who had warded off other collectors and saved it for me.

Sunday, Xena came down from Huntsville with two couples who wanted to see my house. After they had gotten an eyeful, I took them to my office to see my button collection. I proudly showed my fruit buttons, especially the one with the man picking apples, the one showing a lady eating an apple, and another supposed to be Fannie Davenport reaching up for an apple.

After they returned to Huntsville, one of the women who had some buttons herself, sent me a couple of small items. They are apples, green with stem end and the blush on the side. I knew there were such but I had never found any and was especially delighted. I now have buttons with cherries, strawberries, blackberries, pears, peaches, corn, wheat, barley and of course many kinds of flowers to represent the products of my farm, orchard and garden.

FAIRVIEW BUTTON PICTURE

Shortly afterward Lilburn decided to create a button picture of his farm. He tells about this in a family letter of September 1956. I first saw the picture when I visited him in the summer of 1958. I was taken by the creativity of his picture and the color provided by his beautiful buttons. Even though he disposed of virtually all of his buttons in the seventies, his "Farm Project" hung in a place of honor until his death. The letter excerpt follows:

I must tell you about my new "Farm Project." It consists of a water color sketch of the farm, showing house, barns, fields, orchard and ponds — even the cemetery. I had never before touched a brush but thought I would try it. I spent about $15 for water color books, brushes, papers and paints and set about making my picture. The colors are maybe a little harsh in spots, but it was not intended to be anything but amateurish. In the orchard I mounted little buttons depicting apples, pears, peaches, plums, cherries, etc.

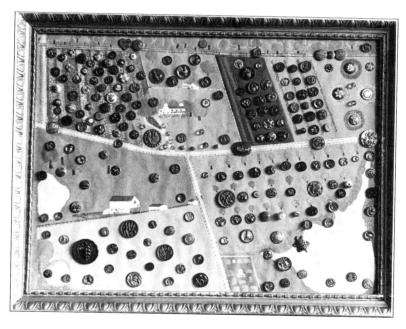

Fairview Orchard/Farm Button Picture

I have an elegant rose garden made of enamel floral buttons and little rose paperweight buttons. There is a poultry yard with

buttons depicting chickens. I have birds in trees. In the pasture
are hogs, horses, a bull (and I have been promised a cow), a goat
and so on. A large part of the farm is given to the flower growth,
as there are so many beautiful little flower buttons of many
varieties. Then I have a grape arbor with many lovely grape
buttons, also a strawberry bed. Strange to say, I couldn't have a
vegetable garden for I do not find vegetables other than corn
depicted on old buttons. In the fields of grain, I have wheat,
corn, oats and other varieties of grasses. To one side is the blackberry patch. Around the ponds are cattails, water lilies, snakes,
frogs, water birds, a turtle and a boat. A dog is chasing a fox, a
peacock struts in the front yard near a rabbit. There is a button
(in the orchard) of a man gathering apples. I believe the idea is
original and I think it will be taken up by others — maybe not
the "farm idea" — but something else.

Nobody Knows Who Invented Buttons

Some of Lilburn's hobby horse rides bring to mind my childhood
thrill of going to the circus and breathlessly watching a daring bare-
back rider of two horses. He galloped them around the ring standing
with legs spread, one foot on each horse, carefully manipulating the
horses' reins as he galloped along to wild spectator applause. Most of
Lilburn's hobby-horse riding was not that demanding physically —
but it challenged him.

A compelling hobby of his, as noted earlier, was history. He had
great curiosity. He wished to know why things were like they are and
how they got that way. Knowing my uncle's propensity for this, I was
not surprised to find an undated manuscript (probably written in
1962) devoted to button history. From the following excerpts I con-
cluded he based talks he delighted in, given to women's clubs, upon
this manuscript.

Buttons have been hoarded and collected in America since
colonial days. The many surviving old button boxes and charm
strings are proof this collecting activity is far from new.

Nobody knows who invented the button. The Egyptians, Assyrians, Chinese, Greeks and Romans were among those who wore loose, flowing robes secured by clasps, buckles, sashes and similar devices. Egyptian excavations have revealed button-like objects, but they are not believed to have been used to fasten garments. They might have been used as seals, or badges of office or rank, or simply for decoration.

It is reasonable to assume buttons were used chiefly for decorative purposes until more tailored styles of clothing required an improved method of closure. Then some genius mothered the invention of the buttonhole. While buttons since then have served chiefly in a utilitarian capacity, they have never lost their decorative appeal nor their use in a military capacity. The earliest buttons of importance were custom-made for the nobility, the landed gentry, and of course, royalty. They were so expensive only people of great wealth could afford them. They were of gold and silver, set with precious stones, miniatures and carvings of ivory.

During the reign of button-conscious Louis XIV, the cost of the royal buttons alone became a drain upon the French treasury. Gold buttons set with the rarest emeralds, diamonds, rubies and other precious gems characterized the extravagance of this monarch. Louis XV was more conservative and content with engraved gold buttons. Next came Louis XVI who expanded the reckless extravagance of his grandfather. He ordered buttons of outlandish size and shape, set with stones of fabulous price. Aside from his satisfaction in strutting peacock-like, he entertained the idea that if he ever had to flee the country, he could don this lavishly decorated coat and wear his fortune across the border.

The earliest button collectors were men because nearly two-thirds of the buttons made before 1820 were made for that once proud peacock, the male of the species. It was a means of combining utility with value on one's own person.

Every art, industry and calling, every trade, profession and pursuit is reflected in buttons. To prove this we might start with the diamond cutter as top man and go downward, or we might begin with the worker in pewter as low man and climb up the scale.

Let's start at the top and go down: painter, sculptor, miniaturist, goldsmith, gem cutter, silversmith, jeweler, watchmaker, tinsmith, whitesmith, armorer, gunsmith, mirror maker, engraver, glassmaker, brazier, cameo-cutter, potter, feather merchant, hair worker, ebonist, lacemaker, tapestry and textile weavers, embroiderer, ivory carver, worker in pewter, and wood turner. All these have contributed to the art of button making. Every substance known in the arts and trades is found in buttons.

Buttons reflect every invention, every pursuit, social and otherwise, every animal, bird, fish and insect known to the makers, and some not known to this day. The frills and foibles and modes of every age are reflected in its buttons. If you collect the relics of aviation, transportation by land or sea, fire fighting, or what have you, you have buttons that mirror that interest.

Perhaps no type of button creates broader interest than picture buttons. They are made in all materials, but predominately of the metals. The pictures on these buttons carry us right into the fields of literature, opera, drama, sport, transportation and industry. Some bring to our minds the fables and fairy tales of our youth. Many suggest the accomplishments of men and women. To name a few: Lord Byron, De Soto, Balboa, King Arthur, Alexander the Great, Lafayette, Sir Walter Scott, Stanley and Livingstone and Emperor Charles the Fifth. We have Queen Elizabeth and Jenny Lind. If one acquires one of those buttons, he may feel impelled to visit the encyclopedia to refresh his memory. The button hobby is also educational.

One of the oldest manufacturers in the United States is the Scoville Manufacturing Company of Waterbury, Conn. Its buttons have been associated with the development of our country, politically and industrially, for the last 150 years. During the War of 1812, Scoville received a contract to manufacture uniform buttons for the Army and Navy. He knew he could make the buttons, but the problem was the Army had insufficient cloth to produce the uniforms. Scoville heard John Jacob Astor owned a large herd of sheep in Manhattan and journeyed down from Waterbury to see if they were ready for shearing. The wool was bought, sent to Waterbury where the company set up and financed a textile mill. From then until 1920 Scoville Wool made various types of military buttons and many different types of uniforms for the American forces.

Among the most famous were some presented to General Lafayette, when he visited America in 1825. Only seventeen were made — as many as could be wrought from a solid gold nugget which had been unearthed in North Carolina. These buttons featured the head of George Washington.

I have long known Texas claims to have everything. I refreshed my memory through buttons that it once had a Navy. It had four ships: Invincible, Brutus, Independence and Liberty. These ships darted about the Gulf of Mexico during the Texas Revolution, preventing the landing of vessels carrying supplies to the Mexican armies. This Navy made a definite contribution to Texas' victory over Mexico. It continued to operate as a fleet until 1843. When Texas was annexed to the United States in 1846, her gallant Navy became United States property. Scoville turned out sets of closures for the Texas Navy in 1837. The buttons carried on the face a lone star, an anchor, and the inscription, Republic of Texas.

Scoville also made buttons in 1840 to further the campaign of William Henry Harrison, running for President that year. There were three distinct types made for that campaign, but all pictured a log cabin. Those early campaign buttons were quite different from the campaign buttons of today. They actually served as buttons, and a staunch political supporter would remove the ordinary buttons from his clothing and attach the buttons of his favorite candidate. No well-dressed campaigner would be without these buttons and they were a common sight during election periods of the time.

Benjamin Franklin was our first Postmaster General who helped design the button still used by the United States Post Office Department today. The Continental Congress appointed Franklin Postmaster General in 1777. Shortly thereafter, he sent a letter of instructions to the postmasters in all the colonies. The letter was illustrated with a wood cut showing a post rider on horseback. In the 1860s and 70s this original of Franklin was used to prepare dies for Post Office Department buttons.

General Zachary Taylor, "Old Rough and Ready," twelfth President of the United States, spent forty years of his life in the Army. He was a national hero having won several battles in the War with Mexico. Scoville made campaign buttons for Taylor's campaign in 1848 bearing his image and the inscription, Rough and Ready.

In 1869 at Promontory Point, Utah, a golden spike was driven into the last tie linking the Central Pacific and the Union Pacific into a transcontinental railroad. Scoville was commissioned to strike off commemorative buttons for this occasion.

Two or three years ago I enlisted the aid of a distant relative in London. She was a retired government employee, eager for something to keep busy with. When I proposed she search the off-the-beaten-path shops of London, she wrote she knew nothing at all about buttons. I sent her illustrated literature on the subject and she studied some at the libraries before setting out for conquest. Now when she finds an item she believes worthy of it, she consults records and sends its history along with the button. When visiting relatives in Scotland and Ireland, she investigates all the button boxes available. These relatives have been quite intrigued and excited about the button hunt. They have been most helpful in making the shops of Dublin and Edinburgh accessible to her. Consequently she has sent me many buttons I would never have found here. She sends the "button transfusion" several times each year, which keeps my button count high

She recently sent me a half dozen from Dublin, dated 1821 which were struck off in honor of the visit of George IV to Ireland. He had just acceded to the English throne. It was the first time a king had paid a visit to Ireland in ages. I found out, however, George IV was such a dissolute king the people must have been sorry to have wasted money on this commemorative button.

My button hunting hobby may have seemed strange to others, as indeed at times it has to me. But it has brought me many new interesting friends and furnished me much entertainment. It has added zest, and someone has said, "Zest is the most universal and distinctive mark of a happy man."

BUTTONING DOWN

For twenty years Lilburn had ridden his button hobby horse hard. His rides had taken him to faraway places in England, France and Italy. He became acquainted with collectors from all parts of the nation. Buying, selling and trading buttons had become a fascinating and profitable — though time-consuming — pastime. Hundreds of thousands of buttons passed through his hands. As his button savvy grew, examples of the rarest and most valuable buttons went onto his display boards. In 1964 — the year of his 80th birthday — his hobby-horse rides began to slow from a gallop to, first a trot, then a walk. In 1978 he put this hobby horse out to pasture. The following excerpts provide insight into his "buttoning down" process:

My oldest and best button friend, Bess Wilson, died of a heart attack at her home in Rockford, Ill., a week ago and my button life has had a big sag ever since. She answered all my questions as to identity and value, as well as keeping me posted about affairs over the country as she was in touch with all the big shots in the hobby.

The State Button Society met the last weekend of April in Sedalia. The President was unable to be there, so as Vice President, I had to take over. My biggest job was to hold a memorial service for Bob Johnson, the banker button collector from Kansas City. He also had just died in his sleep. It turned out to be a real testimonial session. Bob had always wanted me to have another drink whenever we were around the hotel, so when one lady got up and said he was always one who was wanting to lift one's spirits, I thought, "How appropriate!"

Bob was one who early in our sessions asked all the ladies up to his room for a drink. Some six or eight went, and when they got there he said, "What will you have?" One said a Seven-up, another, Orange, and the rest, Cokes. Bob was quite put out! He told me afterward women are that way, that any one of them alone would have taken a real drink, but when together, they all were afraid of what the others would say. He was a good sort whom I never knew well until I read his front page Kansas City Star obituary. Well, we got the memorial over creditably. I sold a lot of my buttons. ...

You may remember my story about seeing the buttons on the blouse of a woman on the boat between Capri and Naples. I approached her to buy them, but she was so sentimental about them she could not think of parting with them. That was nine years ago. The other day I received them, six pretty enamels, as she decided she no longer needed them to remind her of her mother.

In April 1974:

Dear Warren,

I drove to Sedalia Saturday to see who came for the State Button Show and Meeting. There were friends from Iowa, Oklahoma, and Kansas as well as our old Missouri cronies and it was pleasant to visit with them and see the many trays of beautiful buttons in competition. I didn't have time this year to prepare a button tray entry. I returned Sunday afternoon and I was pretty well done in from all the socializing.

Three weeks ago Mildred, outgoing president of the State Button Club gave an outdoor picnic for all members at her beautiful country home. Lillian and I attended and stayed until we should have been chased off with a stick. I took the buttons I had for sale and sold about a hundred dollars worth. Since then I have sold many more to parties who were there. As I do not know what anybody would do with mine, if I should pass out of the picture, I thought I would get dispossessed as much as possible. You can't picture, can you, what these collectors buy -

anywhere from a quarter to $40 per button? I must admit I have sold only one for $40, but I have sold several for $25 each.

A woman from Leavenworth, Kansas, came last week with some samples from a 40,000 button collection she had inherited. She said she knew nothing about them — how rare they were, or what they were worth. Could I help her? She had many wonderful buttons, many I had never seen before, and I was able to tell her she had a small fortune in them. I'd be thrilled to have them. I wish I could sell all of mine, but a liking for them won't let me see them go. I haven't been to the annual state meeting now for two years, but I still keep in touch. I no longer encourage anyone to give me a button. I keep what are thrust upon me. Price of buttons, like everything else, has gone sky high. I know I didn't pay more than $10 for anything.

Warren, I am sending you a long-ago copy of the Missouri Society Bulletin in which is published the story of my day with Lillian Smith Albert in New York. In looking through this 1952 issue of the Bulletin, I note every other contributor to the issue has since died. Naturally, with all these delightful people gone, the button hobby no longer is of much interest to me. I have about arrived at the situation as when Margaret Edwards Simpich, an old New Franklin school girl friend, living in Washington, wrote to me for news of our schoolmates back here, naming those of whom she hoped for news, and I had to tell her, "They are all dead but you and me."

March 1978

Dear Alice,

I had a call while I was watching "Guiding Light" telling me a lady was on her way to see me. I thought I could just kill her for calling at that inopportune moment, but hurriedly got on my visiting britches before she came in the door. When I saw who she was, I was quite pleased. It was Eleanor Marcus of St. Louis, the President of the Missouri Button Society, whom we have known for years.

I think Eleanor was quite impressed with the buttons I still

had. Her idea was to see if she could help me find a buyer. A few
days later Robert Hill called and made an appointment to see the
buttons. He came with a little calculator and as I handed him
each button card, he appraised it and put down the price he
would pay. When finished and totaled up, it shocked me because
I thought he would pay more. However, I let the buttons go
rather than fool with them longer. There is little demand at a
local auction.

As a result I am now buttonless except for my charm string,
my button farm, and some military buttons. When I remember
how I bought so many of mine cheap and so many were given
to me, I figure the score is even. And there were hundreds so
common there is no demand. Hill and I both knew that. I am
relieved to have the buttons out of my hands. But what a glorious
ride I have had on this hobby horse.

Anyone Collect Bed Pans?

*Lilburn loved to play with words, to pun and tease, to be a little
shocking. He may have had this in mind as he referred to "beds
of pain" at the outset of his talk to the Garden Club, only to end
with reference to "bed pans."*

Members of the Garden Club. Madame President. I feel
exalted by your flattering introduction of me as one of Missouri's
most interesting and versatile collectors.

Your attendance brings to mind the adage, "A prophet is not
without honor save in his own country." If you will look about
you, you will see the members from my side of the river are not
here. One of them is my sister-in-law and the other is my farm
neighbor on the north. Where are they? At home, languishing
on beds of pain? No. More attractive entertainment bait was
dangled before them and they have gone to another party.

But I shall not allow this to unhorse me, nor could it when
I have so many other lovely ladies to accompany me on this
hobby ride. Many of you I have known long and learned to love

from afar. As for the rest of you, with me, it is a case of love at first sight.

I think I shall play this afternoon that you, as a group, are a colorful garden yourselves. You Girl Scouts present are the lovely seedlings which soon will bud and blossom. And you club members shall be the established plants: delphinium, campanula, digitalis, lily, daisy, gaillardia, all in full bloom, and without one fading blossom.

I have thought often of what I should talk to you about since your president invited me to come over and bring some fertilizer to stimulate your spirits. She suggested I tell you something about my "Hobbies" and "Collecting." From early childhood I have never lacked a hobby horse to ride. Sometimes these rides made me acquainted with collectors of things I fancied so highly I engaged in their pursuit. So there are many angles we could consider.

Recently I have been reading Douglas and Elizabeth Rigby's delightful new book, *Lock, Stock and Barrel,* a veritable storehouse of information concerning collectors of all the ages, so I have decided to pass on to you some of the thoughts about what is a collector and what makes him "tick."

Let us reflect a little on what a collector is? Here in Boonslick Country our early pioneer ancestors' lives were rigorous. Most of their household possessions had definite essential functions. Beds, dressers, chairs, tables, wardrobes, looms, spinning wheels, furniture, kitchen pots, pans and other household goods were brought from Virginia, the Carolinas, Kentucky and Tennessee. Other such functional things were crafted by skilled handicraftsmen who soon were migrating into the area. Such essentials were not easily replaced. They were carefully treated and passed down from generation to generation.

After the Civil War conditions quickly began to change. Machinery was developed which could produce identical items by the thousands that could be sold. Oncoming generations, lacking the sentimental attachment of their elders were attracted by these bright, shiny new things. They rid themselves of the old.

Much was given to farm hands and servants or traded to them for labor. It was such things as these that first aroused my interest.

As our country has prospered, there is more collecting than ever seen before. It would be difficult to name a pastime which could muster over the centuries and the millennia a similar mass of devotees from children to graybeards, including athlete and disabled, king and commoner, intellectual and uneducated, the poor and the wealthy.

The Rigbys say the roots of this collecting phenomenon are the roots of man himself, nourishing as they do many millions of us through this ancient pastime. How many millions? No one knows, but in the field of stamp collecting, for example, it is estimated there are seven and a half million followers in the U.S. alone. Hundreds of books have been published and scores of special sections in newspapers and magazines are printed solely for the benefit of various collectors. There are 14,000 art and antique dealers who cater largely to collectors, thousands of collector clubs, large and small, local and state-wide, national and international, while in purchasing power, collecting is equivalent to a major industry.

The first prodding in the evolving dramas of collecting appears in that characteristic common to all forms of life, the instinct to live, to gather food to sustain life. The simplest type of collecting is to be found in the gathering and storing of food and other elements essential for survival.

Another type of collecting might be called external collecting. Beasts, birds and insects bring home and store away food that may be needed in times of scarcity. Others gather and hoard many useless objects but to them, things apparently attractive, curious and strange. The grain collecting ants have been a source of wonder since the days of King Solomon. The bee stores honey in combs, and a spider often sews up a reserve of moths, flies and caterpillars in neat bundles on her web. Certain woodpeckers gather acorns and store them in holes which they have pecked into the trunks of trees. Rodents are remarkable collectors. Incidentally, the packrat is credited with having a moral sense in that he always puts something in place of what he carries away.

In the case of man, he has found a multiple use for the simple activity of accumulation. His method of forming a collection represents an intricate web of motives and techniques. The ultimate direction taken by human collecting in its various aspects is influenced by complex psychological mechanisms; by emotional urgencies; and by racial and cultural differences, as well as by basic impulses. His initial impulse to collect food for security has been transformed in many ways and he has turned toward the accomplishment of many ends.

Now having disposed of man's primary need to collect food for security, let us consider other kinds of collecting which appeal to him and to which he turns his attention. Some collect as a means to distinction which gives security to pride in accomplishment. There have been men who have delighted in the hunt, in order to wear about their necks the tusks of wild boars, the teeth of lions and leopards they have slain. The more they could exploit, the happier they were. Others have collected the most gruesome human trophies: heads complete with hair and skin, skulls, scalps and locks of hair. In some societies, the possession of many wives connoted distinction. Have any of you ever seen a display of mounted fish in a den or dining room, the prized evidence of some man's prowess as an Izaac Walton?

Rosenbach doubtless feels secure in distinction as the world's foremost book collector. He seeks "books so rare that they have survived only in a single example." J. Pierpont Morgan felt he had reached the pinnacle of distinction desired as a collector when he completed his collection of the Garland Chinese porcelains, 60 million dollars' worth, regarded the finest in the world.

Some collect as a means to immortality. A man may leave children and they may die or turn out badly. They cannot be counted on surely to perpetuate the line and desired reputation. But a collection can be left to bear its founder's name. It will constitute a lasting monument to his predilections and achievements. And because a collector has identified his creation so closely with himself, he sometimes feels that, like a strong boat, it will bear him through the centuries after his body has returned to earth again.

In our country there are many museums, or wings of museums which bear the names of men whose wealth made such edifices possible, or who have given their splendid collections to posterity. Notable are the Field Museum of Natural History in Chicago and The Nelson Museum in Kansas City.

Henry E. Huntington of California said, "The ownership of a fine library is the surest and swiftest way to immortality." There is the Charles Lang Freer gallery with its collection of notable oriental art, and Folger's Shakespearian collection in Washington.

It is interesting to note one recent exception, that of Andrew Mellon. When he stipulated his great art collection, a gift to the people of America, was not to bear his name so that other collectors might be moved to add to it later, he evoked delighted and surprised gratitude.

Anyone knows that the value of a collectible is governed by the law of supply and demand. If a collection is not based upon too momentary a fad or fashion, it likely will retain its value, even in bad times. It may prove a better investment than the usual stocks and bonds. Not long ago, a label from a match box brought $800 just because a particular collector wanted that particular label to fill out a series in which he was interested. Currier and Ives prints with which many of you are familiar, sold originally for up to $4 according to size. But just one item has been known to bring $3600 at auction.

Have any of you ever found an interesting piece of old china or glass which intrigues you into a trip to the library to examine all of the books on those subjects, to gain knowledge of your possession? Probably you did not find a thing about the article in question but it is likely that, as you thumbed and scanned the pages, you learned something else worthwhile. But if you find that you have something rare, what happens to your aesthetic appreciation?

However, the Rigby's did not explain to my satisfaction, nor can I tell you, why Mary Smith has the impulse to collect old butter dishes, while Cousin Susie Snow feels her happiness depends upon her collection of salts and peppers. Why on earth does Mollie have her mantel full of elephants of every conceivable size and color? Why does your little boy come home, his face glowing with pleasure, his pockets crammed with "finds" from, perhaps, the town dump? He has not just picked these up. He has discovered them, chosen certain ones, rejected others, for reasons close to him. He brings his collection home to show you. He feels he can trust you with his confidence, or else he gloats over them in secret until such time as he can show them to his friends. Certainly he expects his audience to be duly impressed and to admire his cleverness in finding and recognizing so much of value.

Why does old Mr. Joe Brown collect baby shoes, and Mrs. Annie Carson of DeWitt, Mo., moustache cups? And why does Harry Jones have no impulse to collect at all?

As far as hobbies could carry me, I have ridden them most of my life. I have even changed horses in mid-stream. I collected stamps first, then came postcards, photographs of pretty girlfriends, this of course, as a means to knowledge and aesthetic appreciation, bottles and jugs, clocks, pressed glass, flowers, lamps, old locks, brass door knobs, music, complete card-indexed records of every marked grave in my native Howard County, history, bustles, but not bed pans!

Chapter Eighteen

RIVERCENE

Rivercene, the magnificent mansion built by Steamboat Captain Joseph Kenney on the north bank of the Missouri River attracted Lilburn's attention as a child. It continued to fascinate him for many years. When Captain Kinneys' three daughters who inherited the place had financial difficulties, he befriended them in many ways. A few of his columns about Rivercene follow:

Rivercene, now a bed and breakfast inn

No place in the Boonslick Country has been publicized more than Rivercene across the river from Boonville. The supply of stories seems inexhaustible.

Captain Joseph Kinney who founded Rivercene in 1869, died in 1892. His 22-year-old son, Noble W. Kinney, a student of agriculture at the University of Missouri took over management of the farm. His ambition was to convert it into a fruit and vegetable farm and wholesale the products. He had made such progress by the second year of his operation it showed prospect of becoming one of the best arranged places of its kind in Missouri.

Mr. Kinney said that one hundred acres were to be devoted to staple vegetables. There would be fifty-five acres of potatoes on land rented to Jack Hulett.

There would be ten acres of peas, seven acres of tomatoes, seventeen acres of cabbage, four acres of radishes, four of lettuce and two of celery. Five of the seventeed acres of cabbage would be grown for the northern market and the other twelve acres reserved for shipment to southern points in August and September. Everything else would be grown for northern markets.

There would be seven acres of raspberries and blackberries. Eight or nine acres would be planted to pears.

Mr. Kinney had built a greenhouse ninety feet long and sixty feet wide a short distance southeast of the dwelling. Inside were growing long rows of vegetables. The finest varities of radishes were being sold and shipped daily to points north. Lettuce plants without number, fresh looking, thrifty and truly beautiful would be ready to ship in about two weeks.

Some tomato plants were in crocks but would soon be transplanted in beds and trained up the walls and beneath the glass roof. These plants would bear about the 1st of May before the planting of tomatoes outside to mature normally.

To heat the greenhouse there was a coke furnace. Temperature was kept at sixty degrees. Water, a supply practically inexhaustible, was supplied from a large tank in the yard which was filled by an engine from a deep well nearby.

In February a large number of hot beds three hundred feet long and six feet wide would be seeded.

The *Advertiser's* report said, "Doubtless Rivercene will become one of the best and most widely known farms of its kind in the west and ere long the whole north will be a market for the products of its soil."

But young Noble Kinney was not destined to realize his dream. Declining health for many months of which few knew because he always seemed so cheerful and lighthearted in spite of his infirmities, brought about his death in April, 1895 at the age of 26 years.

No survivor in the family was able to carry out his plans and they were abandoned.

RIVERCENE AND HOT-HOUSE HOGS

In the New Franklin News *of April 24, 1902, an advertisement appeared as follow:*

"Kinney and Odonnell will sell their entire herd of Hot-house hogs on the 25th of April, a number of challenge brood sows, fancy bred gilts and a large number of strictly first class shoats. These are all high grade Poland China hogs. Their object in selling is to handle in the future, nothing but registered stock. Come as soon as you get your dinner."

Kinney and Odonnell were probably the first and last producers of Hot-house hogs in Howard County. The reason they embarked upon the project was the existence of facilities which could be used, an idle 90 x 18 green house heated with a coke furnace and well supplied with water.

Miss Alice Kinney, a sister of Noble, with the aid of advisory pamphlets from the Missouri Department of Agriculture took over management of Rivercene after her brother died in 1895. Assisting her was a young man, Daniel Odonnell who had lived at Rivercene most of the time since 1881 when his father's family, he included, headed for the west in a covered wagon, reached the ferry near Rivercene and found the river blocked with ice.

Capt. Kinney, renowned for his assistance and hospitality on such occasions, allowed the travelers to live in a vacant house on his premises until the ice should break up. The two families became so congenial the visitors remained some time. A daughter, Miss Mary, became a fine teacher in the New Franklin school for several years. Dan eventually went on west with his father but later returned to Rivercene.

Maybe someone at the Missouri University conceived the idea of Hot-house hogs, maybe Miss Alice, maybe Dan. Why couldn't the hot house be used for farrowing and growing pigs? There was plenty of sunshine, heat from the furnace and plenty of water. If vegetables planted there thrived, why not hogs?

I found no account of the 1902 sale but there is a record of an annual one in 1905. "Owing to the inclement weather there was not a large crowd in attendance but those who did come, came for business."

The names of the buyers of the pens were listed in the paper. there were 21 pens of which Horace Kingsbury bought 14.

The only other Hot-house hogs I ever heard of were raised scientifically in Alaska by the University of that state, sponsored by the the University of Iowa.

The project of Kinney and Odoennell was quite primitive compared with the one in Alaska.

RIVERCENE'S TREASURES AUCTIONED

When the treasures of Rivercene, the old Joseph Kinney home in south Howard county were sold in 1948, the auction was memorable. Many people learned that fine household goods need not be a hundred years old to be classified as antiques which bring amazingly high prices. The late Opal Melton in her column, "My Say" in the Cooper County *Record*, described the event well. Excerpts follow:

"The weather was Missouri May-time at its best, the sun bright and the air brisk. A wrap felt good if you sat in the shade and the sun felt fine when you moved into it as rays slanted down from the west. And the crowd! Estimated at six hundred. A more intellectual and cultured group of that size seldom assembled in one body in the great out-of-doors. It was predominantly feminine and largely Missourian.

"The place and the people created an atmosphere I liked. The great brick and walnut mansion built in 1869 by Captain Kinney, owner of a fleet of steamboats, was filled with treasures from our own country and far lands. Many of the materials were brought great distances by steamboats and unloaded at Rivercene's private dock just in front of the building site. The eleven mantels of gleaming Italian marble. The two walnut doors to the west parlor weigh 250 pounds each.

"Under the spell of the great house, the maple and tulip trees, the furnishings, a low-voiced audience, antiques sold high. You could understand distinctly every word of the auctioneer.

"A great deal of credit for the successful auction goes to the publicity from a half page feature story in the *Kansas City Star* and to the hundreds of visitors from all over the United States who have seen the house and its furnishings since it was opened in 1948 to the public.

"While Eastern dealers doubtless helped to keep prices up through a day of spirited bidding from ten in the morning until five in the afternoon, I noted that some of the most expensive pieces went to wheatpoor Kansas and not a few to Missourians.

"Mr. Charles van Ravenswaay, historian, author, collector, authority on old homes and Director of the Missouri Historical Society of St. Louis was one of the few Boonville buyers."

Antiques leave many people cold but once bitten by the bug, it takes money to treat the fever. Rivercene during the auction was a likely place to get bitten.

Chapter Nineteen

FROM FRINGE-TOPPED SURREY TO PLANES IN A HURRY

Most baby boomers and their children have little awareness of the amazing changes advancing technology has made in our manner of living. Lilburn's almost hundred-year lifespan allowed him to observe these changes first-hand. In addition, his history hobby horse rides reinforced his recollections. A careful researcher and observer, he frequently shared some of his findings as a featured speaker at meetings of clubs and organizations.

An example is "From Fringed-Topped Surrey to Planes in a Hurry," given at a Boonslick Historical Society Meeting in 1957. This talk was spiced up with some of the folklore stories he picked up on his rides.

A father and son from the backwoods ran smack dab into the wonders of modern transportation. As they came to a river there was a motor boat cutting its way through the water. Amazed, the boy asked, "Pappy, how come that boat run without no paddles?" The father shook his head and replied, "Well son, I don't rightly know." Farther on they came to a railroad as a sleek diesel powered streamliner glided by. In further astonishment the boy asked, "Pappy, how come that train run without smoke?" Again the father said, "Well son, I don't rightly know." Then they came to a highway where cars were whizzing past and the boy exclaimed, "Pappy, how come them buggies run without horses?" Again the father shook his head and said, "Well son, I don't rightly know."

As they sauntered along, the boy said, "Pappy, I guess you git tard me askin' you so many questions?" "Naw," said the father, "I doan git tard. You go right on. You won't never larn nothin' lessen you ask questions."

In preparation of this paper, I have asked many questions but I don't rightly know that I have "larned" enough of the right things about transportation to entertain you and justify your attendance.

Transportation is a subject as long, as wide and as deep as the sea. In a material sense it has been a vital factor in the life of every nation on earth. Spiritually, it is a part of life for every individual. But tonight I am concerned with the ways people have devised to move themselves from place to place. I mean to scratch the surface of this vast subject and review with you some changes in transportation and the reactions of people to them which have come under my observation during my short three score years plus.

I don't recall ever riding in a baby buggy but I remember my delight when, as a little boy, I rode behind my father, my arms tight around his body, on old Jim, the family saddle horse. Bigger thrills were mine when a new world was opened up for me by my first long train ride to St. Louis. No kid ever leaned out of the window farther than I watching the wonders unfold along the railroad right-of-way. In the city was the flurry of a first street car, and the hotel elevator with a lift so sudden, it astonished my stomach. Recently in a large city I rode in a modern elevator lined solidly with beautiful walnut wood. Immediately after the operator closed the door, she opened it again. I thought she had done so to admit some belated passenger and made no move to leave. She looked at me in a way that said, "Get out," but said, "Your floor, please." In no sense had I been conscious of movement.

But all this excitement was nothing compared to the thrill of riding my own horse across the river on the ferry, dressing it up in shiny black harness and hitching it to a new made-to-order, all paid for, high seated runabout with hard rubber tires which I rode home in to conquer the social world.

Until I got this outfit, my courting wings had been clipped. Now they grew out fast and I could "fly the coop." There were never enough evenings for buggy riding. No evening was long enough. How welcome daylight savings would have been.

My next big thrill in transportation came when a dealer left a Ford car for me to have and to hold. It afforded faster, though perhaps no fuller joy-riding, and it extended my horizon immeasurably.

At that time, adventurous car owners were making a journey called "the circle drive." It took one through three counties: Howard, Saline and Cooper. It had to be made when the weather was pleasant and dry as a bone, for if you got caught in the rain, the mud would hold you like a rat in a trap. Usually two or more cars went together, strung along in caravan fashion. There was the feeling of safety in numbers such as pioneers appreciated when they traveled the Santa Fe Trail years ago. Of course there were no Indians on the circle drive but mechanical accidents could scalp your joy. If one car was overtaken by trouble, another could come to the rescue.

After ferrying the river at Glasgow, the caravan chugged on to Gilliam and Slater, exploring the main streets. Usually someone who had made the trip before was able to point out the imposing homes of the bankers. In Marshall, Eastwood Avenue with its stately homes, set far back from the street amid magnificent trees, was traversed slowly and the cars circled the spacious town square before heading toward Arrow Rock for a casual view of the Old Tavern.

Then came the homestretch toward Boonville with everyone hoping there would be no flat tires or other delays, for there was a deadline to be met, the six o'clock ferry back to Howard County.

A girl from Mississippi was visiting near my home when the Ford car entered my life. And she was the first girl to enter my Ford. I had done everything I could to make her visit pleasant for me, and when she was about to leave for home, it seemed the ultimate would be to give her "the circle drive." And so I did, ever mindful that the Boonville ferry was a must at six o'clock. I don't recall ever hearing anybody say what should be done in the event one missed the ferry. You just didn't miss the ferry.

You know how, after an enjoyable occasion, we are prone to indulge in retrospection, to analyze and assay bits of conversation? Well, after this girl had gone home and had, no doubt, changed Ford cars, I pondered something she had said as we were riding along a tree-bowered road unspoiled by highway builders. She had said, "This is a chahmin lane, so shady an' cool. The clustahs of wild roses along heah a'e just beautiful. Don't you evah get ti'ed drivin' so far, so fast, an' feel like restin' a little?" I had assured her, "I never get tired when I am with you," but was thinking, what is a new Ford for but to drive far and fast? We made the ferry. As I have just said, I was brought up to make the ferry. But I have wondered ever since, if I had missed the ferry, would I have "made the boat?"

Back in 1929 I crossed the Atlantic on a boat loaded with 1200 mules bound for Mediterranean ports. It took twenty-one days. There were all kinds of thrills connected with that trip. A notable one was of a burial at sea of a mule that had died. A bigger thrill would have been to bury the other 1199. In 1954 I stood again on the shore of the Mediterranean and marvelled that in only twenty-one hours I had just flown over from New York, with two hours to idle in Ireland and four to loaf in Paris. Such is the magic of modern transportation.

There has always been competition between forms of transportation. Each type has had its heyday of usefulness and popularity until supplanted by some other. Travel by steamboat and by buggies and wagons drawn by horse-power was superseded by railroads. The latter are being supplanted by gasoline vehicles until they must rely upon long, cross-country hauls for passengers and freight for survival. And now airlines are arch competitors of automobiles, trucks and buses. It doesn't seem possible that airplanes might ever supersede ground vehicles, but who, fifty years ago, ever dreamed that the world would be literally run over by automobiles as it is today. Fifty million of them in 1956. Changes come mighty fast.

Everyone is familiar through personal experience, reading, radio and television of the refinements of up-to-date transportation but it is only when we look back into earlier days and make comparisons that we realize what superior advantages we enjoy today.

Perhaps it will be revealing for you to listen in on a repetition of reminiscences of some old men who found horse and buggy days interesting. There is Hank Brady, a railroad engineer, Pat Bradford, a farmer and Lem Pickens who ran a livery stable until driven into the early automobile business, all retired. But each is still quick on the mental trigger and alert to current events. In fact, current events are springboards from which they dive into the pools of memory and bring up souvenirs to be re-examined.

The other evening they sat in comfortable chairs in a shady yard in town when Johnnie Cutter, local "cool cat," rolled up the street in his sleek two-tone convertible, honking blatantly as he approached the house next door. Needless honking, for Judy, his current "warm plate," becurled and beruffled, had run out to the curb and was waiting before he brought his car to a momentary pause. Nonchalantly they watched her open the door, swing herself in slamming it shut. In a burst of speed, they were gone.

"By golly," exclaimed Hank Brady, the railroader, "that gal swung onto that car like a brakeman hoppin' a train! And Johnnie," he continued, reminiscently, "with that horn brings back the days when I used to blow the whistle of old 906 to let my girl know when I was gettin' in or out on my St. Louis run. We had a sort of courtin' code. I could blow the whistle sweet to tell her I loved her. I could make it sound sad and wet with tears when I was pullin' out. And when whistlin' in, I would blow it impatient - like so as to remind her I could hardly wait to get off the engine, wash up and get out to her house to take her buggy ridin'. She lived out of town a piece and I couldn't get out there in a wink like Johnnie breezes in here."

"I got a horse and buggy at Lem's livery stable," Hank continued, "generally an old mare named Maud and a right nifty looking rubber-tired buggy, black and shiny. I was always so anxious to get out to my girl's I felt like whippin' old Maud into a run, but she had her limitations and I just throttled her down to a trot, nine or ten miles an hour. When I got out there I tied old Maud to the hitchrack and hurried into the house."

"Mabel always looked ready to go when she met me at the

door and invited me in but if she was ever in a rush, she never let on. I always talked to her old folks awhile before we started out.

"When we left the house, she waited at the end of the walk until I brought up the buggy, turned old Maud to cut the wheels, and got out. As I held the lines tight in my right hand and she put her foot on the step, I took hold of her arm with my left hand and squeezed it a little to save words as I eased her up into the buggy. As she smoothed her skirts about her, I climbed in and settled myself in what was left of the narrow seat of the HMT, clucked to old Maud and away we went."

"I'll bet you didn't go gallivantin' to the four ends of the earth like Judy and Johnnie," interrupted Pat Bradford, (whose voice was high-pitched). "Why they are going sixty miles down the road to a street fair. Beats all I ever heard of. Judy's ma wasn't a bit in favor of it and raised old Ned but Judy raised more old Ned than her ma, so her ma had to give in."

"No," continued Hank Brady, "we didn't run all over creation. As a rule we didn't have any destination, didn't need any. We didn't think anything about having no place to go. But now and then we drove several miles into the country where they had dances they called 'moonlights'. Funny, they used to have them in the dark of the moon as well as when it was shinin'. To the music of fiddle, banjo and guitar, each fellow transported as many girls as possible around the platform, waltzin' and two-steppin', between the dances he had with the girl he took. I used to wish I could dance every one with Mabel like the boys do now, but it wouldn't have looked well. Young fellows now don't care how it looks. Those 'moonlights' were mighty nice affairs and the ride home was always pleasant and cool, joggin' along smellin' the smells of night, damp and willowy along the creek and hay curin' in the fields."

Lem Pickens spoke with quite a drawl. "Speaking of racing," he said, "nobody could outrace Mrs. Sue Lee. She would poke along the road on purpose until somebody tried to pass her, then she would lean out of her buggy and say, "You think your horse is better than mine?" By then, she had touched her horse with the whip and was way ahead pulling the beatenes' cloud of dust you ever saw."

"She put it all over me once, that way," chimed in Pat Bradford.

It seemed Hank Brady couldn't drop the subject of old Maud and he continued, "Old Maud wasn't much trouble to guide and she went along quietly unless a horsefly or something bit her. But in one way, she just beat all. If I got careless, thinkin, more about Mabel than I was about the lines, and let them hang loose, she would switch her tail over them and clamp it down tight like a vise, throwin' me completely out of control. The old mare seemed to take delight in it.

Of course I had to stop right there and free the lines. There were two ways to go at it. One was to hold to the dashboard with the right hand and lean forward, careful not to lose my balance, and forcibly lift her tail with the left. The other and safer way was to get out of the buggy and work from the side. But by then, she acted like she had lost her taste for the joke and lifted her tail herself. I wanted to kill her for putting me to all that trouble and embarrassin' Mabel like she did."

"Speaking of horse and buggy riding," began Lem Pickens, "I shall never forget the time Cousin Sallie asked ma to go with her to spend the day with their cousin. I took ma to the crossroads where Cousin Sallie picked her up and told me to be back there at 5 o'clock when she would drop ma off on the way home. But things didn't work out according to Hoyle. You see, she was driving old Lucy, a mare with a suckling colt. But lately, the colt had become such a nuisance tagging along, always trying to get its dinner, Cousin Sallie left it at home that day. Well, the women had such a nice visit but when they got ready to start home, old Lucy was so restless from not seeing her colt all day long, they couldn't get into the buggy until somebody held her bridle to make her stand still. Only by being right agile did they make it at all.

"And speaking of that old mare reminds me," he continued.

"You remember old Kate, the mule Mrs. Francis used to drive to her buggy?" She was gentle as a lamb but slower than a turtle. Remember how Mrs. Francis had to whip her nearly every step to keep her on the go? But that wasn't old Kate's worst fault. Whenever they got to the edge of town, old Kate began to bray, "Haw-hee-haw," as if to let everybody know they were coming. And she kept it up right through town if Mrs. Francis didn't whip her extra. She wasn't proud of driving a mule anyhow and this braying just humiliated her the more. But she said she would rather suffer humiliation than to whip old Maud in public and be frowned on by the ladies of the Society for Prevention of Cruelty to Animals."

In the heyday of railroads, the Katy ran three passenger trains each way, daily, through Howard and Cooper Counties. It was possible to enter a Pullman parlor car in Chicago and ride through here to Texas without a change. On the other hand the service did not please everyone. One disgruntled passenger, speaking of one train, said that whenever the engine whistled, it had to slow down, it didn't have enough steam to whistle and pull three coaches at the same time. But whether the service was good or bad, the time had come when nobody relied upon any other mode of travel between towns along the railroad.

The trains had all the comforts of the day to make travel pleasant. The passengers rode in blissful ignorance of better things to come. There were coal-burning engines with firemen always shoveling fuel into the fireboxes. Smoke and cinders which poured through the windows, open in summer for fresh air-conditioning, were accepted as a matter of course. An extra handkerchief was carried as an accessory for removing cinders from the eyes. Open windows were hazardous. Passengers with young children made them sit next to the aisle lest they throw something valuable out, or worse still, stand up in the seat and fall out themselves. Aunt Catherine Kingsbury, starting on a trip to Virginia, sneezed inadvertently before a window just north of Fayette and lost her teeth. In dismay she cried, "O' conductor, stop the train! stop the train!" The conductor chanced to be within hearing distance and pulled the signal rope before he knew what had happened. When the train jolted to a sudden stop, there was nothing for him to do but start it again. She got off at Higbee and caught the next train back to organize a searching party, or failing in that, arrange for a restoration.

The trains consisted of several coaches. Back of the engine and tender was the combination baggage, mail and express car. Next to it came the smoker, upholstered in wicker or rattan. Here, men enjoyed their pipes and cigars without offense to women and here they preferred to ride when traveling alone. In the front seat the "butcher boy" kept his stock of goods. He made rounds through the coaches between towns, offering white sheets of chewing gum with fancy pictures attached, motto candy, licorice, fruit, small novelties and magazines for sale.

Back of the smoker were one or more parlor cars upholstered in luxurious red or green velvet (mohair). These were occupied by women and children, and men who chose to remain with them in preference to an escape to the smoker. It seemed a little effeminate for a man to ride in the parlor car unless he was with his family or accompanying what we today call "a date."

In all coaches the seats originally were straight-backed and double but they were reversible so an arrangement for persons to sit facing each other was possible. But the time came when a reclining chair service was installed in parlor coaches on trains which made night runs. This delighted the public who acclaimed it was a great step toward the comfort of the passengers. It became common for a traveler to wait for a night train so he could recline. These chairs proved so popular that within a month, all parlor cars were fitted with them and passengers reclined with utter abandon both day and night.

Heat was supplied by little stoves in corners of the coaches. Temperature was subject to quick changes because doors and windows were opened often. There was a tank of drinking water on the wall at one end of the coach, with a common drinking cup. It was before germs learned to travel.

It was smart to remain seated while the train was in motion

lest the lurching throw one down. But, for the benefit of those who must move, leather loops were suspended from the ceiling to assist one through the aisle. You could not tell when a man passed through the car whether he was drunk or sober. And it was wise not to go from one coach to another, platforms being open and the couplings over which one must step did a real rock and roll. However, gentlemen who excused themselves from the women in the parlor car and went forward to the smoker, watched their steps and made the transfer safely if not with the skill of the train crew.

At the towns along the railroad on a sunny Sunday afternoon, many people, dressed in their best clothes, weary of the doldrums of life in a little town, strolled leisurely down to the depot to see the trains come and go, curious to see who might get off and who might depart.

When the weather was pleasant, people congregated on the platform to visit. In colder weather they sat on benches or stood around the potbellied stoves in the waiting rooms until the station agent bustled around locking up his office. This was the signal the train was due. Everyone then filed out on the platform to see the train come down the track, the engine small in perspective at first, but growing bigger and bigger as she bore down toward the depot, bell clanging and smoke pouring from her stack like black hair brushed straight back. Instinctively, everyone drew away from the rails as she breezed by the platform like a snorting black beast with a body odor of steam and hot grease, and came to a panting stop.

Back at the parlor cars, those expecting guests wore glad, welcoming expressions as they pressed toward the Negro porter who had set down his little step and was assisting passengers to alight. There were cries of recognition, hand-shakes, hugs and kisses in keeping with the fervor of the greetings. Then as these people moved away, chatting happily, the departing ones, some with sober faces, pushed toward the porter, said goodbyes, and once up the steps hurried inside the coach to a seat, if possible, by a window on the depot side. Here postscripts of conversation could be said to those still waiting outside, and a final goodbye might be said when the conductor shouted, "All aboard."

Fifty years ago, students at the colleges in Fayette arrived by train. Many had to change cars in Moberly and "lay over" there. An official from the colleges was there on the day of great influx to shepherd the lambs and keep off the wolves until they were on the train, Fayette-bound, where upon arrival they would be reasonably safe within the fold. Their arrival was an occasion considered worthy of a reception by a brass band. It played lively airs as the students got off the train and attended their satchels, telescopes and valises. A committee from the Y.M.C.A. was on hand to welcome them and offer any assistance necessary. Then, with a rousing march the band led the procession of new students, on foot, up Main Street toward the colleges, circling the square enroute. Merchants stood outside their stores projecting personality as best they could through greetings. Doubtless they looked with appraising eyes for potentially these boys and girls constituted a shot in the arm for business.

Imagine if you can, anyone strolling anywhere today, and of all places, to the railroad depot. It is a very desolate spot. Bill Vaughan of the *Kansas City Star* said recently that about the only place where a voter can feel safe from shaking hands with a candidate is at the depot. The trains which were such a blessing, the pride and joy of people fifty years ago, no longer pound the rails in Howard and Cooper counties. Some of us need to travel thirty to fifty miles for even a sight of diesel-powered domeliners which move only on main lines. These palace cars move with as much grace as a woman who has learned to walk with a book on her head. Inside are all the refinements of a modern home and the ride is so smooth that one can thread a needle. The railroads are providing every luxury to induce you and me to ride the rails instead of highways and skyways.

The first automobiles I can remember were driven by Fred Arn of Boonville and Perry Lewis of St. Louis. The Arn car had a high seat from which one looked down upon humanity, and a bar for steering instead of a wheel. There was a little bicycle bell which tinkled terror into the hearts of pedestrians. Perry Lewis, reputedly wealthy, drove his large car, a Stevens-Durea, over dirt roads from St. Louis to visit his Howard County relatives. A hippopotamus on the street today would not attract a larger, more curious crowd than Mr. Lewis' car did when he stopped in New Franklin.

Early motorists gave no end of worry to all who drove horses which were not accustomed to the contraptions and cut all kinds of capers at the sight of them. If the driver in a buggy had any warning of the approach of one of these automobiles, he pulled quickly to the side of the road as far as possible, leaped out and grabbed his horse by the bridle with both hands and constituted himself a weight to keep the beast from rearing up, all the while muttering imprecations upon the driver of the car. It would be difficult to say which was scared worse, the drivers of the buggy or the men and women in the automobiles, of what the horses might do. Sometimes they were quite docile and did nothing. It was usual for the farmer, before venturing out upon the road with a horse and buggy, to phone up and down the party line to find out whether any autos had been on the road that day, and if so, where were they, and were they heading toward or from home.

Automobiles had not been in use long before matters of licenses, speed limits and general safety became issues. In 1907 the legislature passed a bill establishing a $5 license fee for each automobile. Speed limits were in force and a party in St. Louis was fined $100 for exceeding the limit of nine miles per hour in effect in the city. In the country, one could speed fifteen miles per hour with impunity so far as the law was concerned.

The papers of that time ran pertinent editorials, such as this one: "Why the automobile is charged for passing through a county when a wagon of any size pays nothing, is hard to understand. It must be due to prejudice against the automobile in the county but this will pass. In former years it existed against the traction engine. Anything that a horse does not understand, frightens him.

"Autos are new on country roads away from large cities. The automobile has come to stay, not the one operated by some incompetent or reckless person, and perhaps not the evil smelling oil wagon now in common use. But the principle of the invention will last. Its use is rapidly growing and it has a use outside of pleasure. It will rapidly grow in popularity and not only result in good highways but to a great extent, supplant the horse and beast of burden.

"The laws are aimed at reckless drivers. But these fools will soon grow weary of such a plaything and endeavor to attract attention to themselves by balloon ascensions or something of the kind wherein the public will have the satisfaction of knowing that only their valueless selves will be in danger."

A man in New Franklin was driving a Model T Ford with his wife and some other ladies. They were chugging along when one of them became uneasy and inquired how fast he was driving. He replied, "Not very fast, about fifteen miles per hour." Horrified the guest exclaimed, "Fifteen miles!" and addressing the man's wife, said in a pleading tone, "Oh Jennie, make him slow down."

If you owned one of the high, hideous but efficient Model T Fords, do you recall the operating routine? You climbed in by the right door for there was no left hand door by the front seat, and reached over to the wheel and set the spark and throttle in the position of the hands of a clock at ten minutes to three. Then, unless you had a self-starter for which you paid extra as did Floyd Capito in 1914 (and he believes he had the first starter in the county) you got out to crank. Seizing the crank in your right hand (carefully, for a friend once broke his arm cranking) you slipped your left forefinger through a loop of wire that controlled the choke. You pulled the loop of wire and revolved the crank mightily, and as the engine roared, you leaped to the trembling running board, got in, moved the spark and throttle to 25 minutes of two. Perhaps you reached the throttle before the engine faltered into silence, but if it was a cold morning, probably not. In that case, back to the crank again and the loop of wire.

But with the passing of years all this was changed. Automobiles were made with such precision that motorists hardly knew a spark plug by sight, many never even lifted the hood to see what the engine looked like. People left the shovel, the towrope and the log chain carried for emergencies at home. As cars were closed, bodies were swung lower and balloon tires came in. Paved roads and filling stations became so plentiful that the motorist sallied forth for the day without fear of being stuck in the mud or stranded without benefit of gasoline.

Villages which once prospered because they were "on the railroad" languished with economic anemia while villages on automobile highways blossomed with hot-dog stands, repair garages, restaurants, antique shops, motels, trailer camps, and night clubs.

Railroad after railroad has abandoned its branch lines as revenues dwindled under competition of mammoth interurban buses and trucks which snort along the concrete highways.

Every car manufacturer is creating new styles, new lines in their 1957 models which will make our present automobiles look obsolete. They are beautiful with luxurious appointments. They are also higher in price. But when were car prices not going up? In 1914 a Ford could be bought for $514 and if a certain number of cars were sold within a limited time, the dealer could refund $50 of that amount to each purchaser. Of course each buyer did get his $50 refund but whether he would or not hardly entered into the purchase. He liked the car and would have it regardless of price. Manufacturers are putting the new cars on the market today in the belief, proven sound, that if Mr. John Q. Public wants a car he will buy it regardless of price and unmindful of the interest he may have to pay on deferred payments.

We have become so accustomed to the accomplishments of modern transportation that nothing amazes us any more. We accept it all as a part of our American birthright. Or perhaps it is because it is completely beyond our comprehension. In September, Capt. Irvin C. Kinchloe piloted a Bell rocket X2 to an altitude of nearly twenty-four miles. Lt. Col. Frank K. Everest flew the X2 1900 miles per hour. Late in the month, Capt. Apt drove it even faster but unfortunately it brought him death in a crash from a mere 3000 feet. Since then, a missile has been fired into the sky eighty miles before it reversed its course. A lot of people have signed up for the first trips to the moon.

My mind is just as confused about these things as was that of the boy who wondered about boats without paddles, trains without smoke and buggies without horses. To "larn" I shall be obliged to ask a lot of questions and I hope you rightly know the answers.

Chapter Twenty

How I Became a Columnist

At the bottom of this manuscript Lilburn had written, "This talk was given before the annual meeting of the Missouri Writers Guild the last time it was held in Columbia." No date was given, but probably about 1975. At the time, he was Secretary-Treasurer of the Guild. Then in his eighties, he was writing a weekly column for the Boonville Daily News.

Lilburn Says...

"Our members would like to know the secrets of how you became such an interesting columnist when you were eighty years old." President Calahan said when he invited me to talk to you today.

I remonstrated. I told him: with no journalism background, I was - if anything - a rank amateur and would not feel at home addressing you clever, successful members of the Guild. When I read in the Guild News of your accomplishments, generally consistent sales of stories, poems, books and plays, I feel sinfully covetous of your talents. And pitifully aware of my limitations. As for my literary achievements, if any, I must say they have been done "by ear," just as some people play music. I have never heard of any rules for constructing a column by ear.

Despite my protests, I found myself on the program. So - I'll tell you some of the events I've dredged from my memory which culminated in my column-writing.

The most remarkable thing about me producing a column, is that the idea of doing it never entered my mind. During the past sixty years I unknowingly was gathering material for it. You wish to know how the idea got into my mind?

First, let me say I've discovered that the two necessary ingredients to writing a column people enjoy reading are: to have a pinch of ability to write and plenty of ideas to write about. Uncolumnly conscious for sixty years, I was trying to improve my ability and fill my memory storehouse with ideas.

As for learning to write, I began during an early romantic period by subscribing to a correspondence course in letter writing offered by Pretty Girl Inc., with daily lessons. I learned the art of choosing the word to express exactly the thought I had in mind. The course yielded me nothing I could sell but there were fringe benefits, until finally, rejection slips caused me to change schools.

In college, I entered a contest for $20 in gold offered for the best essay about "The Weird and Uncanny in the Writings of Hawthorne and Poe." Although there was another contestant, I won. I was so delighted I felt inspired to devote the rest of my life to writing about weird and uncanny things. To be able to do this I planned to enter the Missouri School of Journalism in the fall.

However, the opportunity to become a self-made rich banker in a small town changed my plan. I began at the bottom as janitor (they call it custodian now) and carried in fuel to feed the pot-bellied stove and fetched six buckets of cistern water from the home of a widow a block way. I could have gotten it closer, but the bachelor bank president wanted to shower the widow with attention. Of course, I had no idea at the time he would be good material for a column now!

I had anticipated extra time in the bank to improve my writing expertise but I was very busy writing names and figures in big ledgers. I never got anything ready to send out for publication except semi-annual statements of the condition of the bank. They were always accepted. Having continual acceptances made me very vulnerable in later years to rejection slips.

Some of the bank customers were interesting characters and memories of them were preserved in my storehouse. There was Mrs. Bodgett, who came in twittering a request that I make out her check for fifteen cents. She had to pay her washer-woman, she said, and added, "It's a constant drain."

And Jim Lowe, an old man who moved to town from the hills bringing polecat liniment for "rumatiz" to sell, always attracted our customers to listen to him as he sang a warning:

> *O boys, let the girls alone*
> *An' give 'em plenty of room.*
> *If one you wed, she'll knock you on the head*
> *With the bald-headed end of the broom.*

After twenty-five years as a banker, I was not rich, so I took my insurance business and moved across the street. Policies written sold well with few rejections. It was also necessary at the time that I take over the management of the family farm where fruit was the main crop, chiefly apples. Customers who came to the sales shed to buy apples also supplied many ideas which were deposited in my memory bank. It was amazing, the politeness of one husband and wife, each insisting that the other should choose the variety to be bought, each saying, "It doesn't make me any difference, you choose."

It was well I had a competent secretary in the insurance office, and an efficient overseer on the farm, for I was bitten by an antique bug infatuation. The only thing which seemed to help me was open-air riding over the country buying antiques to refurbish my century-old house. Little did I dream I was gathering material for a column decades later!

There was the old lady who wouldn't sell me a table. She said, "You are such a good friend I couldn't sell it to you. I'd give it to you if I didn't want to keep it myself." I used many schemes to soften her into a sale, but to no avail. Finally in response to a wild thought, I asked her to "lend/lease" it to me. And she did. Most of you are too young to recall when our government "lend/leased" so much that it seemed an individual was unpatriotic not to do it.

Something happened in 1937 which really put me on the main track of literary effort. A local historical society was being organized. I had always been so busy with other things I hadn't had time for history. However, I was induced to attend the dinner meeting. The dinner was fine but the proceedings following it bored me. I was sleepy, wishing I were home. And suddenly, in the time it took me to raise my cup for a sip of coffee to keep me awake and set it down, I had been nominated for president and elected by acclamation. I had been "framed" by the late Judge Roy Williams, whom many of you will remember. I didn't appreciate it and told him as kindly as possible what I had heard that Jonah told the whale the second time he met him (and the whale had lost his appetite). "If you had kept your big mouth shut, it never would have happened."

However, in later years I never missed a chance to thank the Judge for railroading me into an active role in the society. It opened a whole new field in which literary fruits were growing, like research, publication of historical stories, the recording of every marked grave in the two hundred fourteen cemeteries of Howard County. I had recorded everything about my father's life of ninety years in the community he could remember. I was saving all the informational sap I could get from older men and women whom I tapped as if they were sturdy old sugar maple trees.

About this time, Mr. Ernest Kirschten, of the editorial page of the *St. Louis Star-Times*, invited me to write him some letters about life as I had known it on our farm for his editorial page. Surprised and delighted, I labored over eight or ten of them and sent them to him. In due time all of them appeared on the editorial page. Could a benefit have a better fringe than that? And he made the fringe longer by writing, "I cannot tell you how delighted all of us on the *Star-Times* editorial page have been with your letters. They brought an authentic and enjoyable taste of rural Missouri to us city dwellers. We hope you got as much pleasure out of writing them as we did from reading. I sincerely trust you will continue to find time to send more."

It occurred to me that if they were that good, he could at least send me postage for mailing them; in fact, they should be worth money. I did no more letters for Mr. Kirschten and we never heard from each other again.

Later, I realized how foolish I had been to chop up, like a common dandelion in my yard, an opportunity to cultivate any potential for writing. It might have improved my style so I would have made a better showing by the time I prepared a manuscript and sent it to my friend, Fred Simpich, the Associate Editor of the *National Geographic Magazine*. Not that I had hope of the magazine using it, but I knew Fred would give me his candid opinion of its merits.

The first part of his reply was like a gentle massage to my spirit. He wrote: "You choose your material with skill that borders on genius. If you could write it as well as you pick it, you would be another Thornton Wilder. Your manuscript holds all the elements of another 'Our Town' or 'The Bridge of San Luis Rey.' Wilder could take your copy and make a big seller out of it."

What pride I felt! But it fell immediately as I continued to read: "In its present form I could not suggest any publication that would use it. You will have to do it all over using specific rules of story writing. I hope this does not hurt your feelings. I could write you a glib letter telling you how swell your stuff is, but that wouldn't help."

I did appreciate his candid criticism. I wasn't a bit surprised by what he wrote about doing it over. However, Thornton Wilder and I have never gotten around to it yet.

It was a wonderful balm for my spirit to be told I could gather good firewood, even if I couldn't burn it in my fireplace because it didn't have a proper draft.

Meanwhile, the State Historical Society of Columbia and the Missouri Historical Society of St. Louis published some articles which I had prepared and given at their meetings. Of course, they pay nothing to ward off starvation, much less for riotous living. But as one editor assured me, "It is my experience that the satisfaction of seeing one's name in print, fringe benefits and other compensations outreach monetary reward." After my experience with Mr. Kirschten, I never questioned the truth of it.

However, upon occasions when checks have come for something I have written they are so delightfully tangible.

About this time, the Missouri Writers Guild had a fall meeting in Boonville near my home, because I think it was the home of their president, Ellston Melton. A speaker for one of their sessions failed to appear and Mr. Melton asked me to pinch-hit for him with a talk I had just given for the Historical Society. I did so and attended the additional sessions. They were such pleasant people I wished to join them.

In due time, I filled in an application with a puny list of publications . . . and was advised to send one more ("Surely you have one more," they wrote). As you well know, nothing for which only fringe benefits have been paid is acceptable. They were so kind they said if I didn't have a third something to send, they would hold a special board meeting to consider my membership.

I was accepted after a period of suspense and have enjoyed being a member ever since.

By now you should have insight as to my many sources of ideas for a column. In regard to how I started writing it, I must say it was by chance. The *Cooper County Record* is published in Boonville weekly by Ellston Melton, a member of our Guild. For many years, his wife, Opal, wrote a delightful column laced with subtle wit, under the heading, "My Say." One week she casually mentioned the expression "filling the pulpit." It reminded me of an unused story in my files which I had written about myself when, as a youth, I had heard our preacher announce: "Next Sunday, Bro. Marvin will fill the pulpit." I mailed it to Opal Melton, thinking it might be of timely interest. Since it is my first column, I would like to read it:

> "Since my earliest years, announcements of church services have intrigued me. When I first heard a preacher would

"fill the pulpit next Sunday," childish curiosity really turned on. I wondered what he would fill it with and went to see.

"I well remember my disappointment when the pulpit was as empty when he pronounced the benediction as it had been when he announced the first song. My mother explained all preachers, through the grace of God, try to fill the pulpit with a spiritual something which is invisible. Through the years I have seen many who came to New Franklin and labored hard to do it.

"Some, young and vigorous, had new shovels provided by divinity schools. Some middle-aged had well-worn scoops. A few old ones had little but calloused hands.

"But none could accomplish it without the help of the congregation, help for which he was always begging. Help which some were reluctant to give because they had paid him to do this work and expected him to do it all by himself.

"When called upon, the women were right handy with spades of prayer, but only a few men would dig with them.

"Every one of the preachers got so discouraged each year about filling the pulpit, he sent for an evangelist reputed to have a drag-line of excellence and personality to help him. But even the two of them couldn't get it done without a lot of local help.

"The church members were exhorted to pray in public as well as private, to go to anyone the audience thought to be in need of soul salvation, to flex their spiritual muscles by responding to many other propositions.

"Those who felt in need of prayer should stand up. Those who felt themselves saved already might raise their hands . . . to restore brotherly love, men should visit their enemies.

"Brother Shook asked one night that all in the choir who wanted to go to Heaven to go down and stand around the pulpit railing. Everybody went but Bella Scruggs, who stood like a lone tree on the prairie.

"The congregation suffered shock. They had known Bella ever since she was born, an only child of indulgent parents. She had had everything she wanted, of course, but that would not be like going to Heaven!

"Generally at the end of a revival the pulpit would seem filled, but after the evangelist with his drag line had been gone a while, sunken places would appear and sooner or later, the problem would have to be tackled anew.

"I was older but no less curious when an evangelist announced he would preach the next night on "It Wasn't Done in a Corner." The church was packed with those who wanted to know what wasn't done in a corner.

"Squire Doolin hoped to goodness it had nothing to do with Battle Axe plug.

"His sermon was based on John 18:20. "I spoke openly to the world, I even taught in the temple where the Jews resort and in secret I have done nothing." His sermon was eloquent but even so, some of the congregation went out feeling a little "let down."

"At a funeral, Rev. J.A. Snarr chose for the spiritual reading the story of the death and raising of Lazarus. He always read with an inherent flair for the dramatic and stressed, "Lord, by this time he stinketh for he hath been dead four days."

"Completely carried away by his presentation of the story, some of the audience were thinking it really had been four days since Mrs. Bud Grabitt had died, when it fact it had only been two. Squire Doolin stopped short of reaching for his nose with thumb and forefinger, while others sniffed and were brought back to reality by the fragrance of the flowers on the casket."

I was surprised and pleased to receive a note from Melton, the editor, advising me, "The enclosed pittance is a mere gesture of appreciation for 'Filling the Pulpit,' which we plan to run this week in Opal's space. We hope you will not object to our using it or be offended by the small pay. It is my experience and observation that the satisfaction of publication and fringe benefits outweigh monetary rewards. We would welcome frequent contributions from you. It would give variety and change."

For a while I was "Guest Columnist" until Opal, wishing to be relieved of the responsibility, turned the column over to me. It was Ellston and Opal Melton who planted the idea of me doing a column and helped it to grow.

Two years later, Mr. Melton suffered an illness which necessitated changes in the format of his paper and the method of publishing it. The use of my column was curtailed. It was at this point that Wally Lage of the *Boonville Daily News* invited me to do a column for his paper, writing, "I have enjoyed them. Please begin as soon as possible and send as often as possible. I'll run them as often as I get them, but I want to be sure we don't alienate Mr. Melton. At the end of the month you will receive a check." (We didn't alienate Mr. Melton.)

As far as the "ups and downs" of writing the column (as mentioned on the program) there are many "ups" but no "downs" worthy of mention, but I try to keep it as natural as possible.

My column "goes to press" each Monday on the editorial page with the heading, "Lilburn Says," along with a picture of me, sometimes a different one each week (fringe benefit). I was pleased with the one which appeared last week. It looked more like Rock Hudson than any used before!

The monetary rewards, the checks, for writing the column are tingly tangible, though they don't ward off starvation or send me reeling into riotous living. But they are not to be despised. On the other hand, the fringe benefits feed my spirit and make it fat.

Human nature being the same always, almost daily I read something in the papers which reminds me of a story filed away in my vault (my office was once a bank) which looks like a pack rat's nest.

You must agree with me that I had no "ups and downs" getting the column in the papers. But preparing the column is something else. The original draft of the idea is no chore, but revising it, making phrases concise and choosing words which convey the exact meaning I wish to express is difficult for me. Which brings to mind especially the use of the word which carries one's thought.

Last year in a contest among the daily newspapers in Missouri, judged by members of the Oklahoma Press Association, the *Boonville Daily News* won seventeen out of twenty-some honors. Perhaps you can imagine my pride when I learned that my column had been mentioned honorably. But there was a notation which mentioned two of my columns specifically, one as a "knee slapper," and further comment, "The key to his writing is the fact that he tells it all and does so in a low-key literary style."

I wrote to some friends who had gone to the Journalism School and the former editor of a magazine and asked how I should react to the statement that I write with a low-key style.

One wrote that it must be just a sneaky term that has crept into use, she had never heard it when she was in school, but she had heard it at a church meeting when someone announced, "Let's keep it low-key."

Another said, "I would assume that 'low-key literary style' must mean you don't go in for elaborate stylistic tricks, artificial forms or bombast. Perhaps they mean 'he tells it like it is, man, he tells it like it is.'"

I enjoy all kinds of people - excluding no one. I don't feel important - I just enjoy the fringe benefits that come with being a columnist. I wondered if I would ever have enough benefits to make a fringe for my literary shawl. As time passed, I found benefits of various sorts, and together they fringed quite well on my shawl.

Not along ago I failed to get copy to the *Daily News* office for a column in a Monday edition. I think it had never happened before. Later in the week, when I visited a lady in the hospital, I was greeted with, "What's the matter with you? You didn't have a column in the paper!" The pleasure of knowing someone missed it was immeasurable, greater than my regret at having been delinquent.

Fathering a child column born every Monday on the editorial page, ushered into the world by Dr. Daily News, is fringeful, an honor duly cherished. What a fringe benefit!

Being told by Sallie Strithum and Wanda Clickfast and others, "I enjoy your columns and cut them out for a scrapbook for my grandchild" warms me like coming into a warm room during our energy crisis.

It is intriguing when someone I have never seen before greets me with "How are you, Mr. Kingsbury?" Or a clerk in a store equally strange to me asks: "What can I do for you today, Mr. Kingsbury?"

Sometimes there is a chance for me to apologize for my non-recognition. It is good to be absolved when told, "Oh, we have never met, but I read your column and see your picture in the paper."

It makes fringe when Johnny Wiggleberg crushes my hand in greeting and says, "O boy, (imagine being called that), did I get a kick out of reading your column last Monday!"

Imagine Biddie Lustrop calling to say she had just read my column in which I wondered if there was anything new under the sun except pantyhose maybe, and warning me not to go too heavy on research to find out.

And an old Boonville girl, Elizabeth Carey of Smithton, wrote a letter to the *Daily News* and added a postscript: "I do enjoy Kingsbury." That was a bright spot in the fringe. Sadie Crakwell, in a reckless mood, inquired, "Why don't you publish the best columns in a book?" And Kittie Bushwhack and Tommie Creature, more reckless still, said some of them are as good as things in the *Readers' Digest*.

So the editor was right about my "fringe benefits and other compensations" outweighing the monetary reward.

But the weight of the fringe on my literary shawl will never throw me off balance. It gets trimmed sufficiently. Threatena Woodscare anonymously called to warn me, "If you don't quit writing about our people, you are going to be blown up."

I was in a Boonville store where I was not acquainted with

the clerk who waited on me. I didn't think he knew me. Wishing to pay for my purchase by check and feeling the need of establishing my credit, I asked him, "Do you ever see 'Lilburn Says' in the *Boonville Daily News?*"

"Yes," he replied forthrightly, "but I don't read it."

Lilburn wrote more than seven hundred columns between 1968, when he was 84 years old, and his death in 1983.

The letters, articles and texts of talks he gave provided abundant fodder for him to masticate into columns which often titillated his readers. Some of these have been included in previous sections because of their relevance to topics dealt with. Here we have reproduced a selection of columns reflecting Lilburn's deep interest in the history and culture of the Boonslick Country and insight into the eccentricities and activities of its people.

Lilburn drew from many sources for his column. Some were triggered by items he came upon when reading long ago paper files. Others came from stories he remembered hearing, and some stemmed from personal experiences. The following column is a blend of those three.

I FELL FOR IT

Ninety years ago, according to the *Boonville Advance*, the Boonville Council of the State Barbers' Association completed arrangements for entertainment of the delegates who will attend the annual convention in this city Monday and Tuesday, January 17 and 18, 1884.

The manager of the Opera House has offered the use of the house free of rent. Our citizens have subscribed freely to defray the expense of entertaining their guests. There will be about 200 barbers from over the state in attendance.

. . . Jackson Monroe, undertaker, gives special attention to preparation of remains for transportation. Customers from Howard County will have all ferriage charges paid and goods delivered on ferry boat if preferred.

. . . And there was a large sign over one business house on Main Street, viz: A.M. Koontz' Cheap Store.

In 1942, the late Judge Roy Williams of Boonville talked of "Early Days in the History of Boonville" to the local Historical Society, and related an interesting story of Jacob Wyan, an early merchant. The Judge quotes Mr. Whitlow (presumably Mr. R.W.) as saying it was a large frame building painted green with a gallery all around it. But there was something more interesting than Jacob Wyan's general merchandising, Judge Williams related.

"There were three chums in Virginia (from whence Jacob Wyan had migrated) named Jennie, Mary and Nancy. Wyan, after making his start in Boonville, went back to Virginia and married Jennie; they had a daughter and she named the daughter after her chum, Nancy. Jennie died. Mr. Wyan went back and married Nancy. They had a daughter and named her Mary. Nancy died and Mr. Ryan went back and married Mary. They had a daughter and named her Jennie. He was a master at keeping his stock renewed."

. . . Another good story in which a woman was involved was told by the Judge:

"In 1838, the first warlike preparations were made as the Mormons had encamped in our beautiful state. Three companies were organized in Boonville, a member of which was my grandfather, and tradition in the family has it he did not want to fight the Mormons as he had nothing against them, but my grandmother said, 'It is all right to kill any man who has more than one wife, and Marcus you must go.' Marcus went. The Mormons surrendered, however, and the soldiers returned."

The *Boonville Daily News* has some of the finest reporters in the state gathering news from all over the counties. Yet, something can happen on their very front door step, practically "under their noses" and they might not know of it.

On the 23rd, High Street was parked solid with motor vehicles. I double-parked my car with the motor running and hurried in hastily to deliver a package. In like haste, I departed, missed a step on the "stoop" and fell sprawling on my right shoulder on the concrete sidewalk.

An inventory indicated no broken bones. I could use my right arm below the elbow and lift the right upper arm with my left! I didn't see a soul (witness) except the driver of a school bus who had pulled up behind my car and stopped. I didn't see him as I carried my shattered hulk to my car, loaded it and drove home.

After a week of hospitalization at home, a kind letter arrived which fixed my resolve to build another column. The letter:

Dear Mr. Kingsbury: Too often I've missed telling someone I'm pleased with them - or love them - or admire them - or miss them, and although we are strangers, I don't want to miss telling you how much I enjoy your column each Monday. Thank you for writing it. Sincerely, Sallie Saidit. (Not her real name.)

Sallie, my appreciation shall never allow me to think of you as a stranger.

JOURNALISM SCHOOL GUINEA PIG

By 1974, Lilburn had developed such a reputation as a historian, genealogist, collector and interesting personality that he had been extensively interviewed and written about. He had become a prime target for students in the University of Missouri's Journalism School featuring-writing classes. He writes about all this in the column reproduced below.

Instructors at the Missouri University Journalism School assign special work to some of their students to test their progress.

A collector friend of mine told me of one young woman who was directed to call at her home, gain an interview, take pictures inside and then write a story about her personality. It was to be based on furnishings and their arrangement in the house.

My friend said, "I'm afraid it didn't go so well. The young lady didn't seem to share my enthusiasm about old things, my flower decorated copper wash boiler to hold magazines for instance, my stained maple syrup bucket which contained my knitting. Not to mention my coal hod emblazoned with the colorful head of a Landsdown sheep, a sort of trademark in my family.

"However, tea and toast seemed natural to her though I do not think she had the least interest in the rarity or the aesthetic value of my tea leaf china on which it was served.

"As for personality, I think she concluded mine was mixed from rearing a large family during my earlier years and going overboard about antiques in my later ones.

"She took many pictures but I permitted none of me. I heard her instructor spurned all of them but one. He criticized it, saying it was 'too busy' (too many things in it without a central figure, me!)"

During the last three years I have had many journalism students wanting to experiment with me. Each asked for an appointment for an interview and taking pictures. Each assured me that through cooperation I might enable him to produce a story which would stimulate his instructor to give him a higher grade.

I had wondered the first two years why I was chosen as their victim. By the third year, I had concluded it was due to my prestige which comes unsought and without effort to everyone "who lives to a ripe old age."

Mark von Wehrden, the affable young man who asked me to help him in 1973, got exactly what he wanted. Confidently, he had drawn his own plan, inches by inches, for a full-page story in the *Columbia Missourian*. If accepted as he anticipated, it would prove his proficiency in this special line of work and keep his grade up to its usual A status.

Mark was a hunter who needed no bird dog to flush up a covey of facts in an interview or to point telling camera shots. He hunted in my office, on my home premises, and during a Sunday service at my church. When he heard I was headed for Al and Bettie Crow's home in Boonville to be a host at their part of the Celebration of the Festival of Leaves, the young man begged to go with me.

Everywhere he had asked me to forget he was around. This seemed difficult at the time. I didn't realize how well I had complied with his request until I saw the 35 pictures of me, practically all of them shot from ambush.

Robert Burns wrote:

O wud some power that giftie gie us
To see ourselves as others see us!
It wad frae monie a blunder
frae us and foolish notion.

In the quarter page "close-up" of me "in repose" in the *Columbia Missourian*, the tip of my tongue is peeping out from between my lips. Have others always seen me like this? In a series of three pictures taken at Betty Crow's home, first, I am meeting an attractive woman, our faces serious; second, more serious and her upper arm is tight in my grasp; third, she has escaped and our faces register delight.

Maybe, and I hope, seeing myself as others see me will "frae monie a blunder and foolish notion" frae me.

Promiscuous Roller Skaters

In this age of permissiveness it is laughable that a skating rink would have caused a rash of pimples of displeasure on the spiritual face of some good old Methodists of New Franklin. But it did, in 1912.

Kincaid and Sprinkle had been licensed to set up a skating rink on vacant lots on the south side of the business block, in a large tent. From its opening, it attracted good crowds, young, middle-aged and numerous elderly. Beginners afforded onlookers seated around the sides of the rink much amusement when their feet slipped out from under them. The town was hungry for such sport.

Mrs. Flossie Fluke, director of the Methodist choir, has been a devotee of roller-skating in her teens. She was among the first patrons and after a little practice found she could still do the fancy skating didoes of her youth.

It all seemed very worldly to some of the Methodists. There was much talk about it. The wife of our minister dropped into the rink one night to see if what she had heard about the place was true. Her visit was short. On her way home, she stopped to tell Mrs. Burr, a Methodist woman who worshipped from afar, about it. Every ounce of Mrs. Burr's overweight was shocked.

The next day our minister felt impelled to tell Mrs. Fluke that his wife cried all night after seeing her "skating promiscuously with all those men." And to leave a deeper impression, he added, "Mrs. Burr thinks it is just as bad as dancing, holding hands as you do."

At the Wednesday night prayer meeting our minister brought up the matter of the rink and asked for free expression of opinions. The majority kept silent, but one brother present spoke from his heart. "There are three things I must contend with in this town, the pool room, the skating rink, and the dance hall where they are doing that awful turkey trot. The girls raise their skirts until their stockings show."

To improve the spiritual complexion of her critics, Flossie Fluke gave up skating but was present regularly sitting on the onlookers bench, sometimes with tears in her eyes. Buck Dempsey would dance by and entice her. "Come on in, the fallin's fine." When the good Methodist girl, Miss Sallie Hoan, heard this she remarked, "Of course, he meant falling from grace."

A Three-generation Household Goods Sale

This is a story I recorded about a household goods sale held about twenty-five years ago:

It was a cold morning for a sale. A sharp wind got right under one's clothes and laid a chilly hand on his backbone if he had not dressed against such an invasion. Hundreds of foresighted people had come prepared to stand out in the weather for hours. This was an auction of household possessions accumulated by three Elliott family generations.

The goods for sale were displayed in a row which circled the big house. The house itself was empty except the big sitting room. It had been left intact with a hot log fire in the fireplace so that guests might come inside for warmth. Chairs and other furnishings including a Seth Thomas clock marking time on its shelf, would be moved out and sold last. Thus the traditional hospitality of the family would be extended to the very end.

Outside the crowd milled around before the sale began. Many were visiting as at a homecoming. But most of them were inspecting things of especial interest. One woman was hovering over a brass hanging lamp with clear glass prisms. She confided to her friend, "I'm going to buy this if it doesn't go over $7. My husband gave me the money for a birthday present and I want to put it in something I can always keep."

An expression of a "Gone with the Wind" lamp, its bowl and global shade splashed with red roses, conflicted with the opinion of another plain-spoken woman who declared, "I wouldn't have the gaudy thing in my house. But I don't doubt it will bring several dollars." A third woman put it, "Several dollars your foot! They've got a standing bid of $40 put on it."

Men passing along the line experimented with everything with a movable part. They opened and shut the door of the bird cage, turned the wheel of the cherry seeder, and worked the old hand corn planter. The women thumped glass bowls and goblets and listened for tones to establish age and quality. They examined silverware for hallmarks. They lifted and replaced the lid on every covered glass and china bowl.

Someone asked a lady who stayed in the sitting room if she were not interested in buying anything? She replied she wanted nothing but the Seth Thomas clock which would be sold last. She was just waiting where she was comfortable. No matter what was bid against her, she was going to have that clock.

The sale was halted while someone whispered in the auctioneer's ear that one of the ladies feeling chilled had gone into the sitting room, collapsed and died.

The auctioneer removed his hat, announced the unfortunate happening in his saddest tone and said, "Let's have a moment of silent prayer out of respect for this good woman." And with almost his next breath, his hat back on his head, he cried, "How much am I offered for this elegant 'Gone with the Wind Lamp'?" It blew the price ceiling at $45. The light in the face of the woman who hoped to get the brass hanging lamp for $7 went out long before it was knocked off to another bidder for six times as much.

The patient woman in the sitting room got the Seth Thomas clock she was determined to buy. The sale was over by late afternoon. Before sundown every article of household goods which had encircled the house had vanished; the yard was as clean as if it had been swept with a broom.

Except for grass in the yard, flattened by human feet, one would not have suspected it had been the scene of feverish auction activity all day long. And if there had been curtains at the windows and smoke coming out of the chimneys, one not knowing better might have run in again to sit a while with Charlie Elliott, the last of the three generations who had lived there.

SOME NURSING HOME FRIENDS

Two or three years ago I was in the hospital able to walk in the halls. A nurse told me of a patient down the hall who had asked her to tell me he would like me to come and see him, that he had known of me for a long time and he wanted to meet me. When she told me his name, I realized it was a gentleman clock collector whom I had planned for some time to go and see.

Upon sight I instinctively liked him. We had a pleasant visit. I left his room with the intention of furthering our friendship. A couple of days later I went back. He was gone. I could learn nothing from the nurses except he had been moved and they did not know why or where.

Last fall, after another stay in the hospital, I stopped at a convalescent home for five weeks. I soon learned my erstwhile acquaintance was there, helpless, with his wife pushing him through the halls in a wheelchair. I was told he could hear conversation but was unable to respond to it in any manner. His eyes were like windows with the shades drawn.

One day his wife asked me if I would like to come in their room to see him. He was in his chair. As I sat down by him, I grasped his hand as if greeting and continued to hold it while relating the meeting I had had with him in the hospital and liking him so much.

For a moment, like light flicking on when you open the door of your refrigerator, recognition registered in his eyes and he squeezed my hand until it hurt. Then he was gone again. It was the most moving moment I had ever experienced.

Recently, I read what a gentleman wrote of nursing homes. "A nursing home is a community of men and women with memories and experiences they treasure, people who were once a part of the neighborhoods and churches the rest of us inherited. In short, people are like the rest of us except they are older than most of us and living through complications that very probably await you and me."

This is a very good view of the patients of a nursing home and one I had entertained as a visitor. I think one can never appreciate, until he becomes a resident himself of a nursing home, the personnel who make things move like clockwork. From administrator down to the newest recruit, they were the most attentive, kind, loving group of people I have ever known.

One of the oldest ladies used to sail into the dining room unaided, as straight as a flagpole, every curl of her hair in place and in a different dress every day. She reminded me as she glided to her table and sat down of a ship sailing in and docking at the wharf. We became friends.

She walked the halls for exercise and sometimes finding an empty chair would sit down to rest. One day I found her thus and I rolled my chair up by hers tete-a-tete fashion for a talk. She spoke fluently of the days when she lived in the country before disabilities had forced her into the home. This occasion was on Sunday before the election. She said:

"When one loses her sight until she can't see the food on her plate, can't hear well, and has her troubles as I do, I think it would be a blessing if I could pass on. And I am ready to go any time." After a pause, she continued, "But I do hope I'll live until after election day to hear that Ronald Reagan is elected President."

LIFE BEGAN AT FORTY

As far as pressed, blown and cut glass are concerned, life for me began at forty. Of course I knew something about glass, of glass panes in the windows of our houses. I knew I had eaten ice cream out of glass dishes of beautiful colors at Aunt Fannie's. But I didn't know the difference between a tumbler and a goblet in water glasses. I knew a little about cut glass. Once I was commissioned to pick up a cut glass vase at Gemelich and Schmidt's store in Boonville and bring it back to New Franklin on a train. It was a present for one of our teachers. Between the store and the depot, my feet slipped from under me and the vase went to pieces in the fall. To this day if anyone asks me where the Christian Church is in Boonville, my first thought is to reply, "On the corner where I broke the cut glass vase."

But I learned a lot about glass one day when I went with a knowledgeable friend to an auction in Columbia. It was held in the back yard of a private home, people crowded the lawn. My attention was attracted to a prosperous looking prominent social matron who held the spotlight as she seated herself in one of the chairs to be auctioned, near the table on which many articles were contained. She asked someone to put a hassock under her feet and thus esconced she was ready to meet the best bidders of the day.

Bidding was brisk and things brought prices which astonished me. Each time an article from the table was offered, the pompous matron commanded the auctioneer, "Let ME see it." She ran her fingers around the top and base, looked at it intently and rubbed the bottom of it before she handed it back so the auction might proceed.

To my friend I said, "What is that old junk they are selling?"

"Pressed glass," he replied. Conversation ensued between us.

"Who pressed it?"

"A lot of factories made it years and years ago, some of it is very old."

"What do people want with it?"

"Antique collectors use it with their old furniture. They feel if adds atmosphere to their houses."

"Why does the pompous lady rub each piece like Aladdin used to rub his lamp?"

"She feels it to see if it is proof."

"What's proof?"

"A piece of glass is said to be proof if it has no chips or cracks, is in perfect condition. And she feels the bottom of it to see if it has a pontil."

"Heaven's sake, what is a pontil?"

"The pontil is a rough place on the bottom, all the old blown glass had them."

"Why does she look at it so closely?"

"To see if it is three mold. Three mold is much more desirable than two or four."

"Well I wouldn't give a nickel for any of it."

"Let's see if we can go into the house, she may have a lot more glass inside," said my friend, tired no doubt of answering my questions.

We walked into a room in which glass things in many colors were displayed, red, blue, lavender, purple, white, green and yellow. I was delighted to see it. "Plenty of atmosphere here," remarked my friend.

I was really "taken in" by one bowl with bumps that looked like warts on it and remarked, "I wish I had this bowl, I am going to buy it if I can. Where do you suppose all this stuff comes from?"

"Mrs. Reeker goes all over the country looking into peoples' attics and cellars. They are tired of it and she is able to buy it for practically nothing. Some of it, they give her the stuff just to get it out of the way. That bowl you want probably didn't cost her a quarter."

I learned that once around the turn of the century a grocer had given my mother a berry set, a purple bowl with six sauce dishes, a sugar and a creamer. It was purple with gold trimming and is today called the Croesus pattern. The set now retails for $194.50. She became tired of it and when somebody indicated she would like to have it, it was given away. Goodbye atmosphere!!!

A Fine Old Hen

One of the most gracious collectors I have seen recently is a woman in her eighties, as spry as a cricket. She goes to the newspaper office every workday. She boasts of 1800 pitchers in her collection. She also has a collection of hooked rugs of her own making. And, in what she called her "hen-house," she had glass and china chickens of all sorts. She told me when she acquired the hen, which was her favorite, she had to choose between a new dress and the chicken. She sacrificed the dress. "Mr. Kingsbury, she said, "I have never regretted my decision." When one leaves, the strongest impression is of her gracious personality - of what a fine old hen she is - rather than of pitchers and rugs.

Santa Passed Me Up

Christmas trees are such an inseparable part of our Yuletide celebrations we can hardly believe they were ever unknown in this country.

A German immigrant who had come to this country in 1824 trimmed the first tree of which we have record. He was Charles Felton, a political refugee who was the first professor of German literature at Harvard University. He married Ellen Lee Cabot of the famous Cabot family of Boston. They had one son, Charles Christopher, born in 1830 and two years later the first Christmas tree was trimmed for him in the Felton home.

According to Ellen Cabot Felton's memoirs of her husband published in 1844, "Every Christmas since Charles was two years old, his father dressed a Christmas tree for him after the fashion of his own country. This was always the happiest day of the year for him. He spared no pains, no time in adorning the fine spruce tree and making it as beautiful as possible.

The memory of the first Christmas tree impressed upon my mind was a beautiful one at Clark's Chapel in 1890. Both of my parents were born, reared and married near that church and were members as were their children. After their marriage they moved to the home where I now live, 1 1/2 miles north of New Franklin. But their church membership remained at Clark's Chapel until 1890 when Rev. J. Marshall Dempsey, a popular evangelist influenced them to become members of the church at New Franklin. Although we as a family attended services at Clark's Chapel every time there were none in New Franklin, our names of course were no longer on the membership roll.

We went to the Christmas exercises at Clark's Chapel. They were good but naturally I was impatient for the time when the Christmas treats would be distributed by Santa Claus. I thought he would never get around to finding a treat for me. And since I was no longer one of Clark's Chapel children, a fact unfortunately I didn't realize, he never did. Nothing ever "came upon a midnight clear" louder than my weeping and wailing which accompanied Santa Claus' "Merry Christmas and Happy New Year" as he retreated down the aisle.

Never since then have I suffered a greater emotional crisis. I have never forgotten Cousin Mamie Smith, the young woman who sacrificed her sack of candy to shut up my protesting mouth. Long ago she moved to the place where it is said good people wear crowns with stars on them. There must be an extra bright one in hers for being kind to a squalling brat on Christmas Eve.

Chapter Twenty-One

FROM A COLUMNIST'S SCRAPBOOK

This column in the Cooper County Record *Annual Frontier Issue of 1972 shows the excellence of Lilburn's memory and the sharpness of his observations. Such boyhood trips instilled in him a life-long interest in Boonville and its people.*

INNOCENTS ABROAD

A trip from my home to Boonville, a rare occurrence when I was a boy, left indelible impressions on my mind.

South of New Franklin I was curious about rough spots in the dirt road. My father said they were outcroppings of old logs which supported a plank road built with proceeds from the Franklin Lottery, chartered in 1833.

To reach the ferry we had to pass the Kinney mansion. I was curious about it as I had been told Captain Kinney had built, wonder of wonders, a fish pond in the attic. I felt uneasy, too, having heard it was haunted and restless spirits walked its spacious halls.

From the moment it came into view until we had passed it I never took my eyes off this great blue-gray house with rows of fig trees growing in tubs which bordered its brick walks.

Once past it, I had a feeling of relief at not having seen a spirit, mixed with disappointment at not having seen a living soul.

From there the ride toward the river was exciting because there was always a chance of missing the boat. We knew it left the Howard County side on the half hour.

To a country boy, anticipating arrival in the city, it was like having the doors of Heaven shut in his face. Delay would shorten his time for enjoying the "ivory palaces" of Boonville.

I was always elated when we arrived just in time to be the last one on. There was nothing more satisfying than driving off ahead of everybody else as soon as the gangboard was down.

I recall two business establishments in Boonville. One of them was Mr. Dan Wooldridge's drug store where my parents bought such things as quinine, Hotetter's Bitters, penetrating oil, antikamnia and extracts of lemon and vanilla.

On one side he had a combination of museum and zoo. I have no recollection of ever seeing the other side where he must have had his stock of goods. I would beg my parents to leave me there while they shopped elsewhere.

In a glass-walled tank there was a live alligator about three feet long. The sight of it called to mind a horrible picture I had seen of an immense one with wide-open jaws crawling stealthily toward a woman completely unaware of her danger.

Since I was perfectly safe, I enjoyed looking at and being so close to this one. At the side of the tank was a sign, "Don't Devil The Alligator." Mr. Dan could pick it up, hold it in his arms and talk to it. It never opened its jaws an inch. When he had put it back in the tank and gone to wait on a customer, one of two men who had been watching, talking low, said, "Dan handles the alligator better than he does things at home."

There was a raccoon, the first I had ever seen in captivity, a squirrel, a rabbit, some frogs and a terrible looking snake. There were coins, arrowheads, some live canaries and a cardinal, some stuffed birds, rattlesnake skins and rattles. All sorts of curious things. I think of it now as Boonville's Smithsonian.

Mr. Dan was tall with a smiling face with reddish whiskers on its cheeks. He wore a black silk skullcap. I knew where he lived—on Main not far from the business houses. It was a house of unusual architecture.

When my father came for me, I would have been loathe to go with him except for knowing we would be headed for the other place I remember so well, Wagner's restaurant. It was the most popular place in town for food.

More than once, over those dishes of ice cream, my parents reminisced that when as children they came over the water to

Boonville, their chief delight was ginger bread at Mrs. Beck's bake shop.

Shoppers' time flew. The chief concern of all late shoppers who stayed as long as possible was to make the last trip of the "Joseph L. Stephens."

The possibility of missing it hung over their heads like the Sword of Damocles as they picked up packages at Wagner's, and buggy whips hung over the tails of their horses.

Captain Porter always seemed concerned to get everybody who had come over back to Howard County. He seemed always to know just who had not shown up. When time for casting off came, he rang the boat bell to urge stragglers within hearing distance to hurry-hurry.

Those already there and impatient, griped at the delay until the latecomer would round the corner.

After standing on the bow of the boat watching it cut through the water, and the ride through the tunnel of willows to the county road, the day's excitement was over.

A BIG DAY IN BOONVILLE – THE HANGING

The two column excerpts that follow describe the last hanging in Boonville. The gallows platform has been preserved and may be seen at the Headquarter grounds of Friends of Historic Boonville - at the old Cooper County Jail.

The quiet, prosey little city was filled with a hurrying, anxious crowd, dense throngs of people congregated to gratify morbid curiosity.

At 10:30 o'clock the sheriff formed his guard in front of the jail, forced the crowd back, and a wagon carrying the wooden coffin was backed up to the jailyard gate. In a few moments, the bailiffs in charge of the prisoner filed slowly out of the jail door, the doomed man guarded by one on each side of him walked erect and with firm step though gloomy countenance. He was placed in the wagon, took a seat on his coffin and slowly the awful and the solemn procession commenced the march to the gallows.

The guards surrounded the wagon and in their rear followed an array of reporters, physicians and others who had the privilege to occupy the area around the gallows which had been encircled by ropes and set apart for them.

In due time the fatal spot was reached. The scaffold was erected in a semicircular valley surrounded by a grass hill, the place being known as the Old Fair Grounds.

The wagon drew up under the gallows, the prisoner alighted and bade farewell to his friends in tears and convulsive hand shaking. The scene was very sad...he ascended the gallows where he was surrounded by ministers, the reporters, the sheriff and his deputies.

He wore a bouquet of flowers hanging on the lapel of his coat which he deliberately unpinned and tied to the railing.

During this time the immense crowd, estimated at 6,000, crowded up as near as permitted by the guards.

The doomed prisoner faced the crowd and spoke (at length). He then said, 'Farewell ladies and gentlemen, I must go. I must die. It is a debt we all have to pay.'

The black cap was here adjusted, the prisoner's arms and legs pinioned. At 11:58 the drop fell and a dull thud seemed to announce that all was over. But to the horror of all present the rope broke and the hooded form fell prone upon the ground. Quietly he was drawn up again and apparently in fourteen minutes respiration ceased and in twenty minutes life was pronounced extinct and the body was cut down.

Thus ended the tragedy of John I. West (convicted of murder) whose trial has for over seven months been progressing in our midst and once more the majesty of the law has been vindicated.

In the July 31, 1934 issue of the *Boonville Daily News* there was an article by Charles van Ravenswaay concerning interviews he had with elderly citizens who remembered April 16, 1879, the day John I. West was hung.

He learned that the prisoner, though convicted and sentenced, hoped until two days before he was hung to be pardoned by the governor. Although he had admitted killing the man, he claimed that he had done it in self-defense. There had been no satisfactory evidence which was conclusive of his guilt otherwise.

Two days before the hanging was scheduled, John I. West made a full confession of the murder for money which yielded him thirty-fivecents. Why?

An old man related that in anticipation of the hanging excitement, a group of men had arranged for an excursion train to be run from Sedalia to Boonville to accommodate those from Pettis County who wished to witness the event. Fearing that the governor might pardon West and ruin their business project, they arranged to slip a gift of whiskey to the prisoner in the jail. And it was while drunk that he made the confession.

Many citizens of Boonville were indignant, mortified that this occasion took on the aspect of a Roman holiday. For instance there was the silent resentment of Miss Amanda Kelly, daughter of Boonslick pioneers, who lived on High Street at the time. She related that as she sat on her front porch disgusted at the continuous stream of people passing her house on their way to the Old Fair Grounds, a very fat woman, dragging a little girl by the hand had stopped to catch her breath at Miss Amanda's gate. Seeing her sitting on her porch, she asked:

"Ain't cha goin' to the hangin'?"

Miss Amanda sniffed and replied, "No, I am not going to the hanging."

"Well I do declare!" continued the visitor, "I thought everybody would be goin' to the hangin'. I know I wooden miss it fer anything. I ain't never seen a man hung an' I wooden want Ruby here to miss it."

Van Ravenswaay concludes:

"It was the last public hanging Boonville ever had."

THESPIANS ARISE TO SAVE HALL

By L.A. Kingsbury
Daily News Columnist

Thespian Hall c. 1868

In connection with the current move to restore Thespian Hall, a
story which was published in the March 9, 1950 issue of the Globe-
Democrat *of St. Louis is of interest. It reveals that this is not the first*
time an effort has been made to "lift the face" of this old building.
The story appears under the headline, "The Silent War in Boonville."

There has been bitter language in Boonville recently. Thespian Hall, the oldest surviving theater west of the Alleghenies, is
the cause of the whole trouble.

The old timers who want the theater left alone, left just the
way the American stage looked, back in the old days, are ready
to oppose the young folks who take further steps to turn the
theater into a museum.

The old folks are proud to live in the historic town where

guns blazed during the Civil War. Thespian Hall, the last frontier theater, was used for quartering troops as several battles were fought just outside its front doors.

In 1937, it looked like the younger folks were going to have their way. It was about the time the Fox Midway Theaters in Kansas City which purchased the old building in 1930, announced plans to replace it with a modern motion picture theater. A public meeting was held and the Thespian Hall Preservation Committee was organized with representatives from nearly every civil and social order in town.

The General Assembly of Missouri appropriated $30,000 for a new modern picture theater but when the old timers kicked up a lot of dust, only $15,000 was left and that was to be used just in case of emergency where the building might be in danger. And so the two-story structure of Greek Revival design with four Doric columns still stands.

Today the theater is called The Lyric. But the old folks still call it Thespian Hall. At least the name Thespian Hall has a more significant attachment.

Back in 1838, the Boonville Thespian Society was organized by sixty professional men. These gentlemen of wealth had been attracted to Boonville from Virginia, the Carolinas, Kentucky, and Tennessee by the thriving trade with the west and southwest. Their acquaintance with singers and actors in St. Louis, New Orleans, Philadelphia and New York stimulated their latest interest in theatrical productions and led to the organization of the all-male dramatic society. Boonville was literature conscious. Editions of Shakespeare and Johnson were common in most homes. Eighteenth and 19th century plays were read throughout the town.

But, many Boonville ladies and gentlemen were not kindly disposed toward the bunch who were inconsistent in their practices. While most of them were substantial church members, they did a lot of things on Sunday, such as attending the circus, dancing or trading with the steamboats. They were no longer wanted in the houses of worship. So when they formed their theater group, they had strikes against them. 'Play actors' were considered immoral and theaters were 'homes of the devil.'

But the theater went up anyway. It cost the members $16,000, and on July 3, 1857, the new building was finished. In the ceremony which launched the theater, the mayor addressed the assemblage as follows:

"This monument will stand for the liberality and good taste of our citizens. The building of the hall . . . vindicates our public spirit and generosity . . . it proclaims a sentiment worthy of the enlightened age in which we live. . . ." When the building was completed the State Legislature voted the property tax exempt.

"When the war came, the Thespian Society was destroyed. The different loyalties of the members ripped it apart.

As early as 1898, there was talk of removing the historic building. The theater was dingy after so many years of usage. Audiences complained that the chairs were uncomfortable and the building was 'out-of-date.' But here and there were heard the laments of those who remembered the earlier years of glory. A writer in a local paper wrote: "It has been the scene of innumerable shows, many festivities and much oratory. During the war, it was occupied sometimes as a barracks, sometimes as a hospital for sick and wounded soldiers."

Several years later, the building was saved from destruction and the interior was brought up to date. Thespian Hall, with its Society dissolved, was rechristened "The Stephens Opera House"!

The new Opera House was the stage for many famous Shakespeare plays, heavy and light operas. Gentleman Jim Corbett and his minstrel troupe appeared here. Its opening had been a gala affair with the women of town and out-of-town arrayed in silks, satins and diamonds, the men in evening dress, arriving in closed carriages which scurried from one address to another trying to get everyone there on time. The new Opera House was converted into a motion picture house in 1940.

Today, there is no such argument as wanting to tear down the old building. But there are opposing factions in the town. The old timers who fifty years ago were young folk, who wanted a new theater, now are fighting to keep the almost century-old theater. The younger set wants to see a museum established.

"The Fox Midwest Theaters who purchased it want to make a historical monument out of it. They have made the proposal on the condition that the theater will become public property through state or federal purchase on acquisition by a historical society.

"The company wants permission to use it as a setting for a summer season of plays and light opera, a form of revival which has been successful in many middle-sized towns of historical note."

Thespian Hall has been restored by Friends of Historic Boonville. They conduct programs there which attract many visitors.

Thespian Hall today

What to do with dem Bones

An early incident in the Clark's Chapel community's history is told in this column.

Silas Bushnell was not related by blood or marriage to any of the Clark's Chapel clan, but his family fit into the community like a stave into a barrel. Silas was fifteen years older than Lida, his second wife, but they were a congenial couple. Of course there were occasional rifts. Once when bustles were in style, Lida bought herself one of the largest.

Silas was not opposed to bustles but his wife was a dumpy woman and he considered Nature had endowed her amply. He asked her to take back the big fine bustle and exchange it for a smaller one. Lida forbore tears and wore what she considered an insignificant little dab with wounded pride. She felt downright conspicuous among the big-bustled women of Clark's Chapel.

This was bad enough, but a more serious problem arose of which the neighbors were unaware. One night Silas awoke and finding Lida awake, confided to her he had something special to tell her. He said for a long time he had cherished the desire to bring the remains of Maria, his first wife, to Howard County for interment. Maria had died of childbirth among strangers in Kentucky on their pilgrimage to Missouri. He felt saddened whenever he thought of her being way down there with no one ever going to her grave to put a flower on it.

Lida was shocked speechless. For twenty years, she had thought she was the sole mistress of his heart and now he was asking her to make room for another. She drew her warm feet away from his. Long after deep breathing told her Silas was asleep, she pondered the matter. Silas did not mention it again for several days and then finally asked Lida how she felt about it. She refrained expressing her real feelings and told him to go right ahead. In due time all that was mortal of Maria arrived in a plain pine box. Silas was in a quandary. How should he dispose of it?

Lida too was not unmindful of the explanations she would be obliged to make at the church mite parties and sewing circle.

So when Silas, upset by the dilemma, suggested the box should be stored in the attic for awhile, she readily agreed.

Silas carried the box upstairs and put it in a dark corner behind an old trunk. He was unaware that Cassie, his oldest child, saw him. At least for now his mind was at rest, knowing Maria's remains were safe under his own roof and devoted Lida was at his side.

He was a busy man. The months rolled by into a year and Silas all but forgot the box.

One rainy day, Lida heard an unusual commotion in the attic where she had sent the children to play, as the weather was bad outside. She mounted the stairs two flights up to quell the disturbance. Quietly she opened the attic door and there, to her astonishment, she saw her oldest child Cassie, dressed in an old oversized green velvet dress which she herself had in her trousseau and that had been packed away in the old trunk for many years. She sat on an improvised throne, playing queen. Her curls were caught up with a beautiful silver comb for which Lida was unable to account for, until she saw a neat bone in Cassie's hand which she was using as a scepter. Each of the younger boys, subjects who must have decided the queen was ruling them with an iron hand, showed their resentment by threatening, each with a bone in his hand, to pull her off the throne.

"Oh, no," groaned Lida inwardly as she realized the children had found the box of Maria's remains. Unseen, she closed the door and retreated silently. When Silas came in from work, Lida lost no time in reporting the shocking scene witnessed in the attic. She declared emphatically that the time had come to bury Maria's bones. He agreed and assured her he would make arrangements the next day.

The next day, something occurred which in the end brought a solution to his problem. His Uncle Thomas who lived with them stumbled on the porch steps, fell, and broke a hip. The family was greatly distressed and did everything possible to promote a recovery but in spite of their concern, the old gentleman died.

He was buried in the family lot in Walnut Grove Cemetery in Boonville. While he lay in state, Silas was inspired by an idea which would help him in putting Maria's remains to rest.

After the funeral service when Uncle Thomas' coffin was lowered into the grave, a plain box was put on top of it before the grave was filled. Silas did not expect this would go unnoticed by some, especially Miss Tutie Whittle, whose keen eye could see the wink of a fly and delight in telling it. Sure enough, she sought out Silas and Lida before they left the ceremony to extend her sympathy. Then inquired, "What was in the pine box?" Silas and Lida replied without batting an eye, "Just some of Uncle Tommie's keepsakes."

Today the greensward is smooth above him and nothing marks the spot where old Uncle Thomas and young Maria await the resurrection.

THE CHURCH'S EVOLUTION

This column concerns phases of evolution witnessed by me in the life of the Methodist Church of New Franklin during the last sixty years. It does not seem that long since the new, past, and present church was built and dedicated. At that time there were several pairs of parents who brought their children to Sunday School and stayed for the following church service.

Today there are some families who follow the old custom of accompanying their children. Others bring their young to Sunday School and return to pick them up when it is over. They do not often appear in church. In general, Sunday School languishes. Aside from the primary department there is only one class, that of mature women.

There was an evolution in which women's hats disappeared. The first woman who entered the sanctuary bareheaded created quite a sensation. She was viewed by many with distrust. Never before had she shown the least sign of being a hussy. But it wasn't long until someone else followed her example, then others until one wondered if the practice would become general.

Another evolution began with the appearance of the first woman in church wearing pants. Such dress had created a good deal of critical attention on the streets. Nobody dreamed a woman would appear in church without her skirt.

The transition from skirts to pants is taking longer than the elimination of millinery. It is not yet complete. But gradually pants are being embraced by more and more ladies.

Then there is the evolution pertaining to men wearing coats. Until a decade or so ago, I never saw a male member, and certainly not a pastor, coatless at a Sunday church service. As a young "twig" my parents bent me in the way they thought I should grow. Consequently, never in my life have I attended a church service on Sunday in my shirtsleeves. Wearing a coat for an hour or two at church is about the only thing I do in this modern world that distinguishes Sunday from any other day. Perhaps the twig grew with a crazy twist which makes me wince when I see a preacher take off his coat in the pulpit, lay it aside, pull down his vest front and back and resumes his effort to save my soul.

What an old fogy I am! But, if and when, I want to be buried with my coat on.

MY LEPER MISSION

Not so long ago something happened which presented me a first opportunity to administer missions personally.

Flosserfina Faller, an inmate of the far distant leper colony of Culion on one of the Philippine Islands, saw my name in a magazine. She wrote me a letter, using excellent penmanship and very good diction, saying: "I write something to let you know my very wish to have your friendship that I may have someone shower my poor family with sunshine and cheer. I am suffering from lingering illness modernly termed Hansen's disease. To help let the weary long days pass in our miserable condition of being confined in an island isolated from parents and other loved ones, I thought to look for a friend through correspondence. Reading letters will mean a lot for we do imagine we are being visited personally. I would like some religious literature and will you be kind and communicate with me?"

I replied, enclosing a dollar bill as if I were putting it in a slot machine to hear another record.

And in reply to my many questions I received in due time a liberal education concerning leprosy, the colony and much personal information concerning Flosserfina.

She and her husband Valentin had come to the colony when their parents were no longer able to pay for their medicine. They were allowed to marry and had four children who were "non-Hansen." They lived as a family in a small napa house on the seafront. There was no danger of the children becoming infected.

The government afforded them the essentials for living. Neither parent was able, because of infirmities, to earn anything additional. So there was no money to buy extra things of which they read in American magazines. I soon learned that Flosserfina would rather have money than religious magazines.

A storm damaged their little house. It needed repairs before the rainy season began. She wrote, "I beg of you send a little sum, possibly twenty-five or thirty dollars. I honestly believe this may be too much for you though I hope you have the heart to do it."

She wrote that Valentin, sick in the hospital, wept as he kissed the money when he opened the letter. Never have I known money to buy more. The roof was repaired. Bamboo flooring was renewed and the walls were shored up, neighbors doing the labor gratis. And there was enough left to buy Valentin some gourmet food like Ovaltine, fresh bananas, tins of milk and Quaker Oats!

Valentin died. Flosserfina sent me a picture of herself and the neatly dressed children among the floral wreaths beside the coffin.

She worried about what would become of the children were she to die. She wished so much I would bring them to the United States and adopt them so they would have a chance in life.

Soon she wrote her last letter to me advising me of her severe illness, likely terminal. Then eight-year-old Mercie wrote that her mother was so sick in the hospital, always crying for her father; of how she cried and cried to see her mother there, wondering what she would do if she could never go back home; the doctor said there was no hope.

A year passed. I wondered what had happened to the children. I wrote an inquiry to the superintendent of the colony telling him of my experience with the Fallers and that the little girl, Mercie, had written of the impending death of her mother in the hospital.

He replied that the children were fine; that Flosserfina had not died; she had married again soon after Valentin died. And as for any illness which confined her to the hospital, she had not been there except on the occasion of the birth of a baby by her second marriage.

All I know for certain is that Valentin is dead.

DISHONEST SHENANIGANS' STYLES CHANGE

As I have said before, there is nothing new under the sun. However, the style of dishonest shenanigans seems to have changed. We read in the newspapers today of many, but those of the 1880s have a little different twist.

For instance: the church is the last place you would expect an operator, but as soon as the pastor had pronounced the benediction, John Doe fell over in a fit. Of course, this enlisted the sympathy of the people. On the inside of his coat was pinned his name, and the home of his relatives with the injunction that should he die in one of his fits, the people should have the body sent home. But he suddenly recovered and prevailed upon the congregation for enough money to get back home. It took about $20. Doubtless he gets that much every Sunday. Then he pulled out for another town to have another "fit" the next Sunday.

When the Fayette Court House was being built in the 80s, a fellow named Madison who worked on that job boarded with Mrs. M.C. Jasper. He played the "brick scheme" on his landlady. Departing, he indicated he did not have enough money to pay his board bill and take him to Kansas City. He agreed to leave his large valuable valise and contents for one week's board. However, he did so with the understanding that he should have his grip just as soon as he sent his money for the board. The landlady became suspicious and opened the valise. It was chock full of nice bricks taken from the new courthouse building. The fellow, doubtless, is laughing at his shrewdness.

A half-dozen "horse traders" have been in town for a week past and relieved several boys of their ready cash. It is said to be done in this way. The horses they carry along to trade are so trained that when they are traded off they suddenly become lame, fall down or get sick and balk. The one getting them is glad to pay a few dollars to the traders to take them back.

RING CENTRAL

In the spring of 1908, Samuel Burgin came to New Franklin with his family, one daughter and several sons. Old issues of the New Franklin paper reveal that he rented "the upstairs over the post office" for living quarters and the switchboard of Howard County Mutual Telephone Company. By hard work through the summer, building lines and installing phones, there were 11 phones in as many business places and two lines from the country with 23, making 34 on the system. It was put in operation in September.

Sam Burgin's young daughter, barely in her teens, Avanel, recalls how busy she was keeping house, cooking for the family and running the "switchboard" to "plug in" those who wanted to use their phones.

My father did not get on the "party line" running by our farm at first. He had to weigh the benefits against the cost. But before many weeks passed we were on with eight other families, each with a different "ring." Ours was "four longs and one short."

There was an unwritten law against eavesdropping. But we soon learned with so many on the line, one had to listen in to know when the line became idle so he could "ring central" immediately to get use of the line ahead of someone else. In a sense one was forced to eavesdrop!

The present generation cannot realize the favors asked of the switchboard operator, commonly known as "central."

It was not unusual for a farm wife to ring central and say, "My son is in New Franklin, would you mind looking out the window and if you see him, tell him to bring me a spool of No. 40 white thread?"

Not long after we "got on the line," my mother was taking a sponge bath one night. During the procedure she had occasion to move an oil lamp. Setting it down, she missed a table and it fell to the floor setting the house on fire. Miss Ruth Tuttle who was helping with sewing and staying in the house and my sister Anna Rose were upstairs when Mother screamed "Fire!" and "Bring me some clothes to put on!" My sister called central and asked her to yell out the window that the Taylor Kingsbury home was on fire.

My sister, after calling central, with supernatural energy had pumped cistern water into a washtub, carried it into the house, put out the fire, got my mother some clothes and called central again to ask her to announce to the world that "Kingsbury's fire is out."

A LONG AND TWO SHORTS

According to the Boonville *Advertiser* of January 22, 1880, people in town were a little slow in appreciating the benefits of telephone service. The editor relates:

"The manager of the telephone exchange at this place who in every respect is truthful and reliable, informs us that if there is to be any further kicking, he is authorized to gather up the telephone, take down the wires, pull up the poles and ship the entire business to Kansas City. This plant has never made any money for the company and had they known what they know now before they invested here, the exchange would have never been established.

"The *Advertiser* considers the telephone a necessity and would regret to see our citizens discontinue its use. Those who cannot afford it of course should abandon it. It looks like our citizens should endeavor to connect other places with Boonville by telephone, enlarging our business territory, rather than to discourage and kill anything which gives us the appearance of modern enterprise."

In another column, he writes:

When telephones were new in Howard County there were "party lines," and much "listening in." Neighbors were all anxious to hear every day how Mrs. Wirt Muckley, who was critically ill, was doing. She had been quite ill a long time. The end was expected any day, Miss Tillie Droopers helped to take care of her.

Whenever the phone rang "a long and two shorts," a lot of receivers came off the hooks in homes of people who wanted to hear Miss Tillie give the latest bulletin. Toward the end, she would say, "Well, last night she laid about the same. She ain't dead yet but she is mighty bad off. Seems like she can't get neither way."

When she passed to her reward, the preacher was trying to comfort Thomas, her son, pointing out things which he should be thankful in spite of his sorrow. But Thomas was unconvinced and told him, " They ain't but one good thing about it an' it was when she did shut off, she shut off easy."

How Styles do Cycle

There is nothing new about the prevalent long hair style. I have a picture of my Grandfather Kingsbury taken almost a hundred years ago. His long hair comes down to his ears. Sideburns and heavy whiskers extend via his chin from one to the other. It makes a hairy halo around his face.

It is nothing new that girls and women wear their hair long. At a "Recherche Musicale" given in New Franklin in 1882 some of the young ladies "were tastily dressed in pure white with their golden hair falling halfway to their waists." Some then wore long curls as did my mother in a picture taken in the early 1870s.

Do you remember when girls and women, not so long ago quit wearing stockings? Well it wasn't the first time. In the 1880s the Fayette Advertiser mentioned them leaving off their hose and said "this knocks the socks off of ye editor."

Many years ago I took to my heart a copy of a portrait of Pauline Bonaparte, sister of Napoleon. I hung it in my home. With her a member of my household I learned what I could about her. I already knew she was a beautiful woman. In 1803 she married Camillo Borghese, an Italian nobleman. She went to live in Rome in one of the most elegant palaces in the city. In later years the Borghese Gardens with its palace became one of the show places of Rome.

I wanted to see Pauline's old home just as if I could come back home and tell her about it. The palace was elegant. Like most palaces in Europe it was full of portraits, (six hundred, I was told).

But the thing which pleased me most and afforded me the greatest surprise was in an alcove with nothing else to detract from it. It was a white marble figure of a beautiful woman semi-reclining on a couch. I recognized her the instant I saw her, Princess Pauline Bonaparte-Borghese. The surprise was that her hair was done a la pony tail! And back home I had thought the style was new.

Today on TV I saw scenes of young people dancing in Paris, body to body and cheek to cheek. A lone woman had her long hair styled pony tail curved so high she reminded me of a young filly at a horse show.

ARE YOU PLAGUED BY MARASMUS?

No doctor ever told me, but in browsing in the dictionary I have learned that I have marasmus. Strange that I had never heard of it when it has afflicted the human race, in fact, every living thing since the creation of earth.

Marking back to 1912 I wrote about New Franklin's first Street Fair. It was held in the wide street, Broadway, between Missouri Avenue and Howard Street. Traffic was directed to side streets whenever the fair was in operation. There was a ferris wheel, a merry-go-round and numerous concessions for food and soda pop and for games of chance.

Seems everybody was there every night. Even old Mrs. D.R. Wayland who claims she never knows a well day, weaving like a shuttle through the crowds. Her unsmiling face made me wish she could throw a bit of confetti or blow a tin horn to get into the spirit of the occasion.

I persuaded Cousin Annie Boggs to ride the horses on the merry-go-round with me and we had a fine gallop through the street. I didn't get up enough courage to ride a kiddish hobby horse until Friday night. It is great to take a person off his dignity and I think all elderly people should indulge in it if they want to keep young.

Mr. and Mrs. Bob Robertson enjoyed themselves at the Jap-ware booths, but they didn't win as many premiums as the Burkhimers did. Mrs. Burkhimer won the prettiest set of cups and saucers on display, a pitcher and a vase shaped like a spit-toon. Lutie, their daughter, won a poodle dog for herself and for all her friends who asked her to throw for them. She was surely the poodle dog winner.

And there was a minstrel show. One night my sister and I were there when a large Negro woman, Annie Mart, came in and sat in front of us. We both had to move to be able to see the stage. A duplicate of her, Alice Biggs, came and sat to one side of us but near Annie. When they got tickled at the jokes, they would laugh loud as they swayed back and forth, saying to each other, "Ain't that a shame." To us, they were better than the stage show.

On Sunday:

The Street Fair is gone. There is no blaring of "Casey Jones," and the street looks very sad. But I rather like the pathos of it. Saturday night when I went out of town, everything was in a whirl. Sunday morning the street was deserted, not even a scrap of paper in sight.

[Incidentally, if you are not familiar with the symptoms of marasmus, Webster's defines it as: "to waste away; progressive emaciation..." As my 90th birthday approaches, I'm aware I have a serious case.]

Looking At "The Old Seminary" Building

The white two-story brick building located in the north end of New Franklin, known as the Old Seminary has acquired the reputation of having celebrated 146 birthdays. I know of no one able to confirm or deny it. The building is one of five brick residences still standing in town which tradition says were built in 1832 by Booker and Washington, two slaves owned by Senator Owen Rawlings.

My mother and father used to talk of going there, he riding his pony and she with a sister, walking from the Clark's Chapel community.

When the Masonic Lodge was granted a charter in 1857, the upper story was used for its meetings. The Odd Fellows also met there. And I have heard older men and women talk of attending meetings of the Sons of Temperance there.

When the Methodists in New Franklin (incidentally, it was the only church in town) decided to erect a one-story brick church, the lodges persuaded the trustees to allow them to build a second story so they would have a new meeting hall. They would run up the wall and put on the roof and would become joint owners of the building. The building was completed in the late 1860s.

In an effort to learn more about the early school I asked all of the old pupils I could find to tell or write me of their reminiscences. The best letter I received in 1950 was from a double cousin of mine who lived in Montana, Lillian Kingsbury, who related:

"Our family acquaintance with the old Seminary began in September, 1874 when Mr. James Moore was the teacher. No janitor, no reports, almost no nothin'. He boarded at Uncle Taylor's (my father) and rode his own horse, a good one. The Dunaways, who both taught, had the next two years.

"And then there was a grand change. Prof. A.P. Barton, a real administrator, had the school for three years. The first year he used the big room downstairs, then the school grew so, the Sons of Temperance were moved out from upstairs. He moved the older class up there, his brother had the intermediate school downstairs, along with Miss Sallie Cook, who taught the primary.

"In the spring of 1881, Vaughan Bonham offered an essay medal. There were six contestants, four boys, Sallie McGavock and myself. The event came off Friday, April 1, 1881, and I was fortunate.

"And then Prof. Barton and his family, a gifted lot, left for Kansas City and he embarked in the practice of law. Mrs. Barton was a fine artist, Ethel, the first child, a gifted musician. Homer, an actor, Ralph, the stormy petrel of the family, associated with writers and even visited Lady Astor.

"The fall of 1881, I went to college. The Seminary was condemned as unsafe, and a new three-room school was built on the west side of North Howard St., where ten years later, a third building, eight rooms and still standing and being used now as a church school, was erected.

"When the school opened in the fall of 1882, Miss Mary O'Donnell was principal, Bessie Morrison of Fayette taught intermediate and I had the primary. My salary was $30 per month for six months.

"We closed with a May Day party in Ferguson's pasture. Mag

Herndon was Queen of the May and handsome Ed Long crowned her, the first time Taylor Bowman ever had a rival."

It is interesting to consider that the "Old Seminary," which was condemned in 1881 as likely to collapse on the school children and was bought by one of the school directors to be made into a residence, has been a safe home for many families since then. A few years ago, she was showing wrinkles and suffering from stomach ache, but a new family fell in love with her, showed it by giving her a face lift and internal operations which have restored her health. She looks vigorous enough to last another hundred years.

WHERE CAN YOU FIND A RHABDOMANCER?

Can you tell me who is a good rhabdomancer in Boonville or Cooper County? No? Perhaps then you can cite me to a good dowser? No? Well surely there must be a water witch?

I dare say most of you know what a water witch is, though some of the younger generation may think it is an old snaggle-toothed woman with a pointed wide brimmed black hat astraddle a broomstick riding above a body of water.

I queried my grandsons on this and they agreed it was a shapely female at the beach wearing a string/mini bra outfit, projecting a "come hither look."

Water witching is an art of finding it beneath the surface of the earth. It is so old no one knows when it originated. Witchers claim and have proven they can walk over land with a forked twig in their hands extended in front of them. When they pass over a vein of underground water, the butt end of the twig will bob up and down or bend towards the earth. Some witchers claim by counting the bobs they can tell how deep one must dig or drill to reach the water.

The forked twig may be of hazel wood, peach, willow or

what-have-you. Some witchers use instead a metal rod. One used the handle end of a buggy whip. Another simply a blade of grass.

The art of being a dowser or a diviner as some call themselves is rare. One cannot buy it. No one can give it to you. It seems like an inborn intuition.

Historians, psychologists, geologists, students of the mysterious have given study to the art of water witching. But nobody has been able to offer a scientific explanation of it.

The Department of Interior of the United States after comprehensive research issued a paper with the following conclusive summary:

"It is doubtful whether so much investigation and discussion has ever been bestowed on any other subject with such absolute lack of positive results. It is difficult to see how the matter could be more thoroughly discredited - further tests by the Geological Survey of the witching of water would be a misuse of funds."

Stephen Wright, retired, makes no pretense at finding underground veins of water. However, he can locate a buried water main or a sewer line. It has been some sixty years since New Franklin laid its first water mains. Not so long ago, the city needed to locate certain outlying ones. There was no chart and everyone who had assisted in laying them had died. Someone suggested Stephen Wright could find them. He did.

His equipment is simple. He cut the long pieces of straight wire from common coat hangers. With one wire in each hand extended before him, he walked over the ground. Suddenly the front ends of the wire drew together as if drawn by a magnet. Stephen said, "Here it is gentlemen." And so it was.

(Note: Before I finished this, a gentleman I had not known before called at my office. I mentioned what I was typing. He assured me he could not only water witch, but do other things with certain equipment. He suggested I get a couple of coat hangers and he would tell me the state of my health. Before he left, the hangers were mysteriously turning in my own hands. I may report in a later column that my latest hobby is water witching!)

JACK THE RIPPER

My brother, Robert Kingsbury, aged 91, asked me the other day, "Why haven't you written something about Jack the Ripper?"

"Who was he and what did he rip?" I inquired.

"He was a tramp who used to come to New Franklin every fall to saw wood for a lot of people who used it for winter fuel. He was called the ripper because he could saw up a cord of wood quicker than anybody else who ever set foot in Howard County.

He never worked for anybody without the understanding that his dinner, all he could eat, was to be furnished as part of payment. The wives who had to feed him agreed that he had the right name for he ripped through food so fast it wore them out keeping it on his plate."

Dr. Moser, aged 97, remembered Jack the Ripper. "He was just like a whirlwind with a cord of wood. He was the swiftest sawer ever known around here, measuring his strokes by the rhythm of his song. And he could eat more and put it down as fast as he could saw wood. Why one time, Paddy Lee hired him, and Mrs. Lee had to fry three rabbits in succession, and he ate every bit of them except the bones before his hunger pains for meat were satisfied.

"One fall another tramp named Willie showed up in town. Willie heard talk about how much Jack the Ripper could eat and he stated openly that he would like to challenge Jack to eat more than he himself could put away.

"Men around town heard of it and some of them thought it would make a fine sporting event. A date was set. Arrangements were made to have the contest in the only eating place in town where any foods that Jack the Ripper selected were to be provided for the contestants.

"Excitement increased as time for the contest rolled around. There was a lot of betting on the outcome. Jack the Ripper's expertise in eating was well-known but Willie was a bigger man than Jack and looked like he could hold more, so many bet their money on him.

"At the appointed time, all available space in the dining room was filled with spectators who had paid a dime apiece to watch the show. The proceeds were to pay for the food consumed.

"Jack the Ripper ordered chicken, rabbit, sausage, coon, ham and eggs, possum and sweet potatoes, hot cakes and sorghum, milk and coffee. Willie and Jack appeared to be running neck and neck as their supporters cheered them on. But Jack didn't seem able to get a swallow ahead and evidently was afraid he would lose the contest. He gave an order for something which was brought in as another course, dessert. When it was set before the contestants, Jack took a big spoonful and began to chew on it. Juice began to run down the sides of his mouth. Willie looked at it, and then at Jack and pushed it away toward the center of the table. His stomach rebelled, and Jack was declared the winner."

"Doc, what was for dessert?" I asked him, curious to know.

"Well, now it seems funny, but I can't think what it was to save my soul. Ask your brother Robert if he remembers," replied the doctor.

I asked Robert what enabled Jack the Ripper to win the "Eat the Most" contest.

"Sure," he replied, "It was axle grease."

SITTING ON THE FRONT PORCH - WATCHING ALL THE FOLK DRIVE BY

If you live long enough you will remember many things that afforded you pleasure in your earlier years. One I recall is the front porch, which in some cases was large enough to become a second living room during the pleasant months of the year. We used to resort to the front porch to find a breeze on a hot summer day.

Electric fans and then air conditioners and TV sets put an end to the front porch for resting and conversation. It is no longer an important part of the home.

In the 1890s when houses were being built with front porches, my father had a large one thirty by twelve feet added to our house. It had spindling columns with a regular gingerbread of wooden curlicues at the top between them.

In later years there was a five-foot long slatted wooden bench along the wall and a wooden bench swing suspended from the ceiling by chains, with cushions, on either side of the front door. There were a couple of old Boston rockers. And available always was a supply of palm leaf fans or paper ones advertising the funeral parlor in New Franklin. It was a good place to relax and watch the world go by. We were familiar with every horse and buggy which passed up and down the road and later the owners of the first automobiles. If your women heard over the party telephone line that someone's automobile was on the road, they never thought of driving a horse on the road until it had come by and gone back up the road.

Morning glories trailed up trellises at the sides of the porch steps. I remember best the years when the Seven Sisters roses bloomed profusely. Then came the Pink Rambler. They never grew where they could interfere with the view of the road.

I remember my mother coming from the hot kitchen with the folds of her apron in her hand to fan herself while she sat in a swing and cooled off a bit.

Sometimes she would entertain her Ladies Aid Society on the porch. Company who came in the evenings were usually entertained there. Occasionally she would be obliged to remark, "The mosquitoes are so bad tonight we had better go inside."

The biggest social event for which the front porch was used occurred when one of my sisters had her wedding ceremony performed there. I undertook the task of decorating it with greenery from the farm. The porch was to be converted into a chapel. I robbed the woodsy farm hollows of long fronds of ferns, transplanted them into hanging baskets with vines. The long garden row of asparagus was bared of its feathery tops to make a railing around the edges of the porch and to ornament the columns and the wooden gingerbread at their tops. A contrivance was rigged up on the ceiling over the spot where the couple would be married.

Just as they were pronounced man and wife, a string was pulled which released a shower of rice.

How long has it been since you saw anyone sitting on the front porch? New houses don't even have them anymore like homes built back in 1832.

On the bottom of the column clipping Lilburn sent me, he scrawled, "One woman called to tell me she was sitting on her front porch when she read the column."

THE TENT SHOW'S IN TOWN

In a letter to Charles in July 1974 Lilburn writes of attending the Writers' Group at Cedar Grove:

They wanted to make me president of this organization until I told them positively I would not be. It is bad enough to generally be the only man at the meeting. The refreshments are always good. I read my column to be sent to the paper about the tent show Ed "Toby" and Iola Ward used to put on here for many, many years to the delight of southern Howard County.

The column follows:

Before the days of picture shows and television, the people of South Howard County were highly entertained by the Princess Stock Company under a big waterproof tent pitched for a week in June in the middle of New Franklin's Main Street.

The company was headed by a married couple, Ed "Toby" and Iola Ward. Beginning in 1915 they came to New Franklin for such a long term of years that when they arrived it was like home folks coming back for an annual reunion. Ed was a stocky, good-looking man with black hair and dark eyes. Iola was a pretty brunette. Each played a part in nearly every show. Toby was exciting as Simon Legree in "Uncle Tom's Cabin," with a terrible looking whip. He was good as the poor old man who was about to lose his farm through foreclosure of the mortgage unless he gave the hand of his pretty daughter in marriage to the villain. And how he could play the part of a villain himself!

Sometimes Iola played the part of a rich girl, sometimes a drudge like Cinderella. But she was at her best when she was a pretty young, innocent girl, like Susie, trying to resist the evil slicker from the city, the trumpet player in the band. After one performance a Methodist lady said she prayed all through it Susie would be able to hold out. Susie was always triumphant in the plays.

To some of the women the plays were so realistic, like "Uncle Tom's Cabin," they shed tears when little Eva made her jerky ascent to Heaven.

There were five or six strong-lunged men with band instruments who gave a very loud concert every night to attract the crowd and signal it was time to enter the tent and get seated before the show began. In 1919 a ticket was twenty-seven cents plus the war tax of three cents. There were reserved seats for those who wanted to be closer to the stage when the hero would shoot the villain, for nine cents plus one cent tax. And for those who wanted to remain for the vaudeville show which followed the play, the charge was an additional nine cents plus onc cent tax. One just remained in his seat until the drummer in the band could collect the toll.

Of course most of the gags of the comedian, sometimes a comedienne, were stale, but the audience was so imbued with the spirit of fun, it laughed as if they had never heard them before.

Such entertainments would be allowed to set up their tents in the corner of Ferguson's pasture just a block from the business section of the town. The change of location made no material difference to Toby and Iola Ward.

But time brought a change which made a difference to many of the Princess Stock Company fans. An advance agent brought the news that Ed and Iola Ward were playing new roles as separates. She was no longer with the company – no longer to be the pretty heroine to be saved from the wiles of the wicked trumpet player!

After each appearance in New Franklin, the editor of the paper always wrote a paragraph of praise, saying the same things each year – it was a clean show with clean people. Through the many years it had come to New Franklin it had established a great reputation among the pleasure-seeking people of southern Howard County and "had played to capacity."

I inquired, naturally, but never learned what was the wedge that split Ed and Iola's log of happiness.

What Should A "Bundle Of Joy" Cost?

A story recently in the *Boonville Daily News* about "bundles of joy" (babies) being so expensive now—as much as $1,000— reminded me of a black woman who lived in New Franklin before hospitals were established. Upon my request, she gave me a list of all the babies she had helped bring into the world between 1894 and 1920—150 of them.

Nannie was in New Franklin at the time of my earliest recollections and was no doubt a native of the community. She was a nice looking woman, always neatly dressed, highly regarded, and treated with great respect. Men and women never knew when she might be needed to help in their homes.

Because of her profession, Nannie was able to contribute to the support of her household. Charlie, her husband, had one empty sleeve, so was handicapped in performing many kinds of work.

Instead of hospital costs which the story says may run as high as $600 in a case of childbirth, there was none where Nannie presided as an assistant to the doctor (if he arrived in time). There was no delivery room at $75, nor $114 nursery charges. The room in the home sufficed for everything, and Nannie did all the nursing.

Not only did she nurse the recuperating mother and care for the baby, but she looked after the feeding three times a day of other members of the family.

She was happy to have earned a dollar a day, $12 for her services.

In due time, the father of the baby got around to paying the doctor delivery charge of $25 instead of today's current price as quoted in the story of $250. One would think the present high cost of bringing babies into the world would be an effective brake on the population explosion.

WEDDING PRESENTS EXPECTED

It is interesting in perusing old newspapers to note the changes in their manner of reporting weddings.

A hundred and fifty years ago the *Missouri Intelligencer* used four or five lines to announce one, giving the names of the contracting parties, the date, maybe the place and the name of the minister or the Justice of the Peace who performed the ceremony.

Many years passed before we find the newspapers handing out compliments to the "estimable" bride and the "dependable" groom, and furnishing some details of the ceremony.

The day came when the newspaper published not only a complete account of the wedding but a list of wedding presents with the name of each donor. This custom of giving wedding presents was established, it appears, in the seventies of the last century. A Clark's Chapel bride of 1872 told me with humor that when she was married, she received only a gold-embossed family Bible and a pickle dish, both of which proved appropriate.

But once established, the custom of giving presents flourished even to this day. And lists of presents were published in the newspapers.

Today no prospective brides would announce their choices of patterns of china, silver and crystal in the local newspaper. But none seems averse to slipping the word to the public through the privacy of a display in the window of a shop on Main St.

Newspaper lists of wedding presents in the newspapers would be of interest to many people who cannot go to the weddings.

The newspaper report of a crystal wedding celebration in 1886 follows:

"The latest social event of the season was the crystal wedding of Mr. and Mrs. W.W. Smith. At an early hour the doors were thrown open and the guests began to assemble. All who are acquainted with the royal manner in which Mr. and Mrs. Smith entertain bear me out in saying this time they excelled themselves a little.

"The supper was abundant, substantial and delicate. Mirth was the order of the night and each guest enjoyed the occasion thoroughly. As the 'wee sma' hours advanced the crowd dispersed, each wishing in his heart, the words echoed from lip to lip, 'Many happy returns of the anniversary. We hope you may live to celebrate in the same manner, your diamond wedding.'"

DID YOU EVER SEE A HORSE IN BED?

Dr. Henry Moser tells me that in 1903 his dental office was over Arthur Cox's store, here in New Franklin. "Jennie Dempsey," said he, "was in the chair and I was preparing a tooth for a filling when the first explosion came. The floor beneath us seemed to rise. There were other explosions before we could get down the stairway to the street."

Arthur Cox had show windows on either side of his front door full of fireworks of various kinds. Roman candles, small and giant firecrackers and an intriguing little thing called a grasshopper. When lit, a series of small explosions would make it jump between them.

It was the third of July and Jim Burch had brought his young son, Frank, uptown to buy him some fireworks to shoot off on the glorious fourth. Arthur was showing his stock, and putting a grasshopper on the counter, he lit it to give a demonstration. But he never dreamed of the demonstration which followed. The "live" grasshopper jumped into a show window and set it afire. Before Arthur could pump and bring a bucket of water to put out the fire, little firecrackers and giant firecrackers sounded like bedlam broke loose.

Mrs. Harris' old blind mare hitched to a buggy was tied to the rack in front of the store. She broke loose and sightless, headed directly across the street and into the plate glass window of Jake Hunter's furniture store where the chief display was a bed made up in the best style to display a spread and pillow covers.

The old mare crashed through the glass and fell into the bed. There she lay, seemingly resigned and satisfied, so trussed by her harness she couldn't move.

Hunter had never had a window display to equal this one.

MAGICAL HACKLEY MAD STONE

News items from the *Fayette Advertiser* in the 1880s concerned rabid dogs and advised everyone to be on his guard.

"A young man named Smith was bitten by one this week. He went to Boonville to have a mad stone applied to the wound."

"The son of J.O. Callaway, bitten by a mad dog a short time ago is, we are glad to report, getting all right again. The Hackley mad stone worked charmingly in his case."

What was a mad stone? Traditionally it was a small, hard object which had lodged in a deer's stomach, and had become coated with a calcium deposit. Its surface was as smooth as satin. It was said it made the animal twice as hard to kill as one without it.

The virtue of the stone was that when applied to the bite of a rabid animal it would draw out the poison and save the victim from hydrophobia. It was effective, too, when applied to the bite of a rattlesnake, even a spider.

Lott Hackley, mentioned above, brought his mad stone from Kentucky when he came and settled in the Boonslick Country in 1824. After he died in 1874 it was handed down through successive generations. It was in Howard County 115 years. In 1939 Hardin Hackley gave it to his own son David who took it to Dallas, Texas. It had been in Hardin's possession for 25 years. He told me, "Of all the people who used the mad stone there was only one who died and he already had a couple of fits before he could get to it."

David Crews and John Lusby, a couple of young farmers residing a few miles of Fayette were bitten by a young mad calf. When first attacked the animal had symptoms of being choked so the boys caught it and attempted to relieve it by thrusting an arm down its throat to remove whatever they might find. They found nothing but in their efforts each was bitten on his hand. The calf continued to froth at the mouth and finally developed a genuine case of hydrophobia from which it soon died. When the young men learned this they lost no time in getting over to Dr. Hackley's, a neighbor, and applied the mad stone. During the ten days following, it never stuck to either of their hands so they felt no serious harm would come from the bites received.

Once when Mr. Hackley exhibited the stone at a Fayette fair, the late Dr. Charles Lee picked it up, examined it closely, shook his head and remarked, "I don't think much of it but if a mad dog bit me and I didn't have anything else, I would sure get my engine hot getting to it."

Nothing To Fear But Fear

Old Mt. Pleasant Cemetery is within a thousand feet of my front door. As yet I haven't played as much a part in its life as it has in mine.

Youthful memories linger of it and the abandoned church by its side. The Baptists and Campbellites who had worshipped there so long had moved to New Franklin and built new churches in the 80s.

On moonlit nights I used to see strange lights over there. Nobody had told me about the reflection of moonlight on polished tombstones.

As for the frame church with its boards cut to simulate rectangular stones and now pecked by woodpeckers, nothing could have induced me to enter its unlocked doors alone.

On the bravest occasions I would speak a few words so we

could hear a spirit repeat them right after me. The church seemed so empty.

But the black men who worked on the farm told me that every night it was full of spirits which came out of the graves in the churchyard to hold a meeting inside.

One of the men made a $10 bet with my older brother that the latter wouldn't sleep all night in the church.

I remember with what misgivings I saw him go down the lane at dusk with a blanket and his shotgun, I doubted if I would ever see him again.

Next morning when I saw him coming back, I ran to meet him. If I had had a fatted calf, it wouldn't have had a chance.

But there came a day when I didn't feel so solicitous about him. He used to milk the family cow.

I used to beg him to let me try. I thought he was very kind to favor me. Before long he was hiring and paying me a nickel every time I would do the chore for him.

When I became proficient he told me he would let me do it all the time! Thus he left me holding the bag. And being the youngest son, I held it for a long time.

I was afraid of the dark. The graveyard may have been the cause of my being afraid of the dark. My family was concerned about it.

Another brother resolved to cure me of this illness. He taught, and we drove to school in a buggy. One afternoon when we got home I forgot to take my books into the house. It was pitch dark before I needed them.

Despite my begging, no one would go with me to get them. To reach the buggy I had to traverse our large yard. Cautious at every step, I was passing a bushy cedar tree when something jumped from behind it and grabbed me in a tight embrace. I was sure in my terror that it was a ghost from Mt. Pleasant until I heard the familiar voice of my teacher-brother. I gasped.

"Why did you do it, why did you do it?" I cried

Before long I realized why. During that experience, something died within me—my fear of the dark. And to this day I am grateful to my brother for the harsh treatment which cured me of my illness.

Did You Ever Have a Leap Year Date?

I can't remember when I last heard of a leap year party. Is it because women now have become so "libbed" that they feel that old-time special attention shown the men would be a waste of time?

These thoughts were induced by reading about a leap year party reported in the *Central Missourian* of Glasgow on the 1st of March, 1888. Arrangements for it were "perfect and satisfactory."

The ladies called for the gentlemen shortly after 8 o'clock and cared for them in the most tender manner, having them driven to and from the party in carriages and bestowing on them every possible attention.

Arriving at the home they were ushered into a blaze of light by their gallant escorts. The evening was spent dancing, card playing and social conversation. At 12 o'clock the ladies escorted the gentlemen into the dining room where a bountiful repast was served and highly relished by all.

When Did You Have Your First Radio?

On November 10, 1922 the *New Franklin News* reported:

"The radio craze is gaining momentum locally. The first set in town we believe was installed early in the summer when Mr. Mecum, son-in-law of Mr. and Mrs. J.K. Dodson was here on a visit. Soon after, Emil Bethke installed one and since then Elmer McMillin, John Agnew and Kelly Munro have installed outfits.

Mr. Wallace Estill we understand has also installed one of the high type machines. The radio is a great thing and is bound to grow in favor as people become familiar with the advantages it affords for keeping abreast of the happenings of the day."

Radios grew in popularity with the speed of a race horse.

Many people became devotees of listening to the news and serials just as today they are to television.

Concerning the radio craze Lilburn wrote of personal experiences. It follows:

Allow me to complain gently about people who will not let hell nor high water interfere with their reception of favorite radio programs. In St. Louis recently I called on some friends I had not seen for a long time. Hardly had we exchanged greetings and launched into the natural exchange of questions about Tom, Dick and Harry, when the hostess announced, "Oh it's time for Bob Hope to come on. We just drop everything to listen to him." And on he came to their keenest delight. Stymied by the comedian, I sat and clocked off more minutes than I should have spent there.

Pat and Sue, whom I visited for the first time in their beautiful new apartment, had a different approach. There was a sudden interruption of a lively discussion about mutual friends when Sue said: "I'm crazy for you to see my new book on antique silver." "Get him that old ship of mine too," added Pat sitting within arms reach of the radio, his fingers tinkering with the dial. As she handed them to me, I heard the announcement from the radio, "Mr. District Attorney" and realized what they were doing to me!

By now both host and hostess were glued to the radio, their faces rapt with interest. They were lost to my world. I could have slipped out without them knowing it. I tried to look at the books but couldn't keep my mind on them because of gunfire on the radio. My hostess suddenly grew more tense and clasping her hands gladly exclaimed, "Oh good, the police are coming, the police are coming!"

My silence was complete until Pat and Sue figured the casualties, seven killed and four wounded. "Phew," sighed the hostess. The radio was snapped off, the books laid aside and visiting was resumed as it had begun.

How Long Did the Candle Burn?

How interesting it was to read the advertisement of Foster's Drug Store in the issue of the *Boonville Daily News* of March 24th!

It told about the "biggest apple pie in the whole world." It was six feet in diameter and six inches deep. It contained twenty-two bushels of apples and other ingredients in proportion.

It took seven men to "wrestle it into the oven" for baking. A hoist was used to load it onto the flatbed of a truck which conveyed it to Bell's Orchard east of Boonville. It was a product to advertise Boonville as the Apple Center of the United States, and was enjoyed by members of Missouri State Orchards Association.

The account of the oversized pie turned my mind backward 55 years to the day in 1920 when the Bank of New Franklin (now the home of Exchange Bank) was opened and one of the most interesting events in connection with it was a guessing contest as to how many hours an immense candle would burn.

The candle was at least six inches in diameter and five or six feet high. It was put on display the day before the opening in the officer's room to the right of the front entrance so that people who had been informed of the contest might view it and begin speculating. The first prize for the nearest correct guess was $10, second, $5, and third, $2.50. That day differences of opinion varied greatly from five hours to twenty-one days.

The formal lighting occurred at 8 o'clock on the morning of the opening. It was a gala day in New Franklin. As cashier of the institution, I had a ball. The ladies were given white and pink carnations, the men cigars and every little boy and girl had a tin horn which produced more bedlam than desired. Everybody wanted to record a guess about the candle, and 743 did.

The big candle burned 161 hours and 59 minutes and 45 seconds. All of its close "relatives" (those who worked in the bank) were at its bedside when it died. And fortunately it occurred in the daytime. The winner guessed 162 hours and 20 minutes.

THE DRESSED UP TOILET SEAT

Zip and Lula Coated have lived in the country all their lives. They are plain people. They have a comfortable home, but nothing pretentious. They have one bathroom, not a fraction more. They have never been disposed to "keep up with the Joneses" and buy every creature comfort that comes on the market. In fact, they don't pay much attention to the market.

Lula recently had a birthday. Her sister, Dilsie Peeling, who lives in the city sent her a present.

When Zip brought it from the mailbox, Lula could hardly wait as she struggled with the wrapper.

Zip, who had sat down in his easy chair to read the *Boonville Daily News* looked over his glasses.

He watched her raise the lids of the box and take out a rectangular piece of material covered on one side with what looked to him like a lemon-colored kitten fur with a half- moon shape hollowed out on one end. Puzzled, she held it up in front of her so that her neck fitted the hollowed out space.

Zip remarked, "Why it don't have any strings to tie it around your neck or waist either! Funny sort of bib!"

"And what would you want with a bib anyway after you get your hair washed?" Lula asked him.

She laid the bib aside and took out what looked like a night cap of the same material. She stretched its band of elastic and put it on her head.

Zip didn't like what he saw. It wasn't Lula's color, it did nothing for her. He resumed his reading until she exclaimed, "This is sure a crazy outfit!"

Then Zip remembered a letter in his pocket that he had overlooked in giving her. She was delighted that it was from Dilsie. She hadn't read far when she exclaimed, "Well, if this isn't the beatenest! Listen Zip! 'I do hope you and Zip will like the present I am sending for your bathroom. You may have to trim the little rug to make it fit closer around the stool. The covers are a little hard to put on the lids but the elastic is givey enough that you won't have much trouble. I ordered a jacket for the flush tank but they were temporarily out of stock and I will send it later. Tillie, my best friend, has a complete set, hers is pink and covers everything but the hole. It is lovely and lends such a nice touch to her bathroom.'"

Lula stopped reading to remark, "How far behind can we get with the new styles?" Then, "It is just too nice to use everyday, we'll just have to put it up in the back room 'til company comes."

"Yes," replied Zip, a tone of displeasure in his voice. "Keep it up ther 'til Pat Nixon comes! I'll have nothing to do with it! It's just one of those womens' lib contraptions to make sissies of us men, to cramp our style."

And so Lula's birthday present reposed up in the back room. She is wondering what Dilsie will say when she comes.

Do You Remember
The Ringing And Tolling Of The Bells?

The following story is in the September 14, 1900 issue of the *Boonville Weekly Advertiser*:

"On Monday the three bells of St. Peter's and Paul's Catholic Church of this city which for the past forty years have announced the time of day, morning, noon and night, and called the people of the parish to prayer and devotion, were taken down and shipped to Trenton, Illinois where they were sold to Rev. Father Dolson, Pastor of St. Mary's Church.

They weigh in the aggregate 4,225 pounds and the Trenton Church paid $844 for them.

These bells will be replaced in about a month from now by three fine new bells which are being cast at the McShane foundry in Baltimore, Maryland. They will weigh 6,225 pounds and will cost $745. They will be noted in F, A and C-sharp, will harmonize beautifully and produce a sweet mellow sound.

"At present St. Peter's and Paul's Church is doing without any bells. The Rev. Kussman says he relies upon the ingenuity of his people to find out the correct time."

My first thought after reading it was of wonder whether these bells of 1900 were in use seventy odd years until the old church was recently razed and replaced by the elegant edifice at the corner of 7th and Morgan Streets. I have been told they were sold at that time.

While ringing of bells has been generally upon joyous occasions, there were and are occasions when they proclaim sadness. As when the church bell is tolled to announce the death of a beloved member, one dong for each year of his age.

And some churches toll the bells after a funeral as the cortege moves away toward the cemetery. But church bells are not rung as commonly as they were in earlier days. The custom has been passing along with many others so significant to older generations. Today people are too busy to hear them.

One beautiful Sunday morning I set out in Nice on the Mediterranean coast of France to see things never available on a conducted tour.

At the foot of a street I continued by climbing in a succession of wide stairways with a succession of straightaways between them to the top of a small mountain. On either side were three and four-storied dwellings in pastel colors. On top of the mountain were the ruins of a castle which in ancient days had been built by one of the Caesars who came to the coast for relaxation. From this vantage point the view was overwhelming.

To my left was the sea, intensely blue, stretching to the horizon, to my right were distant snow-capped peaks of the mountains and before me lay the whole City of Nice along the crescent shaped seashore and extending up the mountain side.

Suddenly every bell in Nice was ringing. There must have been hundreds of them. Already filled with the beauty of the surroundings, this was too much. My feelings exploded.

Another time I had gone by train from London to visit the famous Cathedral of Canterbury. Arriving in the small town I elected to walk from the railway station so that I might enjoy the English architecture. It was New Years Day. Just as I arrived

before this magnificent edifice at noon, all of its many bells began
to ring. It was indeed impressive, extremely so until someone told
me not to think it was to welcome me, but rather the New Year,
repeating what had been done the midnight before.

We left late with the music of Evensong and soft bells ringing
in our ears.

THAT MAN LOOKS LIKE PRESIDENT TRUMAN

Do people like to be told they look like someone else? I
asked a number of men and women. They said it would be all
right if it were someone handsome, pretty, great or good. One
man said he would not mind if told he resembled his father or
mother. Still another suggested politics might enter the picture.
Which reminded me...

Once upon a time I joined a group of people from Chicago
for a tour of Mexico. As the train pulled out of St. Louis I passed
through a car where the director of the tour was sitting by and
talking to Senator Connolly of Texas. Seeing me, the latter remarked, "That man looks like President Truman."

That gave the director an idea. When he introduced me to
the other members of the party he did so as "President Truman."

Although he followed up with my proper name, to the group
I was "President Truman" throughout the trip.

But the fun was not all on their side. At the first hotel in
Mexico, one lady lamented that there was no piano on which the
"President" might play the "Missouri Waltz." Deep regret was
feigned by all. The next night at another hotel when assembled
for dinner there was a piano in the room and being invited, I
went over and played the "Missouri Waltz" in a manner second
only to President Truman. This set the group back a little. Some
thought maybe I was! In London after World War II, I enjoyed
dinner with a friend at an Officers' Club. As we checked our
coats and hats and turned to leave, I overheard one of the attendants remark to one the other, "Did you notice how much that
man looked like President Truman?"

Lilburn with his sister Lillian:
"That man looks like President Truman"

A little later I was enjoying the magnificent scenery along the Amalfi Drive in Italy. I sat by an English speaking Italian and on the reply to his question about my home, I told him it was in Missouri. I had observed that the word, Missouri, usually brought forth the remark, "Ah! Missouri. Independence, the home of President Truman." It did here and the gentleman added, "You look a lot like his pictures." His next words with an appealing tone amazed me, "Please, would you whistle for me the "Missouri Waltz?"

And whistle it I did as we swung around the cliffs with matchless blue Mediterranean below us on one side and fruitful orange and lemon groves and flowers in profusion above us on the other.

And incidentally my attention was diverted by a woman from the Argentine sitting across the aisle, addressing me, "Cawn

Margaret Truman sing?" I knew well how to answer that question safely!

These incidents happened many years ago but the pleasant memories came trooping back into my mind recently when my bus passed the former President's home in Independence on my way to Kansas City.

The very next day at the check-out counter of the grocery store I was behind Mrs. Harry Chipley who turned toward me and asked, "Do you know who that picture of you in the _Boonville Daily News_ looks like?"

"Who?" said I, nibbling at the bait and thereby springing the trap.

"President Truman."

Evangeline Means, President of the Boonslick Historical Society, presenting Lilburn Kingsbury with plaque recognizing 40 years of service to the society of which he was first president.

Chapter Twenty-Two

WHAT A COLORFUL AND GLORIOUS SUNSET

Lilburn's last years may be likened to an adventurous fall day of travel over highways and by-ways passing through rolling wooded country ablaze with Fall color. And what a brilliant multi-colored sunset lit up the sky October 14, 1977 when more than three hundred of Lilburn's relatives and friends gathered at Central Methodist College to honor him on his 93rd birthday.

On the wall centered behind the long, fall-flower-bedecked head table, was stretched a large banner. On it in large, bold, block letters was inscribed:

BOONSLICK HISTORICAL SOCIETY
HAPPY 93RD BIRTHDAY!
LILBURN A. KINGSBURY

Behind the lectern, which was almost hidden by a colorful arrangement of fall garden flowers stood a stoop-shouldered man with a weathered face wrinkled by age. His sparse white hair had receded from his forehead. The brown suit coat he was wearing hung loosely from his shoulders. In the button hole was a partially opened red rose. The harmonizing tie of brown with small red and white stripes failed to draw his white shirt closely about his neck. High on his aquiline nose were glasses through which his pale blue eyes peered intently out at the 250 relatives and friends who had come to wish him Happy Birthday and honor him.

For more than two hours Lilburn A. Kingsbury had been sitting to the right of the Master of Ceremonies, Cordell Tindall, vice president of the Harvest Publishing Company.

As first president of the Boonslick Historical Society, founded forty years earlier, Lilburn had been awarded a plaque reading:

"Boonslick Historical Society Citation to Lilburn A. Kingsbury for Meritorious Service October 14, 1977."

He had listened to a reading by State Senator Warren Wellman, of a resolution passed by the Missouri Senate honoring him as one of "those exemplary individuals who have led truly outstanding and noble lives, lives filled with significant contributions to mankind...[a man who] has established a sterling reputation as a writer, musician, business man, and civic-minded citizen which will long serve as a standard of excellence against which future generations will be measured and found wanting."

The Missouri House of Representatives, not to be outdone by the Senate, also passed a Resolution. It was read by Representative, John Rollins, as Lilburn gave equal attention to its extolling him for the many qualities making him an "exemplary gentleman."

As Robert Bray, Alumni Secretary of Central Methodist College where the banquet was being held, spoke, an incredulous look of amazement registered on Lilburn's line-furrowed face. Bray said:

"Occasionally there are born into a generation men who affect everything and everyone with whom they come into contact. Men whose lives are dedicated unknowingly to the cause of their fellow man. Such a one is Lilburn Adkin Kingsbury, whose life began October 14, 1884. His eventful and humanitarian life is studded with accomplishments and honors. But it is the man himself that best displays the essential qualities of his nature: loving brother and kinsman, devotee of history of the Boonslick Country, loyal Methodist, astute author and journalist, successful horticulturist, competent musician, discriminating collector of antiques, witty speaker and faithful friend to all. These are the many facets which distinguish his commanding personality. Dr. Samuel Johnson once said of Oliver Goldsmith, he touched nothing that he did not adorn. All of us know that the same sentiment applies equally as well to Lilburn Adkin Kingsbury. Another Englishman's words describe the man we honor tonight. John Dryden penned these lines: 'How blessed is he who leads a country life, unvexed with anxious cares and void of strife, who studying peace and shunning civil rage, enjoyed his youth and now enjoys his age. All who deserve his love he makes his own. And to be loved himself needs only to be known.'

"Lilburn, it is my privilege and pleasure to announce to you, for you are probably the only person in the room unaware of the announcement that I am going to make, that in recognition of your lifetime of extensive and significant service to family, friends, church and community, there has been established at Central Methodist College, by relatives and friends, the Lilburn Adkin Kingsbury scholarship endowment fund.

His face still reflecting his surprise, Lilburn continued listening as Joe Howell, President of the College, in accepting the check for the Scholarship fund, commented:

"I can remember on so many occasions as a boy going to funerals and saying, wouldn't it be more meaningful for a family to just get together before a loved one dies rather than after? I couldn't help thinking what a living example this is to see this great family get together, take the trouble, travel the distance to honor such a great man while he can hear those words and enjoy them from now on...this inspired me so that I got together with [staff members] and said what can we do to make tonight a first for another 123 years [the college's age at the time], to bring special attention to the Kingsburys? We have an endowed scholarship, we said, but we have scholarships. What can we do with one of this magnitude? One that will surely provide an outstanding student a most attractive financial assistance to come here and profit from our academic offerings, one that will live forever, one which will never go away?"

Howell then announced the establishment of a Hall of Sponsors Scholarship program with Lilburn becoming the first to have his picture placed in the Hall.

Cordell Tindall, the M.C. then turned to Lilburn saying, "the man we really are eager to hear - the man we came here to honor is Cousin Lilburn. Cousin Lilburn, what do you think of all this?" Lilburn rose and took the microphone. Speaking softly, at first hesitatingly, but as he sensed the warm, rapt attention of his many assembled friends and relatives, firmly and fluently in his twangy, Missouri drawl: he responded:

What do I think? Well, this beats anything I have ever heard of anybody having. I have listened to the comments of Cousin Evangeline and Cousin Cordell and many other cousins and kinfolks. It reminds me of Mandy Brown at her husband's funeral. The preacher was speaking over the coffin of her husband in very glowing terms and Mandy became just a little doubtful. So she turned to her son and said, "Johnny, you go up there and look in the coffin and see if that's your Pa."

All of you have indicated that I have met with success along some lines. But, so you may not go away with a biased opinion, I think it only fair to inform you of some projects I have undertaken which were abject failures. I was very surprised to hear this tape [Djalna] being played tonight. It brings to mind that it was back in 1904 I composed, copyrighted and published that piece of music, dedicated to my second sweetheart. Well, after it was published, I put it up for sale in the drugstore in New Franklin, and after three or four weeks only three copies had been sold. So, I just considered my talents as a musician as a flop. And my second sweetheart married someone else, but I didn't let it get me down.

One Sunday night, after enjoying an all-day picnic I stopped on the way home for the Sunday evening church service. I planned to stay for a wedding which was to follow the close of the service and I just settled down to enjoy the ceremony when an usher touched me on the shoulder and whispered, "You're wanted out in the vestibule." Imagine what I thought when the wedding was about to begin, and now I'd be sent to Heaven knows where and miss it which I was distressed about. But when I got out to the vestibule, the wedding party was all lined up at the end of the church and the grandmother was there, and she said, "Mr. Kingsbury will you do us a favor? Will you give the bride away?"

Well, imagine my surprise and astonishment. I asked her, "How can I give the bride away?"

"Well, all you do is walk in with the bride and when the preacher asks you, 'who giveth this woman in marriage, or gives this woman away?' all you need do is say, 'in the absence of her grandfather, I do.'"

I'd been on a picnic all day, my shoes were not shined, my hair was not combed, and I was in my shirt sleeves. But, you know how women have a way with me, and so I consented that I would do that. And before I knew it, I was flowing down the aisle with a bride on my arm and her little hand just shakin' like this [he fluttered a hand to illustrate] on mine. Well, I had asked grandma if the preacher knew that I was going to give the bride away. She said, "Oh, yes, he knew."

Well, I had heard the marriage ceremony several times and when the preacher got started I kept thinking, surely he'll ask me directly. But do you know, he pronounced them man and wife, the groom kissed the bride and they all but ran over me, leaving me at the altar. Well, I was a failure.

Once, when playing at a revival, (you all heard that I've been going to church for a long time) the evangelist, unexpectedly to me, announced that we will now sing number twenty-three at the conclusion of which Brother Kingsbury will lead us in prayer. It was such a surprise and shock I was struck dumb. Down on my knees by the organ stool, I wished I could climb in through that hole where the pedals were. Well, it was quiet then, it seemed to me, for a long time when the preacher said, "Pray Brother Kingsbury, pray!" It was just like Simon Legree lashed me! "Oh Lord, help him to pray." I think I lost consciousness. I came to, and the preacher was doing what he had asked me to do. Well, I was terribly embarrassed and felt like I had fallen short but I got up and played the next hymn just like nothing had happened.

Well, I'm just amazed that all of you cousins could say so many nice things. I have been pinching myself but I am not yet sure it is I you're talking about. And after having so many flattering things said about me I don't give a hoot about any old obituary. Thank you very much, but I want to extend my thanks for these papers and for the plaque and this book, Loving Remembrances of Family and Friends. I'm just knocked dumb because of the scholarship fund. I have never heard of anybody having anything like that. I just feel that there's nothing nicer that anyone could receive and I'm very grateful to everyone who has contributed to this evening, which is undoubtedly one that comes to a person once in a lifetime, if at all. I hope everyone of you will live to be ninety-three and be given an ovation such as I have received. Thank you!

Chapter Twenty-Three

SUNSET AFTERGLOW

The sunset afterglow lingered on. Publicity generated by the birthday party made him the subject of feature articles in newspapers and magazines with headings such as "A living history book," "Writes it like it is," "Mark Twain of mid-Missouri," "Country gentleman," and "Howard County historian."

His "Lilburn Says" column continued to receive accolades; he was sought as a speaker; and was barraged by requests from people in far-away places seeking information about their early Howard County ancestors.

But by the end of 1980, his marasmus was taking its toll. January 19, 1981, he wrote me:

Lillian and I are fine. I at least am, except for protesting knees when I get up. But they never say a word as long as I am lying or sitting down. Thank God. You know it sounds strange to tell I was 6 weeks in the hospital and five in the Colonial Gardens Home and going on seven now back here. Except for my knees, I have had no physical discomfort other than "sticks" for drawing blood, or inserting feeder tubes in my hand (vein). I continue to hear amazing things from Lillian about my hospital stay. It seems there was a time when they were fearful of hearing the telephone ring, lest it be word that "I had passed on." They brought mail and read it to me and thought I was enjoying it, as I told them to take it home. When I got home and read it, I thought it was the first time. I still haven't found out what they did to me about once a week for which I was billed $118 a throw.

He wrote:

I walked out to the garage, parked the walker, and holding to the side of my car, unlocked it and got in. I started the engine and backed out the door. Washed off the license plates to put on the new little tags which must be placed on the old plates and when Charles arrived we drove my car to town to exercise it. It runs like a top, but has a heavy coating of dust that needs to be washed off. Some warm day, I mean to back it out, put the walker in the back seat and drive it to town myself. Will have to go to Boonville to find an automatic washer.

The prospect of such activities alarmed me as they did other relatives and friends. We tried to persuade Lilburn and Lillian to leave Fairview and enter Colonial Gardens. To such advice from his cousin Louisa Terrel Huggs he wrote:

Dear Louisa:

Responding to the advice in your letter, Lillian and I are always fighting the idea of going to a nursing home because we have always wanted to be "hearsed" away from this, our life-long dwelling place though we know it is good sense to go to a nursing home before one gets to the stage where it's necessary to do so. But at the moment, neither of us has that kind of good sense.

On the last of May, I had been a Mason for seventy-five years and they celebrated the diamond jubilee of my membership in my Masonic lodge. If I could have walked on it that far, I'm sure they would have had the red carped rolled out all the way to my home. Somebody had dug up my past, things I had forgotten. I was amazed to hear listed the vocations and avocations in which I have had time to stick a finger. Three pretty girls sang three old-time songs and one of them placed a lei, fresh from Hawaii, around my neck and made me a sweet-smelling creature. There was a handsome plaque and many flattering words of commendation by this one and that one. I had a great time and I think Lillian did too.

In July 1982 Lilburn wrote Louisa:

Well, things have gone "tolerable smooth" with Sister Lillian and me. I have a feeling our friends think it would be so sensible if we would just sell out and go to a home for the aged, but neither of us has that kind of sense, though we realize that except for the grace of God, circumstance could tie a knot in our living. Here's an example of that fact.

Lillian, who always slept in an upstairs bedroom, is no longer able to climb stairs, so she sleeps in what was the living room when you were here. Her single bed looks very good, dolled up on the north side of the room. One evening she was ill and rolled off the bed, I was sitting nearby in my wheel chair reading. I couldn't get proper coordination of my limbs trying to get her up by any methods we could manage. Finally, she suggested I pull the top mattress off her bed and let her sleep on the floor all night. So the mattress came off, but it was at right angles with Lillian. Then came the job of getting her parallel to the mattress. I finally accomplished that but she couldn't roll up on it. I went across the hall to my room for something and when I go back, she had rolled on to the mattress. In the process of getting the covers on to her properly, I lost my balance and fell backward, cracking my head good on the floor.

My first thought then was "What if I can't get up and use the telephone to call for help?" But I found myself intact, and the situation seemed utterly ridiculous that Lillian and I were both lying on the floor. I got up thankfully, and spent the night in a reclining chair. And Lillian did get up the next morning of her own accord and prepared breakfast as usual. Then she got the place cleaned up just in time for us to act as hosts to friends from Hot Springs and Louisville, together with relatives, they are visiting here. But at the sight of a full house they said they just dropped by to say hello and departed. We love to have visitors and they come from all over, but once in a while I hear Lillian complaining she doesn't have time to wash her hair and do it up before company comes in the morning. And in the afternoon, someone usually comes to interrupt our lessons in modern living as portrayed on television.

Sometime in March 1983, he wrote Louisa:

Since my 98th birthday, unusual things have complicated life for me, unlike what has happened before. I have found what the term "speak in the unknown tongue," which I have heard Biblically, may mean. For only a short time, twice, I have been unable to utter a word that I have ever heard before and twice I have lost the use of my lower right arm, once especially but my voice came back OK and so did the use of my arm after massage. Needless to say how thankful I was. But the worse thing is nothing new, stiff knees which have bothered me for over two years and I have had to resort to my walker because a cane is useless. And I must be very careful with the walker. Have had two bad falls with my body tied up with the walker. Damage is muscular chiefly, no bones broken. I can no longer mount a two step ladder to wind the big mantel clock. I renewed my driver's license for the sake of my morale, but have not ventured out on the highway since the fall of last year. Sometimes I drive around in the yard.

Lilburn's last letter to me was written March 19, 1983. It chronicled the succession of visitors tendering gifts of food - "bestowing welfare" as he put it. He deplored his dependence upon a walker, his inability to drive his car, and his difficulty in writing what he wished. He hoped to write more soon.

With the help of friends, they managed to stay on at Fairview until April 25. Jean Edmonston (Lillian's daughter-in-law) outlined the events. Her mother-in-law suffered a massive stroke which required hospitalization. She and other relatives tried to convince Lilburn he should go to Colonial Gardens Nursing Home. According to Jean, he said, "Why should I? I've been getting my meals when she didn't feel up to it. I'm staying right here."

He did until May 11. Fortunately, when he became ill, a friend was visiting and called a doctor who rushed Lilburn to the hospital. I got regular reports from Missouri about Lib and Lillian. Lillian was still comatose; Lilburn's condition worsened. The doctor thought he had only a short time to live.

I flew to Missouri on June 13 and remained until June 17.
When I went into Lib's room, the head of his bed was raised so
he was in a semi-sitting position. He was pale and gaunt but gave
me a big, warm smile and said,

"Warren, how good it is to see you. How nice you look."

His mind was clear. We argued about Reagan's supply-side eco-
nomics for a few minutes and then he told me, if I could find time,
he would appreciate me reviewing all his historical and genealogical
material, scrapbooks, letters, etc. He said,

"I know you have thought something should be done with
my letters. Take those you want. Do with them as you wish. If
there's any other stuff you'd like, take it also. Other material you
think of historical value and worth preserving, I'd like you to
arrange for the State Historical Society to have. They've told me
they'd access it into their library so interested people can use it."

I promised to do this. The next two days, with breaks only to visit
Lib, I worked my way through the mass of material in his office and
in his study at Fairview. It was an amazing conglomeration which
included card files, correspondence, family histories, family papers,
genealogical records, historical records, maps, plats, architectural plans
and drawings, photographs, reminiscences and anecdotes, speeches
and writings, newspaper clippings and scrapbooks. There were even
shoe boxes filled with what must have been his every cancelled check.
I didn't have time to make critical judgements so discarded only what
obviously seemed of no historical value. Two State Historical Library
staff members arrived in New Franklin early the next morning.
When they saw the pile of material I had piled up in Lib's New
Franklin office, they couldn't have been more excited and happy if
they'd discovered a rich vein of gold.
I worked through the material with them and about seven that
evening, the big station wagon they had driven over from Columbia
was jam-packed with boxes of his memorabilia. I doubt they could

have found space for even an additional newspaper.

After I had seen the Society people on their way, I reported back to Lib at the hospital. He told me he had planned to meet the Society's Director at his office to go over things with him, but had become ill and taken to the hospital the day before they were to meet. He said,

"I'll sleep tonight knowing you have taken care of this for me. Thank you, Warren, for coming."

He looked up at me. Tears were rolling down his cheeks. He held out a hand, I took it. His clasp was firm. Neither of us could speak for several minutes. We just looked at one another. My eyes flooded also. Then, still gripping my hand, he said softly but clearly,

"When we said 'Goodbye' after our mule boat trip (*to Europe in 1928*), I knew it would be a long time before I saw you again. I knew though, it wasn't forever. I don't feel it is now. Somehow I believe there is truth in the old hymn, 'We Shall Meet Again in the Sweet By-and-By.' I have faith we will!"

The pressure of his grip increased, relaxed, grew firm once more. I bent over, close to him, put my free arm around behind his shoulder, hugged him, kissed his cheek.

"Goodbye, Lib," I said, raising my head. I was so emotionally caught up, I had difficulty phrasing the words. Then, "God bless you for all you have done for so many of us. 'Till we meet again in the sweet by-and-by.'"

At the doorway to his room, I turned and blew him a kiss. There was a faint smile on his face. Then his eyes closed. The lines in his face seemed to have smoothed out.

That was the last time I saw Lib. Relatives and friends saw that everything which could be done for him was done. They kept me informed and when he died July 1, 1983, saw his funeral was conducted as he wished it to be. He was buried in the Kingsbury-Smith plot in the Clark's Chapel cemetery high on a bluff overlooking the Missouri River to the wooded hills rising from the other side. Here his parents and many relatives rest in peace. His sister Lillian died July 4; his sister Anna Rose died on July 30.

    I didn't return for the funeral. I preferred to cherish the memory of our poignant parting and our many stimulating visits when he was an active, vibrant man.

    My bachelor uncle's hobby horse rides made him a legendary figure well before the brilliant colors of the setting sun of his life's journey gave way to the darkness of death.

Lilburn in his beloved Clark's Chapel cemetery a year before his death

Chapter Twenty-Four

L'Envoi

In reviewing the excerpts of Lilburn's writings which make up *Hobby Horse Rider*, it seems to me he exemplifies Walt Whitman's poem, "A Child Goes Forth."

...A child
went forth every day:
And the first object he looked upon and received
with wonder, pity, love or dread,
that object became a part of him for the day,
or a certain part of the day.
Or for many stretching cycles of years."

Lilburn truly absorbed the mores and became an important part of the community in which he lived for nearly ninety-nine years. His remains now repose close by his parents in the Kingsbury plot at the Clark's Chapel Cemetery on the hilltop overlooking a beautiful expanse of Missouri River valley - the heart of the Boonslick community. Close by is the beloved Chapel where he played the organ for services.

This book presented much of what became a part of him in the hope it will help preserve the "precious little library" his writings through the years represent.

In his unpublished manuscript written in 1942 Lilburn closed with the following paragraphs. They seem to me to catch the essence of his love and feeling for the Boonslick Country and its interesting people of which he was such an important part.

Retrospect

And thus for more than a century and a quarter, the dramas have gone on with personnel and stage properties ever changing.

Today it is a far cry from Becknell's wagon train outfitting at Franklin, which creaked its way over a Santa Fe Trail, to the automobile which speeds along the farm-to-market road whirling a cloud of white rock dust into the air. There is nothing in common between the crude plow drawn by oxen and that of the sleek tractor which now races across the fields, except the rich earth which both have turned. Race horses tied to crowded hitchracks in front of the church, and pews inside filled with grandparents, uncles, aunts and cousins, are as far removed as play parties, the distillery, slaves and stock.

One senses tragedy in the dramas of today. In the church and in the school on Clark's Chapel Hill, in the homes of the valley, there is no longer a child who is descended from the pioneer men and women who settled on this land, "winnowed the chaff" from busy lives and built a community second to none.

But Mother Earth is fruitful in the valley and after more than 100 years of cultivation of its acres, one may still say, as did Robinson G. Smith in 1840:

"Henry, I want to tell you the truth about this country...the land is so rich you can plant crowbars at night and they will sprout ten penny nails by morning."

Warren Taylor Kingsbury, Editor
Professor Emeritus
Arizona State University
June, 1998